PROGRAMMING THE FUTURE

PROGRAMMING
THE FUTURE

POLITICS, RESISTANCE, *and*
UTOPIA *in* CONTEMPORARY
SPECULATIVE TV

SHERRYL VINT AND
JONATHAN ALEXANDER

WALLFLOWER

NEW YORK

Wallflower Press is an imprint of Columbia University Press

Columbia University Press
Publishers Since 1893
New York   Chichester, West Sussex
cup.columbia.edu

Library of Congress Cataloging-in-Publication Data
Names: Vint, Sherryl, 1969– author. | Alexander, Jonathan, 1967– author.
Title: Programming the future : Politics, Resistance, and Utopia in Contemporary
Speculative TV / Sherryl Vint and Jonathan Alexander.
Description: New York : Wallflower, [2022] | Includes bibliographical
references and index.
Identifiers: LCCN 2022009170 (print) | LCCN 2022009171 (ebook) |
ISBN 9780231198301 (hardback) | ISBN 9780231198318 (trade paperback) |
ISBN 9780231552578 (ebook)
Subjects: LCSH: Dystopian television programs—United States—History
and criticism. | Television—Social aspects—United States.
Classification: LCC PN1992.8.D97 V56 2022 (print) | LCC PN1992.8.D97 (ebook) |
DDC 791.45/75—dc23/eng/20220330
LC record available at https://lccn.loc.gov/2022009170
LC ebook record available at https://lccn.loc.gov/2022009171

Columbia University Press books are printed on permanent
and durable acid-free paper.
Printed and bound by CPI Group (UK) Ltd, Croydon, CR0 4YY

Cover design: Elliott S. Cairns
Cover image: Makkkro/Shutterstock.com

CONTENTS

PROGRAMMING THE FUTURE

INTRODUCTION

I n 2016 and 2017, SyFy aired the single season of Alex and David Pastor's series *Incorporated*. Set in a future in which climate change has produced a world where people live either in "green zone" corporate enclaves, protected from the worst economic and environmental disasters, or "red zone" ghettos that began as FEMA camps, its grim vision is simultaneously banal and familiar. Symptomatic of the speculative imaginary's almost exclusive turn toward dystopian futures in the twenty-first century, *Incorporated* remixes the familiar icons of cyberpunk futures in which corporations have replaced governments, the impoverished must commodify their identities and bodies for income, and a vast swath of the population is simply irrelevant to the existing order. Moreover, much of this imagery and especially the logic of economic austerity that grounds it have become even more familiar to us as a vision of a coming future that haunts the present. These projections of high-tech, commodified, urbanized futures have become something of a horizon of expectation not only because we are immersed in a popular culture that circulates and amplifies them but also because the neoliberal ideology to which cyberpunk responded has migrated, since the 1980s, from the margins to the center of Western democratic political rhetoric.

We begin with *Incorporated* because this series, despite its formulaic qualities, aptly captures and articulates important shifts in contemporary democracy that we seek to make visible in this book. Unlike most of its cyberpunk predecessors, *Incorporated* puts a rationality that privileges profit over any other value at the heart of its narrative. The protagonist, Ben (Sean Teale), whose real name is Aaron, has infiltrated Spiga Corporation in search of his girlfriend, Elena (Denyse Tontz); she is indentured as a corporate escort to secure her father's release from debtor's prison. Part of the reason his debt is so high is that his business assets were lost in a fire, which the fire department did not attempt to stop because premiums for their service had not been paid—although they were present to ensure the fire did not spread to surrounding buildings with up-to-date payments. Without Elena's help, her father's sentence would stretch longer than his life: he is required to labor to pay off not only his original debt and interest but also the cost of his incarceration. On the one hand, this narrative repeats commonplaces of dystopian futures in which predatory corporations wantonly destroy human life in pursuit of profit, but, on the other, it also conveys an uncanny sense of the quotidian, a familiar if exaggerated sensibility. *Incorporated* portrays the felt experience of contemporary debt culture, a reality as calamitous as any speculative dystopia.

This book looks to SF television as a discourse that allegorizes and interrogates the ways that economic crisis has redefined the social and the political in a polarized world. SF television foregrounds issues of governance because of its frequently being set in futures whose novel institutions and norms must be explained. These series extrapolate and intensify contemporary tensions, allowing us to isolate and examine the interactions among a myriad of discursive threads that stand in for political and economic claims that circulate in the public sphere. Analyzing *Battlestar Galactica* (*BSG*; miniseries 2003; 2004–2009) as a comment on the way politics no longer operates according to the logics of democratic modernity, Eva Cherniavsky argues that the series makes these changes visible in "flickering prospects that neither quite emerge into narrative view, but also never cease to exert their centrifugal force on the grammar of modern political subjectivity." The allegory of the series, she argues, is crucial to her project to map and intervene in this changing landscape because it can "pose the problem that we barely know how to think, much less resolve." For Cherniavsky, this problem is what she calls the "unreal" of contemporary politics.[1] We will return to this challenge of the unreal below. Our central purposes in this book are to see how narratives about alternative-world political struggles help viewers negotiate the shifting terrain of identity and belonging and to theorize how SF television's public pedagogy might be radicalized toward new modalities of sociality.

For instance, as we watch Ben/Aaron negotiate the corporate culture of Spiga, we are given a primer in neoliberal rationality and its human costs. Spiga executives are obsessed with protecting their IP, in everything from terminator seeds to the neurons within employees' brains, and the SF technique by which metaphor is literalized is used repeatedly to remind us of the violence behind choices to prioritize profit. Episode titles such as "Cost Containment" (S1E4) and "Profit and Loss" (S1E5) ensure that we connect their violent action sequences to the financial transactions they symbolize. In "Downsizing" (S1E2), for example, a drug dealer tells the Latino youth he is recruiting, "Things weren't always like this. People had homes. Homes that my company insured. Homeowners insurance. Can you believe that?" In "Executables" (S1E7), we see a party celebrating the anniversary of the Twenty-Ninth Amendment to the Constitution, "granting corporations the sovereignty we needed and deserved." Repeatedly we are reminded that profit is more important than people, via storylines that make it clear that Spiga would rather kill its employees than let competitors gain access to proprietary data they know. Ben and his wife must sign a waiver taking on full liability for healthcare costs when they contemplate having a child without genetic engineering. *Incorporated* exaggerates physical precarity—the literal murder or neuro-erasure of employees—but the logic that underpins its narrative aptly captures our real economic and social precarity: as Zygmunt Bauman compellingly argues, all social relations and bonds have been liquefied in an ever-changing world in which we are continually compelled to reinvent ourselves for the next job. Wendy Brown uses the term *responsibilization* to describe this neoliberal project of eradicating the social and notions of governance that include the provision of services to citizens. *Incorporated* and other series that we discuss negotiate, interrogate, and work through the contradictions of living in this neoliberal order, making visible what might be hard to see as one lives through it, at times naturalizing the status quo and at times offering visions of alternative possibilities. That is, SF television is a space of public pedagogy concerning governance.

SPECULATIVE TELEVISION AND
PUBLIC PEDAGOGY

We focus on television as a medium whose recent emphasis on long narrative form, rather than discrete episodes, creates conditions for a sustained immersion in a text's ideologies. Viewers thus inhabit these narratives (and their ideologies) in domestic screening spaces over a duration of weeks and years. Moreover, as television scholars such as Lynn Spiegel have established, television enters the intimate space of people's homes and becomes part of the quotidian more so than do other media forms. Focusing on speculative television allows us to examine sites where displacement in time or onto figures such as alien invaders often prompts a more open and explicit expression of cultural anxieties and preoccupations than is possible in more realist genres. All of the series we discuss also foreground fusions of the political with the familial, and we suggest that this nexus is central both to television as a medium and to the education of desire in response to economic crisis that we trace in our analysis. These series have the potential to shape how viewers both think and feel about contemporary social, political, and economic problems as they are extrapolated into the future. They thus form part of a broader public pedagogic in the education of desire, or how we are taught to conceive, imagine, and hope for the future.

We take our notion of public pedagogy from the work of Stuart Hall and Henry Giroux, who theorize popular culture and media as constituting a pedagogic that channels both thinking and affect along ideological tracks that often support hegemonic norms and values. Giroux, for instance, argues that "under neoliberalism, dominant public pedagogy with its narrow and imposed schemes of classification and limited modes of identification uses the educational force of the culture to negate the basic conditions for critical agency."[2] While we take the force of Giroux's criticism of much contemporary popular culture, we also hope to open up a space of thinking about contemporary SF television that need not see it as "narrow" and "limited" in the "modes of identification" that it presents us.

Along these lines, the work of the cultural studies theorist Stuart Hall has been tremendously inspiring, particularly as Hall recognizes that "in the study of popular culture, we should always start here: with the double-stake in popular culture, the double movement of containment and resistance, which is always inevitably inside it."[3] Like Giroux, Hall fully understands how popular representations can serve to promote "narrow and imposed schemes of classification and limited modes of identification." At the same time, however, Hall maintains that "people have to have a language to speak about where they are and what other possible futures are available to them. These futures may not be real; if you try to concretise them immediately, you may find there is nothing there. But what is there, what is real, is the possibility of being someone else, of being in some other social space from the one in which you have already been placed."[4] While not referencing science fiction or speculative narrative in this passage, Hall's comments about the need for people to imagine different futures—the "possibility of being someone else"—gestures to how pop cultural narratives can provide such spaces for imagining. To be sure, as Hall reminds us, such imagining does not necessarily occur automatically or even compel agency. But the possibility is there—and, given the number of series focused on imagining the future differently, the collective force of such narratives may very well bend toward critical thought, possibly critical agency. Catherine Chaput reminds us in *Market Affect and the Rhetoric of Political Economic Debates*, following the work of Adorno and the Frankfurt School, that the "work of subjectification actively enlists individuals in the process of personality formation; thus, individuals possess the possibility for differently mobilizing those energies."[5] Viewers of series that actively and consistently suggest how the future might be different may thus have the opportunity to mobilize their own energies toward ends other than maintaining the neoliberalized status quo. And while we must acknowledge that some versions of the future seem to cultivate retrograde and nostalgic visions of past nation building, others attempt more complex questioning of what kinds of social structures and relations should be desired. Our book thus maps the landscape of contemporary SF television while also critiquing how desires are channeled in the imagination of futurity.

NEOLIBERALISM, BELONGING, FUTURITY

With the possibilities of such public pedagogy in mind, we analyze contemporary speculative television as a space of political imagining about an ongoing crisis of neoliberalism that replaces democratic values and concepts of citizenship with market logics. We examine how televisual depictions of the future entwine concerns about national security and terrorism with concerns about economic hegemony, demonstrating how deeply the security state exercises its power on behalf of American and corporately driven economic hegemony. In the process, possibilities for citizenship and for individual and collective agency frequently come to the fore as a variety of television series attempt to imagine the ever-changing images of belonging in the face of significant social, political, and economic crises and changes. Through neoliberal discourse, subjects of Western democracies are increasingly encouraged to understand themselves as independent, entrepreneurial agents rather than as part of a social collective. At the same time, since 2016 we have seen a new political crisis in Western nations embodied by authoritarian leaders and openly nativist, often explicitly racist politics, a topic we will address in more detail in our conclusion. Overall, the book charts how SF television both embodies and addresses shifts in the American political imaginary from the 9/11 crisis, through the 2008 economic crash, and into the present moment of entrenched polarization and public health crisis (which promises an economic one to follow).

We contend that popular culture has become central to the public sphere as journalism increasingly shifts toward online and social media modes of distribution, blurring the lines between entertainment and commentary. In the twenty-first-century cultural landscape, news media often emphasize polemical entertainment over thoughtful reflection, but fictional series, reciprocally, use their entertainments to comment incisively on political realities. Given its identity as a genre committed to imagining how the world might be otherwise, we suggest that SF television occupies a place of privilege for thinking about the future of democracy because it is already preoccupied with images of the future. Stuart Hall reminds us that, while cultural forms "create the possibility of new subjectivities . . . they do not themselves guarantee their progressive or reactionary content. They still require social and political practices to articulate them to particular political positions."[6] We take Hall's caveat seriously, but we also maintain that the collective force of contemporary speculative TV narratives bends toward not just a containment (à la Giroux) of identities but rather an ever-increasing interrogation and critical engagement with the structures that bolster and sustain neoliberalized forms of governance. SF's orientation toward the future serves also to orient viewers to seeing and imagining the future differently.

As we follow the shifting political terrain of U.S. ideology into the twenty-first century, our initial focus is on series animated by a sense of American vulnerability that followed after the 9/11 attacks. Inevitably, these narratives of invasion by aliens or imposters transform into ones about how America must be rebuilt in the aftermath. Always at stake, then, is the struggle among competing factions about which America should be restored—that is, imaginatively embraced—as the nation's future. Such series often depict futures in which America had already disappeared even before the external attacks, at times taken over by a cabal of elite insiders who are often complicit with the external agencies of attack. We read these narratives as if they were a kind of litmus paper that reacts to the conditions under which democratic values have eroded, even if at times they are unable to depict the sources of the change they register. Even as they imagine fantastic scenarios of alien takeover or apocalyptic collapse, they emerge from a sense that, in Wendy Brown's words, "neoliberalism assaults the principles, practices, cultures, subjects, and institutions of democracy understood as rule by the people."[7]

Our analyses proceed from the conviction that neoliberalism and its proliferation of market metrics as the only valid mode of governance constitute a crisis for Western democratic forms and indeed for the viability of the future. As David Harvey explains, neoliberalism "proposes that human well-being can best be advanced by liberating individual entrepreneurial freedoms and skills within an institutional framework characterized by strong private property rights, free markets, and free trade."[8] If a market does not yet exist for some social good (water, land, education, health), then the limit of state power, at least according to this theory, should be to create such a market and then cease intervention. Under this logic, politics (democratic freedom) becomes conflated with economics (market freedom), such that governance in the mode of social welfare programs comes to be seen by its opponents as a threat to all-encompassing freedom equal to the threat of foreign invasion. As this new logic swept away the last remnants of a civil order founded on Keynesian theory, so too departed any sense that the role of governance is responsibility for the welfare of its citizens. The election of Ronald Reagan in the United States and Margaret Thatcher in the United Kingdom marked the ascendancy of this new logic, encapsulated by Thatcher in her now-infamous declaration that "there is no such thing as society"—only individuals and their families, who, from this point on, were required to assume all responsibility for their health, longevity, and survival in a free enterprise system.[9]

The texts we have selected to discuss in this book do not represent all or even the most important SF television series distributed in the twenty-first century. Rather, we have selected these examples because, in distinct ways, they all illuminate the ongoing crisis of democratic modernity, which is faltering under the combined weight of, on the one hand, neoliberal accumulation and dispossession and, on the other, authoritarian disenfranchisement and division. While the logics of these two antidemocratic systems are distinct, they also have an entwined history in America over the last forty years, which is one of the reasons we insist throughout this book on thinking through the combined emphases in these series on the political/economic structure and on the individual family unit. We will turn in more detail in our conclusion to issues of antidemocratic and authoritarian strains in recent U.S. politics, but here we want to note their origins in neoliberal economic reforms that dismantled the welfare state, displacing support for those in need from the state to the family. As Melinda Cooper demonstrates in *Family Values*, although neoliberals and neoconservatives had very different reasons for their veneration of the family as the center of social and political life—neoliberals seeking to avoid state programs of economic dependence that might require wealth redistribution and neoconservatives seeking to restore the centrality of patriarchy, white supremacy, and heteronormativity—their shared interest in the family transformed right-wing U.S. politics; as Cooper puts it, "Neoliberals must ultimately delegate power to social conservatives in order to realize their vision of a naturally equilibrating free-market order and a spontaneously self-sufficient family."[10] Similarly, Wendy Brown takes note of the fact that these dynamics that see the family as central are an important technique used by neoliberal thinkers to delegitimize social and economic inclusion: "If there is no such thing as society, but only individuals and families oriented by markets and morals, then there is no such thing as social power generating hierarchies, exclusion, and violence, let alone subjectivity at the sites of class, gender, or race."[11] Crucially, as we will take up further in our conclusion, this neoconservative emphasis on traditional values aligned with the family belies the political history by which social stratification based on race, gender, and orientation become entrenched, normalized, and socially reproduced through economic inheritance. This is a key issue for queer politics precisely because the heteronormative Fordist family is so deeply embedded into U.S. economic policy, where entitlements and inclusion are dependent on policies that police sexual mores and racial boundaries.[12]

The preeminence of neoliberal logic has two main consequences that haunt the contemporary political imaginary and whose trace shapes the narratives we explore in this book, even if most are not as centrally about the economy as is *Incorporated*. First is the way that neoliberal values have become the weft of cultural rationality, generalized to all aspects of life beyond strictly economic matters. Brown points out that the values neoliberalism cultivates—efficiency, productivity, maximization of returns on investment (of money, time, energy, etc.)—have so thoroughly colonized our imaginaries that it is difficult to mount a critique of this political ethos since other rationales for the good life are delegitimized in advance; the good life has come to mean a life of abundance understood in capitalist terms. How, Brown asks, "do subjects reduced to human capital reach for or even wish for popular power?"[13] Democracy becomes a method of problem solving rather than an institution of popular sovereignty, and the citizen is reduced to a shareholder, or merely a stakeholder, with an interest in the outcome of decisions that no longer proceed by law and governance but instead by "guidelines" and "facilitation"; such "replacements also vanquish a vocabulary of power, and hence power's visibility, from the lives and venues that governance organizes and directs." Thus, Brown argues, neoliberalism converts "the distinctly political character, meaning, and operation of democracy's constituent elements into economic ones."[14] In her more recent work, Brown notes that neoconservative elements in contemporary culture articulate their aims in terms of traditional moral values rather than strictly economic ones—that is, the defense of patriarchy, white supremacy, and heteronormativity already discussed—but nonetheless traces the roots of this parallel delegitimizing of democratic politics to the rhetoric deployed by one of neoliberalism's chief architects, Friedrich von Hayek.

The second main consequence of neoliberalism that we trace in this book is linked to the hegemony of financialization in the twenty-first century. Its ascendency, to use Joseph Vogl's term, has transformed the operation of capital such that profits from what Marx calls fictitious capital (dividends, interest, derivatives, and other financial instruments) have vastly outpaced the productive economy, leading not only to the widespread financialization of the economy but also to the market-driven rhetoric that has become our cultural commonsense. As political structures took on the hues of economic ones, the management of risk—the core to financialization—was adopted as a generalized cultural logic. Max Haiven argues that this shift created a context of securitization in which national security risks (associated with 9/11) and financial ones became conflated in popular discourse, producing militarization and surveillance as "two key elements of a broader social transformation towards a paradigm of securitization, one in which collective and social possibilities are reduced to the hyper-individualized calculus of risk."[15] We see traces of this conflation in the series we study and their shift from narratives about external, military threats to America to more recent ones that interrogate how the economic logics that now buttress democratic forms actually undermine popular sovereignty, even as they restore class privilege as the pinnacle of state power.

As the 2008 crash taught us, financialization and the contemporary mode of capitalist profitability are rooted in debt culture. Concomitant with the emergence of neoliberal values in the early 1980s was the expansion of consumer debt in the form of credit cards, alongside the extension of mortgages to a larger segment of the classed population. As many scholars have noted, the expansion of credit in this period served two purposes.[16] First, although initially used to ensure liquidity to the economy through luxury consumer purchases, it quickly became an extension of household income required to pay for necessities no longer provided by the state (such as healthcare or, in the absence of rent controls, housing). Second, as became evident only after the crash, consumer debt has become a revenue-generating product for the financial system, traded via entities such as collateralized debt obligations. While the details of these financial dealings do not concern us here, what is important is how this reality reframed the space of political agency around issues of economic disparity. Yet, as already discussed, efforts to organize political resistance must come to terms with the challenging fact that the same neoliberalism that produced this crisis has also remade social logics such that democratic forms no longer convey the voice of popular sovereignty and resistance.

They too are thoroughly colonized by economic privilege, all the more so since *Citizens United v. FEC* (2010) anointed campaign financing as a kind of political speech. Naming this situation the "derealization" of the public sphere, Eva Cherniavsky argues that "we are living in the midst of a momentous reconfiguration of political order, which seems increasingly to represent either a new stage of capitalism, or, perhaps, the beginning of its end."[17]

Like Brown, Cherniavsky believes that the modern political ethos in which government exists to serve the needs of its populace has evaporated. Long challenged by a Western conviction that capitalism and democracy reinforced each other, belief in the efficacy of democratic institutions cannot sustain itself in a political environment from which the state has conceded to the market. This is what Cherniavsky means by the "unreal" of contemporary political expression, which is "eroding the sense of a common reality in which a national or even a local (not to mention a planetary) 'we' live in simultaneous time and convergent social and material worlds."[18] Instead of the inclusive modalities of classical democratic forms (and the strategy of marginalized groups to petition for recognition and entry into the public sphere), we now have a simulacral form of governance, one of whose principal aims is "the negation of the electorate's attachments to its political forms and institutions, attachments that live on, for the time being at least, only entirely in the register of (still) unresolved disappointment."[19] This simulacral governance does not even strive to produce a consensus vision of reality, which no longer serves any purpose since the state lacks interest in popular convictions about the political and cares only about controlling the collective behavior of its human resources, which are ensured by debt servitude. Thus, "politics is no longer the art of norming mass sentiment to confirm to [*sic*] the priorities and agendas of the dominant bloc—indeed, of a bloc that dominates precisely because it can produce the masses as the political referent for its policies. Politics becomes instead the art of running simulations, of redistributing the political life of the social body along so many nonintersecting planes."[20]

Cherniavsky differs from Brown in that Brown sees the hegemony of neoliberal logic as what consolidates a new kind of social order, one now grounded by the maximization of profit, whereas Cherniavsky sees only proliferating and nonoverlapping realities that do not share any social norm. She calls this mode of governance simulacral because it discursively establishes its frames of reference for profitability in advance of any materialization, and thus for her there is no social norm because the market is not committed to any social relations beyond its own growth and will adopt any strategy that facilitates this—or drop any that does not. Moreover, although not addressed by Cherniavsky and only obliquely addressed by Brown, the question of who constitutes the "we" of any shared political reality is also deeply complicated by a history of racist exclusion in the United States, visible today in the opposing logics of neoconservative authoritarianism seeking to perpetuate traditional exclusions, on the right, and, on the left, the grassroots activism against state violence that has catalyzed around the Black Lives Matter movement, which gained national visibility and support in 2020.

Yet where Cherniavsky thus sees the end of any "consolidating ethos of a social world,"[21] we see instead the intersection of materiality and dreaming, the world as unfinished and open, in Bloch's terms, as we will discuss in more detail in what follows. The unreal of our dystopian present is a challenge that demands we invent new forms of political agency and new strategies of resistance, as Cherniavsky asserts—and one that requires more careful thinking about the diversity of the citizenry and the power structures shaping any coalitions or expressions of agency. Yet we also contend that popular narratives, as much as economic discourse, have the power to project a reality and capture our affective investment in it. The utopian imagination, as theorized by Bloch and extended by the adoption and adaptation of Bloch among theorists, provides one such technique of political resistance. Before exploring what a Blochian and queer utopian imaginary has to offer this particular cultural and political moment, we first need to understand why television is an important medium to present and explore it.

TELEVISION AS MEDIUM AND INDUSTRY

This book predominantly approaches SF television as a genre, and our analyses focus on narrative elements of the series, not on the industry of television. Nonetheless, it is important to situate the series we discuss within the massive changes to television as an industry that coincided with their original release. The twenty-first century was not only a period of significant political change in the United States following 9/11 but also one in which new technologies of distribution—and the changing financial economy of television that they prompted—created possibilities for television narrative that did not exist before. Many of these changes required the development of a new vocabulary in television studies as the distinction between film and television, once central to critical approaches to both media, began to erode. The series we discuss in this book, including *Incorporated*, which aired on the SyFy network, overwhelmingly were distributed in venues marked by industry changes, and this fact is relevant for the kinds of stories they tell. At the same time, we also suggest that SF has increasingly become a more mainstream genre on television during this same period, at least in part because the new methods of distribution and the new kinds of content they enabled allowed television to more thoroughly engage the utopian capacities of SF.

Although American television remained relatively stable in terms of production and distribution from its emergence until the late 1990s, it has transformed dramatically in two distinct phases since then. First was the emergence of cable channels—basic cable, still supported by advertising, and subscription premium services such as HBO—and second, the advent of streaming services and internet television distribution, which began around 2010. These changes to how television was produced and distributed had myriad consequences for the kinds of series that were created, how they were funded, how distribution media enabled new narrative forms, and ways that content creators (networks, channels, streaming services) sought to differentiate themselves in a crowded marketplace. Documenting these transformations in detail is beyond the scope of our work, but we do want to draw attention to how and why these factors have an impact on the series we discuss in this book.[22] What we now mean by "television" is remarkably different from what the term conveyed during the network era, when Americans chose among three mainstream networks and television was an important and centralized mass communications medium. Since the proliferation of channels with cable services, television has increasingly become a niche medium of narrowcasting, a process that has only accelerated with the ongoing rise of streaming services. In one brief decade, streaming has transformed from two aggregating services enabling access to full seasons (Netflix, Hulu) into a competitive marketplace of multiple subscription services all seeking to attract viewers to their platform through the creation of original and desired content, including the launching by the original legacy networks CBS and NBC of subscription streaming services that augment (and not merely replicate) their broadcast offerings.[23]

The need for television content to differentiate among alternatives in the marketplace began with late-1990s competition among cable channels, initially driven by HBO. This shift is significant on a narrative level because the move away from advertising-supported television typical of the broadcast era enabled greater creative freedom and risk taking, allowing the more complex narrative forms and darker themes that characterize what Jason Mittell calls complex TV. The move away from advertisers not only eliminated pressure to seek series whose broad appeal would avoid offending any market segments but also freed up storytelling from the constraints of segmented commercial breaks, which required some narrative hook to ensure viewers would return to the channel after the break. With streaming distribution, even episode lengths become flexible, as there is no longer the need to ensure programs fit into network programming slots of thirty or sixty minutes. Changes in home equipment, beginning with VCRs and later DVRs, similarly shifted television from being an activity in which one watched whatever was on based on an industry-controlled schedule toward one in which viewers controlled the time and content to which they would direct their attention. Similarly, improvements in television design created high-definition, even 3D viewing experiences, eroding the technological differences that once differentiated television aesthetics sharply from those of film.[24] The prestige of HBO and its subscription-only peers further drove a desire for prestige content for which advertising-based channels could demand higher fees and, perhaps more importantly, could brand their channel as appealing to a distinctive market segment desired by the advertisers, part of the overall transformation of the advertising industry driven by big-data metrics.[25] Thus, the success of subscription television enabled greater experimentation overall. The increased interest in sought-out content on the part of both distributors (for network branding) and consumers also led to the rise of the showrunner as a public figure whose creative reputation became significant, much as the director is seen as the defining aesthetic voice in film.

Shifts in technology and political economy were dialectically entwined with changes to storytelling in television narrative, which from the late 1990s began to move away from the repetitive and linear structures of network-era television and toward multiepisode, even season- or series-long story arcs. From the mid-2000s prestige series began to be pitched with distinct endings in mind,[26] transforming some series from an open-ended to a closed narrative format. Other characteristics of this new complex TV included breaking the fourth wall to address the audience directly, metareflective engagement with genre or medium conventions, puzzle narratives that engage viewers in "forensic fandom" in the gap between new episodes,[27] and complex world building that rewards careful attention and often rewatching. What is important for us to stress here is that many of these qualities were well suited to the development of SF television, given the genre's long history of creative and engaged fan practices and its interest in the distinctive social locations of stories as much as in their characters.

We offer this brief overview of industry change to take note of the fact that overwhelmingly the series we analyze here—selected on the basis of their engagement with questions of political futures—were distributed outside of legacy broadcast networks. Of the series we analyze, only *Threshold* (CBS, 2005–2006), *Jericho* (CBS, 2006–2008), and *Revolution* (NBC, 2012–2014) aired on legacy networks, and the latter two already show signs of these shifts—*Jericho* continued in graphic novel form to complete the planned narrative for fans, and *Revolution* is associated with the branded showrunner Eric Kripke. The youth-oriented series *The 100* (2014–2020) aired on the CW, a relative newcomer to broadcast television, created in 2006 when the late-1990s networks UPN and WB merged. Notably, the CW quickly provided access to its content through an advertising-supported streaming service, and it is distributed as a subscription-based service outside of the United States. Most of the series originated on basic cable—*Falling Skies* (TNT, 2011–2015), *Colony* (USA, 2016–2018), *The Expanse* (SyFy, 2015–2017; Prime Video, 2017–2022), and *Mr. Robot* (USA, 2015–2019)—while *Continuum* (2012–2015) falls somewhere in between, produced for the subscription cable service Showcase in Canada but distributed in the United States via SyFy. SyFy is clearly branded for SF content, but TNT bases its brand on action-driven series and an appeal to masculine viewers, and USA uses the slogan "characters welcome" to suggest its unconventional protagonists. Only *The Man in the High Castle* (Prime Video, 2015–2019) and *For All Mankind* (AppleTV+, 2019–) were created by streaming services, but ongoing trends suggest that genre television has recently become recognized as important for branded prestige content, especially following the worldwide success of *Game of Thrones* (HBO, 2011–2019). The other series we discuss in chapter 2 as exemplars of how SF works as a political narrative mode—*Watchmen* (HBO, 2019), *Counterpart* (Starz, 2017–2019), and *Beforeigners* (HBO International, 2019)—all emerge from premium subscription channels. In the following chapters, we focus our analyses on narrative features, but these industry developments and original modes of distribution also have a role to play in shaping the differences we note among them.

In the shift from broadcast to cable to streaming, the increasing range of channel options also meant that even for successful series, the overall share of the audience was lower than for series that aired during the broadcast era, leading to increasing audience segmentation. While this may be desirable from the point of view of advertisers (or network brand promoters) seeking a specific kind of viewer, the overall trend of increased polarization within U.S. politics in the twenty-first century is arguably linked to the dominance of social media and their use of algorithms to immerse users into content that replicates their established taste patterns. This effect of internet media consumption is relevant to the themes pursued by several of the series we discuss here. Nonetheless, although television is less a mass medium than it once was, we contend that it remains a medium that we experience with intimacy, an important factor for its ongoing role in public pedagogy. Although new technologies mean that people can watch television from multiple locations, research shows that, in 2013, 82 percent of television viewing (64 percent of that on a smartphone) was still done at home.[28] Although seasons are now often shorter than the twenty-two to twenty-six episodes per season typical of the broadcast era, we still spend a considerable amount of time immersed in the worlds of our favorite television characters, and streaming has perhaps intensified this connection: Lotz reports that as of 2017, Netflix accounts for 46 percent of all streaming time and also that television dominates film viewership on the platform by a ratio of 70 percent to 30 percent (the data from the second study was compiled in 2016).[29] Our phones are intimate parts of our lives, perhaps even closer to us, given our reliance on social media, than the televisions of the broadcast era, despite the familial sensibility attached to them by early critics based on the medium's presence in the family home. But television remains a mass medium (albeit more segmented than previously) and an important part of daily rituals. It is thus an exemplary medium for exploring dynamics of the Blochian utopic imagination.

IMAGINING THE FUTURE QUEERLY

If television serves as a privileged medium through which to consider speculative narratives of the future and understand their potentially critical force, what tools might aid and animate our analysis? Methodologically, our project brings together work in utopian studies and queer theory to analyze how contemporary speculative television offers opportunities for understanding the education of desire around citizenship in the imagination of alternative social futures. We draw primarily on Ernst Bloch and his notion of anticipatory consciousness, which suggests that even in the most derivative and retrograde visions of the future, the very act of imagining futurity holds within it the possibility of both hoping for and desiring change, that is, alternative personal and political arrangements. Along such lines, Carl Freedman argues in *Critical Theory and Science Fiction* that "it is in the generic nature of science fiction to confront the future, no matter how unpromising a critical and utopian activity that may seem."[30] And while we agree that such confrontations need not necessarily be critical, we hold that the possibilities for a robust analysis of contemporary politics can surely benefit from the genre's imaginative extrapolations. Ruth Levitas calls this approach to speculative work "utopia as method," a way of questioning that is both critique and world building, a dual recognition that we need gestures of interrogation and imagination. Such a stance is both critical and hopeful, leading to what Miguel Abensour calls the education of desire. Levitas uses the literary critic Edward Thompson to gloss Abensour and the education of desire: "In such an adventure two things happen: our habitual values (the 'commonsense' of bourgeois society) are thrown into disarray. And we enter utopia's proper and new-found space: *the education of desire*. This is not the same as 'a moral education' towards a given end: it is rather, to open a way to aspiration, to 'teach desire to desire, to desire better, to desire more, and above all to desire in a different way.'"[31] The possibility of desiring differently suggests potentially useful intersections between speculative fiction and queer theory, both of which have long developed ways of thinking about the alternative possibilities latent in hegemonic cultural forms. Speculative fiction uses tools of world building to focus on how the social might be differently organized, and queer theory thinks genealogically about the formation of desires in social spaces.

Interestingly, queer theory has recently taken up futurity as a generative concept through which to think the workings of ideology in personal and political domains, further suggesting profitable connections between it and speculative modes. Theorists such as Lee Edelman, in his polemical book *No Future*, see the investment in futurity as one of the most pervasive hegemonic dimensions of heteronormativity, which requires that we sacrifice our current pleasures and possibilities so that we can ensure better futures for children. Such "better futures," though, rarely include expansive notions of intimacy and love but rather focus on the maintenance of socially stabilizing family norms. Other queer theorists, though, have seen in imagining futurity different possibilities for cultivating ways of thinking about social relations, even citizenship. José Esteban Muñoz works directly with Ernst Bloch's theorizing about anticipatory consciousness in his book *Cruising Utopia*, in which Muñoz develops what he calls a queer utopian hermeneutic: "A queer utopian hermeneutic [is] queer in its aim to look for queer relational formations within the social. It is also about this temporal project that I align with queerness, a work shaped by its idealist trajectory; indeed it is the work of not settling for the present, of asking and looking beyond the here and now."[32] For Muñoz, the value of such a hermeneutic is that it would be "epistemologically and ontologically humble in that it would not claim the epistemological certitude of a queerness that we simply 'know' but, instead, strain to activate the no-longer-conscious and to extend a glance toward that which is forward-dawning, anticipatory illuminations of the not-yet-conscious." The accompanying gesture in such humbleness, a Blochian openness to the anticipatory, is the casting of a critical gaze on the present and its seemingly sedimented ideological (and intimate) formations; as Muñoz puts it, "The [critical] purpose of such temporal maneuvers is to wrest ourselves from the present's stultifying hold, to know our queerness as a belonging in particularity that is not dictated or organized around the spirit of political impasse that characterizes the present."[33]

Muñoz's intervention parallels the move of other queer theorists who are trying to find a way to move beyond *No Future* and create ways of thinking about the past, present, and future that are not bound by the organizing structures of contemporary capitalist life. Many begin with a pointed rejection or "opting out" of such structures in the present. We take the phrase "opting out" from the title of Mari Ruti's monograph *The Ethics of Opting Out: Queer Theory's Defiant Subjects*, in which Ruti worries through Edelman's antisociality and embrace of "no future." Ruti argues that one of the major hallmarks of contemporary queer theorizing, even encompassing theorizations such as Jack Halberstam's turn to failure as generative and Elizabeth Freeman's critique of chrononormativity, is the desire to opt out of organizing structures of life that emphasize and actively promote "capitalist accumulation, normative ethical paradigms, the cultural ethos of good performance and productivity, narcissistic models of self-actualization, the heteronormative family, and related reproductive lifestyles."[34] The danger in "opting out," however, is a fixation on negativity and critique that fails to forward a more generative sense of the possible. As Ruti puts it, a "politics of negativity [is] devoid of any clear political or ethical vision: it wants to destroy what exists without giving us much of a sense of what should exist. . . . I am more inclined to look for 'real-life' referents for my theoretical paradigms than those who believe that theory is—or should be—an imaginative activity wholly divorced from the exigencies of lived reality."[35] Ruti's gesture toward referents in "real-life" and her interest in "what should exist" open up ways of thinking queerly not just as a mode of critique of the present but as a method for thinking critically about futurities, however tentatively such thinking must necessarily be.

Such a gesture parallels the best Blochian approach, which moves dialectically among past, present, and future. Douglas Kellner summarizes Bloch's method in ways that echo Ruti's interests in both "real-life" and her desire for an ethical vision. In "Utopia and Marxism," he asserts the following: "Bloch's is a philosophy of hope and the future, a dreaming forward, a projection of a vision of a future kingdom of freedom. It is his conviction that only when we project our future in the light of what is, what has been, and what could be can we engage in the creative practice that will produce the world we all want and realize humanity's deepest hopes and dreams."[36] Such an interest in creative practices that have as their goal the realization of "humanity's deepest hopes and dreams" animates both our interest in contemporary SF television as well as our analytical approach combining queer and utopian studies.

What do the two approaches collectively help us illuminate? Bringing together queer theory and utopia studies allows us to consider the importance of the education of desire for this moment, as well as a recuperation of "hope" as a critical term. Many SF series of the twenty-first century, while certainly products of the marketplace and its demands for entertainment, also perform a public pedagogic—not only informing viewers about some of the complexities of contemporary citizenship and agency but also prompting them to question critically prevailing social and political formations and their relationship to larger geopolitical issues. In the process, they also invite viewers to imagine futures in which those relationships might be different. Or, in Muñoz's words, they cultivate the "work of not settling for the present, of asking and looking beyond the here and now."[37] Similarly, scholarship on speculative fiction is premised on the notion that, at its core, SF is about a critically estranged view of the ideologies that structure our social world and the capacity thus enabled for imagining change. In *Shockwaves of Possibility*, Phillip Wegner contends that "utopianism is fundamental to the very narrative dynamic of this vital modern practice" and argues that what Fredric Jameson calls the "desire called utopia" is foundationally a desire for the narrative effect offered by SF as a mode.[38] Joining scholars such as Istvan Csicsery-Ronay Jr. in understanding SF as a mode or way of perceiving reality rather than a set of icons or type of content, Wegner suggests that speculative fiction is thus a way of "engaging with the world" rather than merely describing it. Similarly, we see the narratives of the SF television series we discuss as ways of conceptualizing and responding to shifts in experiences of citizenship in the twenty-first century.

This approach also allows us a more sustained and robust ideological critique of the enmeshment of the personal and the political—and what Ernst Bloch calls the warm and the cold streams, a materialist and economic analysis that's intertwined with a cultural and affective set of critiques. For instance, contemporary SF pays attention both to the quotidian and larger social structures—and the intertwining of both. Many SF series focus on the impact of apocalyptic futures on families, so much so that the figure and function of the family as a sociopolitical unit comes to the fore as a "problem" needing interrogation, understanding, and perhaps reformulation. Given queer theory's frequent focus on how desires are normalized through heteronormative family structures, a queer approach to thinking about the family—and what desires are sustained into the future through the (re)imagination of the family—seems fertile ground for analysis.

How so? Rosemary Hennessy has documented in *Profit and Pleasure: Sexual Identities and Late Capitalism* how "scholarship on changing state and family formations within and across the global north and south has drawn attention to sexual regulation as a feature of national identity and changing sexual practices across national formations of public and private life."[39] Hennessy posits a metonymic relationship between family as a unit organizing personal intimacies, energies, and investments and larger sociopolitical structures and controls on populations. Public and private life often mirror each other so that gender and sexual roles come to reinforce social and national expectations for behavior, socialization, and relationality. Even seemingly "liberal" changes and developments, such as the legalization of gay marriage, serve to reinforce the kinds of traditional pair-bonding and closed circuits of the nuclear family—an arrangement upon which individuals are becoming increasingly dependent for the kinds of social security no longer offered by governments because they are now dominated by neoliberalized mandates of privatization. Given the relationship between family and larger socioeconomic and political structures, some queer theorists argue that a reimagination of social relationships at the macro level entails a reimagination of them at the micro or familial level. Hennessy asks how such might be workable in the pursuit of what she calls "utopian aspirations": "Is it possible to forge a sexual politics that is attuned to needs and the pleasures of wellbeing, that attends to the insights of those who have passed, and keeps alive a horizon of possibility among the living? A politics that does not confine the erotic but leavens it with the inexhaustible common of collaboration?"[40] Other theorists boldly answer such questions. In *Warped: Gay Normality and Queer Anticapitalism*, Peter Drucker argues that realizing a "utopian vision" of queer anticapitalism should look toward "more conscious, more open, more collective ways of organising domestic life. This utopian vision should include ways for queers to join in creating economic alternatives, in a world in which both community *and* individual autonomy flourish." For instance, Drucker suggests that "we will have to combine experiments in polyamory with measures to expand legal options for households and reverse the privatisation of care."[41]

Speculative television and its depiction of future families offer an incredibly fertile ground for imagining alternatives to familial structures that metonymically suggest alternative—and more collective—arrangements at macro sociopolitical and economic levels. Their revisioning offers viewers an opportunity to reflect on personal changes that might affect larger structures. In *Market Affect and the Rhetoric of Political Economic Debates*, Catherine Chaput argues that "the market structures civil society as the capitalist milieu and cultivates its political subjects as naturally self-interested economic agents. If we want to reinvent civil society according to community-based interests, then we need to mobilize affect according to different governing circuits, ones aligned with collective rather than individual interests that, over time and through spontaneous circulation, produce different aggregate expectations."[42]

Alternative families, including extended notions of kinship and relational networks, may serve as powerful reeducators of desire, inviting viewers to consider multiple ways that communities of care and intimacy might reanimate more sustaining, supportive, and *hopeful* social structures. Indeed, many of the series we examine offer a deep questioning of normative family relations as the ground upon which alternative visions of sociality and citizenship are predicated. This focus on the family is another reason why television is the ideal medium for this analysis, since the family has long been at the center of this medium, with even series set in workplaces tending toward affective storylines that understand coworkers as an alternative kind of family structure. In contrast, the print tradition in SF has often been understood to focus on world building rather than on characters as does realist fiction: the genre thus often draws its themes from the structures of the world in which the story takes place rather than from the interior experiences of its protagonists. It is thus an ideal genre to interrogate systemic structures of oppression and exclusion, but at times it pays scant attention to the implications for individuals in this focus on the systemic. Finally, the fusion of SF with the television medium, like the fusion of utopian studies and queer theory, allows us to keep our analytical focus on the intersection between social structures and processes of subjectivization, both at the large scale and in their effects on individuals, families, and daily life.

THE FUTURE, PROGRAMMED: CHAPTER OVERVIEWS

We begin our analysis in the first chapter by setting up the framework by which we argue that SF television is in dialogue with contemporary political structures and notions of civic identity and participation through an examination of the entire canon of Star Trek series, as well as the important contributions to speculative TV made by both the original *X-Files* (1993–2002) and its reboot (2016, 2018). Perhaps the best-known SF television series—and now an extended franchise with multiple film cycles, spinoff novels, action fictions, theme park events, and more—Star Trek is in many ways the paradigmatic narrative of both the current transmedia landscape and the affective investment that people make in cultural texts. From Gene Roddenberry's *Original Series* (1966–1969) to the newest *Star Trek: Discovery* (2017–), this franchise has been imagined in dialogue with the contemporary political ethos and has often sought to make progressive interventions into the popular imagination.

While the various Star Trek franchises seem to remain committed to the possibilities of liberal governance, other series, notably *The X-Files*, mobilized a growing interest in conspiracy theories to fuel viewer interest in a series that narratively cast doubt on the reliability of governments to fight for, much less tell, the truth. Such a series also built on a long history of SF texts that symbolize social alienation through literally nonhuman characters. By looking at how these series projected a future out of these divergent historical moments, this chapter shows how SF television allegorizes and responds to contemporary ideologies of citizenship and belonging.

Chapter 2 offers an analysis of the importance of *Battlestar Galactica* (miniseries 2003; 2004–2009) in this history. A celebrated rebooting of the 1970s original, Ronald D. Moore's version has been credited with launching a new era of SF television imagined as political narrative. We first lay out the groundwork for the chapter by analyzing what made *BSG* such a distinctive series before turning to several more recent series that we argue show the full potentiality of SF as political narrative: Moore's more recent SF series *For All Mankind* (2019–); the miniseries *Watchmen* (2019), an ingenious extension and recontextualization of the narrative of Alan Moore's 1986–1987 comic book; *Counterpart* (2017–2019), a fusion of SF with the political spy thriller in its story of parallel worlds; and finally *Beforeigners* (2019–), a Norwegian series that estranges our ways of understanding the immigration crisis in its story of temporally rather than spatially displaced migrants. Like *BSG*, each of these series set out to tell political stories through the genre of science fiction, and this chapter thus establishes the importance of SF tropes for such storytelling, laying the ground for our analysis of less explicitly politicized series in the rest of the book.

The chapters that follow each theorize specific themes within twenty-first century SF, providing an overview of how the scenarios and themes that have come to the fore in the genre respond to the defining events of twenty-first-century political life. Chapter 3 begins by focusing on series that depict invasions, particularly of the United States. American television developed after the 9/11 attacks offers multiple examples of invading aliens, often disguised as humans, in narratives that repurpose 1950s-era fears articulated by the film *Invasion of the Body Snatchers* (1956) to twenty-first-century contexts. *Threshold* imagines a branch of the national security apparatus dedicated to responding to alien invasions and voices contemporary anxieties but offers no way for thinking about alternatives to the distressing present reality. *Falling Skies*, which quickly became one of TNT's most popular dramas, returns to older, pulp iconographies of alien invasion, depicting the human survivors of an alien invasion that destroyed human culture as we know it. It takes a jingoistic, nationalist tone and often reinforces xenophobia, especially in a narrative arc about the theft of human children, activating anxieties about reproductive futurity that have long fueled racism in its eugenic forms. *Colony*, which imagines Los Angeles as a displaced version of Baghdad, takes a very different tone. It does not show us any aliens, and we feel their effects only in how the occupation disrupts daily life. The trauma concomitant with being an occupied nation is expressed through the conflicts within a single family, each member of which chooses a distinct way to negotiate this crisis, from outright rebellion to feigned collaboration to reluctant complicity.

Chapter 4, "American Civil Wars," takes up the motif of a conflict between a proper "real" America and a debased "fake" one—whether this is because a conspiracy of insiders has taken over and diverted systems of governance or because changes in the timeline have resulted in another historical outcome. As the ongoing vicissitudes of capital make it increasingly clear that democracy and capitalism have no necessary or even certain connection, mythologies of U.S. identity struggle to sustain themselves in social contexts in which profit has evidently been prioritized over people. *Jericho* uses the tradition of apocalypse stories to imagine wiping the slate clean of the conflicted America as it exists today and then seeking to build something more unified in its stead. Built on a tacit recognition that neoliberalism has fully oriented systems of governance toward the protection of property for an elite minority, these series strive to recuperate the ideals of American democracy by suggesting that the true ethos of the country remains with the people. Going in a very different narrative direction, *The Man in the High Castle*, an adaptation of Philip K. Dick's alternate history about a Nazi victory in World War II, disturbingly reveals how much our real twenty-first century resembles one imagined as the result of such a Nazi victory, pointedly illustrating the stark split between extreme left and extreme right factions. In contrast, a Canadian series, *Continuum*, offers a substantive critique of corporations replacing civic control and also makes the thematic of public pedagogy part of its diegesis, tracing the transformation of the protagonist, Kiera (Rachel Nichols), a security officer from this future transported to our present who is initially invested in seeing her future as the correct path of history.

The following chapter, "Desiring a Different Future," considers series that seek to offer complex visions of future worlds in which the anxieties explored in earlier chapters—about invasion and occupation, about the fragmentation of a shared civic space, about the erosion of democracy by economic forces—persist but are set in worlds that assert the importance of diversity and that privilege globalized over nationalist perspectives. We attend to series that ask how we might imagine shared community across a range of political orientations, whether these be ethnic identities or geographical allegiances. They thus shift our focus toward the intersection of economic structures and waning resources in a context of global environmental crisis, foregrounding how challenges such as climate change and pollution require us to think beyond the governmental reach of individual nation-state structures. *The Expanse* imagines a solar system widely colonized by humans, with each of its political entities (Earth, Mars, the Outer Planets, the Asteroid Belt) having a distinct political and social identity. It simultaneously demonstrates the necessity for some kind of panhuman social order to ensure peace and reveals the obstacles, primarily resource inequity, that stand in the way of such solidarity. Taking a slightly different angle of view, *The 100* makes its primary conflict an intergenerational one and similarly dramatizes a number of competing visions of how best to rebuild society in the wake of its collapse, with no clear "right" answer apparent in these struggles. Overall, these series speak to the affective experiences of displacement, disruption, and changing logics of civic belonging.

Our final chapter takes as its paradigmatic text the near-future series *Mr. Robot*. Centered on a disgruntled hacker who seeks to collapse the financial system, as emblematized by E Corp (openly glossed as EvilCorp), the series both offers an open and pointed critique of the injustices of neoliberalized capitalism and a vision of revolutionary action against it. The series' critique of capital is complicated, however. As we learn near the end of the first season, our protagonist, Elliot (Rami Malek), suffers from multiple personality disorder, and thus he is both the main agent of the hacking attacks against American capital, Mr. Robot, and the person seeking to divert Mr. Robot's agenda to ensure continued stability. In Elliot we see the two faces of the divergent American ideologies explored in a series about splits between real and fake Americas. Elliot's ambivalence exemplifies the predicament of the American economy since the 2008 crash: on the one hand, deeply aware of the damage this system does on a daily basis; on the other, compelled to "bail out" and perpetuate this system because its real subsumption of daily life means that, at least in the short term, its failure would cause even more damage than its continuation.

We conclude, then, by asking how all of these series have both expressed and educated our desires vis-à-vis future modalities of democracy, especially its concomitant economic structures. What negotiations sustain us in this period without—or, ideally, before—revolutionary action? What compromises are we willing and perhaps even encouraged to accept? In his work on utopia, Bloch differentiates between abstract and concrete utopias, preferring the latter. Abstract utopias are mere wish fulfillment, the desire not for a better world but merely for a better position within the structures of this one. Concrete utopias, in contrast, educate our desires toward truly transformative visions, understanding that the better world emerges not merely from improved personal circumstances but from widening the opportunities for diverse peoples to thrive. Such radical change does not come without disruption, struggle, and even cost. In *Mr. Robot* we find traces of such a desire to "reboot democracy," but the question remains as to whether these popular narratives can truly educate our desire toward structural social change or if they merely express our dissatisfaction with the world as we find it. Bloch would argue that the mere existence of such narratives, however abstract, speaks to a powerful desire for change and alternatives, for a hope that we might still have time to change course and build a better world. Ultimately, this book argues hopefully for television and SF television in particular as a medium and a genre that can cultivate thoughtful and affectively rich approaches to thinking—and feeling—critically about the future. Understanding television as a powerful formation of contemporary artistic endeavor, we hope to illuminate how the very best SF television grapples with history, our current socioeconomic and political situations, and our very best possibilities for creating livable and just futures.

1

THE CHANGING SHAPE OF
SCIENCE FICTION TELEVISION

BEFORE 9/11

This book is predominantly focused on SF television of the twenty-first century, but to understand something of its distinctive shape it is first necessary to look at its immediate precursors in the ethos of the 1990s. For our context, 9/11 marks an important periodization not only because of its substantial influence on American culture but also because within SF television it signals an important shift in attitudes toward governance. The 1990s television landscape was dominated by the return of the Star Trek series to the small screen and by the massive success of *The X-Files*, and both took very distinctive attitudes toward governance. While Star Trek renewed the sense of liberal optimism cultivated by Gene Roddenberry during the countercultural era, it also often signaled the distance between its Federation of Planets and divisive, twentieth-century "Earth" politics, implicitly (if also inconsistently) voicing a left-wing critique of imperialist elements of U.S. policy. *The X-Files*, in contrast, openly embraced a left-wing suspicion of government motives and methods that were an extension of 1970s political struggles, openly referencing the Watergate scandal by using Deep Throat as the code name for the shadowy figure who provides the show's protagonists Mulder (David Duchovny) and Scully (Gillian Anderson) with information about both the government conspiracy to hide the existence of aliens and the plans of a secret cabal within the government, the Syndicate, to facilitate alien colonization. Neither series easily navigated the resurgence of conventional patriotism following the 9/11 attacks.[1]

The failure of the brief reboot of *The X-Files* epitomizes how much had changed between the 1990s and the late 2010s: popular among the continued series fanbase, it offered a mélange of beloved episode types (monster-of-the-week, conspiracy theory, strange new technology, metareflections on genre icons), but the series' conviction that "The Truth Is Out There" could no longer speak to the chaotic and polarized world of online social media. This shift is acknowledged in "The Lost Art of Forehead Sweat" (S11E4), which all but reveals that the series could now be enjoyed only nostalgically—times had changed.[2] Yet the importance of *The X-Files* to the 1990s ethos—as a marker of the difference ushered in by 9/11—should not be underestimated. It emerged just at a time when the rise of niche cable networks was changing the television landscape, but it aired on a mainstream network, Fox, and adhered to the then-standard formats of a twenty-plus-week season and a predominance of standalone episodes over a season- or series-long narrative arc. But unlike much television of the time, the series was founded not merely on a premise (which builds on popular myths about Roswell and the 1951 "coverup" of alien contact) but on a specific project, Mulder's commitment to find this truth, which gave the series an overall story arc through which the audience would gradually learn further details about this larger conspiracy. Such arc narratives, now dominant in television, were only just emerging in the 1990s, and genre television led the way.

The X-Files offers early anticipations of several themes that we will theorize as dominant in SF television today. It was much praised at the time for its reversal of stereotypical gender dynamics, making the male partner the "hysterical" true believer in aliens and the female lead the "rational," rigorous scientist. It also fused its government conspiracy storylines with family melodrama: Mulder's obsession is rooted in his belief that his missing sister was abducted when they were children; the mysterious government provocateur and black-ops agent who is their most consistent antagonist, the Cigarette Smoking Man (William B. Davis), is ultimately revealed to be Mulder's biological father; Scully is abducted by the Syndicate and experimented upon, part of a storyline about human-alien hybrids, and when she later has a child by IVF, he too proves to be a result

FIGURE 1.1 The "Smoking Man" from *The X-Files*: "Musings of a Cigarette Smoking Man," season 4, episode 7.

of secret experimentation with human genes. Although the level of suspicion the series cultivated regarding the U.S. government could not be sustained in the immediate aftermath of 9/11, the underlining premise that there are elites within structures of power that manipulate systems to ensure their own advancement at the expense of others continues to structure narratives that try to grapple with persisting inequality. Most importantly, *The X-Files* established SF narratives as a way to process concerns about governance.

STAR TREK AS SYNECDOCHE: UTOPIAN LONGINGS

We focus on the Star Trek series as a synecdoche for how the themes of SF television change over the decades because the series has been televised for much of the medium's history. It enables us to mark shifts over the decades that influence how the same narrative world is differently imagined as contextual and historical contexts change, and its developing narrative tracks changes in political cultures and developing modes of televisual narration.

The first iteration of Star Trek, often referred to as "TOS" or "The Original Series," was largely the brainchild of the writer Gene Roddenberry, and while it only ran for three seasons, from 1966–1969, its subsequent syndication and fan uptake transformed SF television, leaving an imprint on nearly all speculative storytelling following it, its success spawning several series "franchises," major motion pictures, and an extensive fan culture. As of this writing, the Star Trek meganarrative has been unfolding for fifty-four years, with multiple new series currently in production and continuing to develop, expand, augment, and even challenge some of the foundational characters, story arcs, and values of the original series. Roddenberry's genius in creating Star Trek might be attributed to his ability to use episodic televisual narrative to forward a version of liberal humanism that seems roughly American in its outlook and spirit while also making room through encounters with "aliens" to challenge its characters' beliefs and values while not undermining them. The spacefaring mission of the USS *Enterprise*, as famously articulated in the opening credits of every episode of the original series (and in slightly modified form in *The Next Generation*), is "to explore strange new worlds. To seek out new life and new civilizations. To boldly go where no man has gone before!"

While the characters of the Federation starship understand—and often practice—their exploration as a peaceful endeavor, one of building and expanding human and humanoid knowledge, their exploration of the galaxy seems at times structured on a vaguely colonial ethos.[3] The attraction of such an ethos is perhaps unsurprising if we remember that the original *Star Trek* first aired during the late 1960s, a time of American imperial expansion bolstered by a sense of the need to bring "democracy" to the developing world, a period of rapid scientific and technological development, and the ongoing (and at times intensifying) threat of the Cold War. Projecting into the future the hope for a world unified and at peace, human differences are set aside in the pursuit of knowledge and exploration. The appearance on the deck of the *Enterprise* of a Russian officer, Mr. Chekov (Walter Koenig), promised a post–Cold War world while putting Iowa native James Kirk (William Shatner) firmly in the captain's chair. *Star Trek* is to be commended for figuring a diverse community—including a major role for an African American actor

FIGURE 1.2 The multicultural crew of *Star Trek: The Original Series*.

(Nichelle Nichols); an "alien" science officer, the Vulcan Mr. Spock (Leonard Nimoy); and an Asian American navigation officer, Mr. Sulu (George Takei)—working collectively for a common and putatively peaceful cause. On the other hand, however, the quasi-military rankings on the *Enterprise* and the ship's substantial supply of torpedoes and phaser banks suggest an unsettling comfort with couching a peaceful and egalitarian mission within the fortified armaments of a military machine—a situation akin to that envisioned by twentieth-century Americans as "global peacekeepers." *Star Trek*, as diverse as it might be, seems to forward a very midcentury American ethos: peace and freedom bought with the protection of militarized science. The result is a diversity in casting but not necessarily in cultural outlook.

One of the original series' most famous episodes, "City on the Edge of Forever" (S1E28), written by the science fiction author Harlan Ellison and first aired on April 6, 1967, plays out some of these contradictions. In this episode, the crew of the *Enterprise* investigates a time anomaly and arrives at a planet with a strange portal protected by an eerie voice calling itself the Guardian. The portal allows one the ability to travel back in time to any point in history, and Mr. Spock sees an opportunity to record the data flashing by on the portal's "screen" as a way to expand significantly the Federation's knowledge of history, particularly parts of human history not heretofore recorded and thus lost to time. Drama ensues, however, when the ship's physician, Dr. McCoy (DeForest Kelley), is accidentally injected with too much of a powerful medicine and runs, screaming, into the portal. Almost immediately, communication with the *Enterprise* is lost, and the team realizes that McCoy must somehow have changed history so that the "future" they are in no longer occurs. Kirk and Spock decide to go through the portal to find McCoy and prevent this from happening.

Kirk and Spock find themselves in New York at the beginning of the Great Depression, and they are appalled by the terrible living conditions, which contrast with the postscarcity society of the Federation. They find food, housing, new clothing, and even employment in a local mission for the homeless, run by a social worker named Edith Keeler (Joan Collins). Kirk and Keeler start to become romantically involved, even though Keeler knows that something is "odd" about her two new charges. But Keeler too is somewhat odd both from the perspective of Kirk and Spock and of the Cold War–era viewers of the episode; she represents views from a progressivist pre–World War II America that envisioned a move toward socialism, a move largely derailed by the war against the Nazis and the subsequent Cold War. In a speech she gives to her mission's residents, she envisions a world in which people work together to eliminate poverty and hunger, eventually traveling to the moon and beyond. She is describing, essentially, the world of the Federation.[4] Through his ongoing research into the history of the time, however, Spock, a cold rationalist, realizes that Keeler's vision won't lead to the development of the Federation: one possible timeline has her conferring with President Franklin Roosevelt to keep the United States out of the looming Second World War, a move that allows the Nazis to win and thus destroys all future hope of the Federation emerging; the other timeline has her tragically hit by a car and dying, but this timeline preserves the future that creates Kirk and Spock's reality. Spock surmises that McCoy must have saved Edith from dying, resulting in the disappearance of the Federation. In a moving scene, Kirk and

Spock find McCoy just as Edith is about to be hit by a car, and Kirk prevents McCoy from saving her. We as viewers are clearly meant to empathize with Kirk's self-sacrifice—a sacrifice that restores not only his history and timeline but also preserves Edith's utopian vision of the future.

While superb science fiction storytelling, "City on the Edge of Forever" encapsulates the contradictory movements of the original *Star Trek* series. Edith Keeler's vision is the right one—hopeful and utopian—and she puts her vision into practice through her work directing the mission. At the same time, however, she must die to preserve that vision, one that, in the narrative logic of the story, can only potentially come to fruition on the other side of a devastating and bloody war (not to mention the first use of atomic weaponry) that will prove America victorious. This episode, emblematic of much of the series, thus forwards a deliberately hopeful politics of peace and cooperation built on a background of militarization that continues to linger in the stories and the hierarchical social structures of the *Enterprise*.

The Next Generation (*TNG*; 1987–1994) renewed the franchise, drawing from the success of the films that had extended the fandom for the original *Star Trek* crew and ultimately supporting four films featuring the new crew,[5] beginning with the crossover film *Generations* (1994), which linked the two casts across time. Like the original series, it relied on an episodic structure typical of television at the time, although it moved toward story arcs in later seasons, starting with two-part season cliffhangers and eventually using paired episodes for any major storyline, consistent with ongoing industry shifts between the 1980s and 1990s. It sought to evoke the original series yet also convey a sense of progress in the ninety years that have elapsed between the end of Captain Kirk's tour and the beginning of Captain Picard's (Patrick Stewart): the pilot episode depicts Picard's initial voyage on the ship, and he gets to know his new crew alongside the audience.[6] As with the original series, the crew is designed to emphasize the inclusive, multicultural liberal future, but without the emphasis on multinational diversity, since Earth is presumed to have been long since unified. This crew includes a half-human/half-Betazoid ship's counselor, Deanna Troi (Marina Sirtis); a Klingon, Worf (Michael Dorn), albeit one raised on Earth by humans; a blind crew member able to see via a technology, Geordi La Forge (LeVar Burton); and a sentient android, Data (Brent Spiner). Season 2 introduced Guinan (Whoopi Goldberg), an

FIGURE 1.3 Some of the crew from *Star Trek: The Next Generation*: "Encounter at Farpoint," season 1, episode 1.

El-Aurian, a race spread out across the galaxy, long-lived, and capable of mysterious insight. Guinan offered a positive representation of an African American cast member but also falls into a stereotype that associates Black people with magic. It also introduces several new species of humanoids, including the acquisitive Ferengi (who embody anti-Semitic stereotypes), whose commitment to profit contrasts strikingly with the Federation's postscarcity utopianism to demonstrate the persistence of countercultural ideals in this Reagan-era series.

Overwhelmingly *TNG* promotes an identification with duty and the high-minded values of the Federation, and although there are ongoing storylines about the crew's personal lives and friendships, they remain in the background for the most part, something that gradually shifts in later seasons. Consistent with any long-running series, the crew does develop and change over time, but their upright identities as Starfleet members never change—even in several storylines where Worf explores his Klingon ancestry, for example, he always defaults to Federation values. The emphasis on duty, honor, justice, fairness, and rule of law that lies at the heart of so many episodes of this series goes a long way to establishing the Federation ethos so important to devoted fans, as considered in the documentary series *Trekkies* (1997). Although the original series was founded on similar values, Kirk was a captain better known for his swashbuckling heroics, often in defiance of policy; Picard, on the other hand, is defined by his equanimity, erudition, and insistence on protocol. The powerful and life-shaping identification with Starfleet values articulated by fans in *Trekkies* captures the power of the education of desire through the public pedagogy of SF television.

TNG balances between updating and expanding the Star Trek world and paying homage to the original: both Spock and Scotty (James Doohan) make guest appearances. Although allegiances have shifted, the Cold War world order framework remains in place, and the Federation's main role is to prevent encroachments by hostile species, chiefly Romulans and the Borg in *TNG*. Although arcs are now dominant in television narrative, *TNG* uses the standalone episode to powerful effect, and several episodes have become celebrated. For example, "Darmok" (S5E2) is a first-contact story that depicts the difficulty of establishing communication with a species whose language relies on allusion.[7] The emotionally powerful and elegiac "The Inner Light" (S5E25) sees Picard experientially living an entire lifetime as a member of a now extinct species, although only hours pass in his timeline. Both "The Measure of a Man" (S2E9) and "The Quality of Life" (S6E9) raise questions about artificial life and its capacity for self-determination. Fans were disappointed at the refusal to include any queer characters on the series, but several episodes do interrogate heteronormativity, including "The Offspring" (S3E16), "The Host" (S4E23), and "The Outcast" (S5E17).[8] Yet there are serious missteps too, most notoriously "Code of Honor" (S1E3), which featured a storyline about a "tribal" race—played entirely by African American actors—who attempt to kidnap the blond, white security officer Tasha Yar (Denise Crosby), thereby reinforcing racist stereotypes about the dangerousness of Black masculinity.

The most memorable episodes of this series, however, are undoubtedly those focused on Picard's encounters with new enemies, the Borg in "The Best of Both Worlds" (S3E26, S4E1) and the Cardassians in "Chain of Command" (S6E10, S6E11). The appearance of the collective Borg, who assimilate all species they encounter in their machine-like hive mind, turning humanoid bodies into automatons, is alarming. Their technological power easily overwhelms Federation defenses at first, and within moments of their initial attack they have managed to kidnap Picard and turn him into a drone spokesperson they call Locutus. Given Picard's role as the moral center for Federation values, there is considerable impact in scenes of him as Locutus announcing the Borg axiom "Resistance is futile." The Borg deem any values pronounced in opposition to their relentless accumulation as "irrelevant," and it is chilling to see the figure of Picard-as-Locutus naming Starfleet values such. Yet Federation victory is made possible by contact with the "real" Picard beneath Locutus, beginning a number of Borg-centric narratives about the inevitable triumph of humanistic values that continues through other later Star Trek series. Picard's encounter with the Cardassians is equally emotionally powerful. Caught while on an undercover mission, he is detained and tortured not merely for information but also to break his spirit: he is repeatedly asked to state that five lights are visible, when only four appear. In the denouement, a Federation victory results in him being returned to the *Enterprise*, but in their final moments together, his captor tells him instead that the Federation has lost and that he must choose between the rest of his life in torment or capitulation to the five lights. The truth is revealed, and Picard defiantly announces "there are four lights" before leaving, but he later admits to Troi that not only was he on the verge of submission but that, for a moment, he "believed" he saw five lights.

As these celebrated episodes demonstrate, authoritarianism is the greatest threat to Federation values, reflecting the optimism of an era that saw the end of the Soviet Union as a sign of the better and more united future to come. The absence of the Federation espionage agency Section 31 and dark Mirror Universe episodes in *TNG* also speaks to its ethos of confidence about the future. Later series, especially *Enterprise* (2001–2005), would increasingly have to contend with the failure of such optimism and the existence of authoritarian and xenophobic ideologies within America, and thus a darker sense of what the future might hold.

STAR TREK AS SYNECDOCHE: UTOPIA QUESTIONED

By the late twentieth century, the era of American imperial expansion may have ended, but not its *cultural* imperialism and colonization. In significant ways, both the original *Star Trek* and *Star Trek: The Next Generation* played out the cultural exportation of liberal humanist values even if the era of land (or planet) grabbing had subsided. John Rieder's point in *Colonialism and the Emergence of Science Fiction* (2008) is well taken: "Colonial geography continues to provide an imaginary framework for much science fiction throughout the twentieth century, especially in the genre of space opera, where the most common of strategies is that of treating outer space, in effect, as an infinitely extended ocean that separates exotically diverse continents, not radically different worlds."[9] However, the next series installment in the Star Trek universe, *Deep Space Nine* (*DS9*, 1993–1999), took something of a detour on the path of ongoing cultural expansion. If the previous two series were still boldly going, *DS9* was boldly, sometimes painfully, staying, its action primarily taking place on one space station at the far reaches of Federation space. *DS9* expanded and challenged some of the Star Trek megatext's familiar plots, character arcs, and narrative assumptions.

In many ways, *Deep Space Nine* deepened Star Trek's commitment to diversity, both in terms of actors hired to play roles and in the characters they represented. The series' cast was famously led by Avery Brooks, the first African American to play a leading role in a nighttime dramatic series on American television. His character, Captain Benjamin Sisko, is a complex and nuanced individual, having lost his wife in the Borg attack on Earth and now raising his son as a single father. He is joined by a strong female first officer, Kira Nerys (Nana Visitor), a Bajoran; a shapeshifting chief of security, Odo (René Auberjonois); a North African chief medical officer, Dr. Bashir (Alexander Siddig); and even a bar-owning Ferengi, Quark (Armin Shimerman). The characters' various backgrounds and races often play significant roles in the creation of dramatic conflict. Even more interestingly, viewers are introduced to Jadzia Dax (Terry Farrell), the chief science officer, who also happens to be a Trill, a humanoid species that lives in a symbiotic relationship with an entity called a symbiont, which is transferred from one Trill host to another, remembering all of its past lives. The symbiont (Dax) moves from one gendered body to another, so people who knew Dax in an earlier body might have known them as female *or* male. For instance, Sisko knew Dax when it was in a symbiotic relationship with an older Trill man; now, reunited with Dax, Sisko frequently refers to Jadzia, an attractive young woman, as "old man." The Trill species thus allows for some interesting expansion of consciousness around the fluidity and constructedness of gender. In all of these ways, then, from race to gender, *DS9* continued to push boldly on frontiers of identity. Critics and scholars noted such early on; Robin Roberts discusses how "*Deep Space Nine* advances the depiction of sexual orientation, including an intense lesbian kiss[, and in] its use of Odo, a Changeling, who, like Data, functions as an isolate among humans, the series explores issues of race."[10]

The primary narrative conflicts of *Deep Space Nine* center on darker dimensions of interstellar politics—politics that paralleled, in the 1990s, growing social unease in the aftermath of the Cold War with the legacies of colonialism. The station, Deep Space Nine, is situated near the planet Bajor, which, when the series opens, has just been liberated from the rule of the warlike and brutal neighboring Cardassians. The station too had been under Cardassian jurisdiction but, after the liberation of Bajor, is now run by the Federation (we see Sisko take command of Deep Space Nine in the series' first episode), which will act as mediators and protectors of Bajor as the Bajorans decide if they want to join the Federation. Tensions between the Bajorans and Cardassians, some of whom still remain on the station, are often intense, with violent conflict frequent. Sisko is constantly challenged not just to keep the peace but also to understand the resentments and anger of the newly freed Bajorans, long subjected to oppression. Part of what animates and even underlies the conflicts between Bajor and Cardassia is the proximity of Bajor, and the station, to a wormhole that provides relatively quick access to the Gamma Quadrant, on the other side of the galaxy. The wormhole, much like the fabled Northwest Passage, promises potentially easy access to significant resources, so control over it is strategically, politically, and economically attractive. However, the Gamma Quadrant is largely run by a race of shapeshifters called the Dominion, who have subjugated multiple species in the creation of their own empire; the Dominion uses the wormhole to launch an invasion of the Alpha Quadrant, resulting in a long and devastating war whose story occupies much of *DS9*'s middle and late seasons.

All of these conflicts highlight the devastating legacies of imperial expansion and colonial subjugation, almost all of which are driven by the desire for control over resources. By shifting focus from peaceful exploration to the realities of occupation and its aftermaths, *Deep Space Nine* radically expands the dramatic territory of Star Trek. It also highlights the extent to which, in the aftermath of the Cold War, former colonies and formerly subjugated individuals have intensified their own search for justice and equity. In many ways, Sisko's race, his visual presence as a Black man, and his African American heritage (often underscored through references to his family history in New Orleans, where his family runs a Creole restaurant), highlights not just attention to race but also the problem of racism and its legacies. Personally, Sisko's commitment to the ideals of the Federation is constantly put to the test. Is the Federation's interest in Bajor, for instance, an expression of its humanistic commitment to value and protect Bajor's people, or is it politically motivated by having control over the wormhole and thus gaining a substantial advantage in this part of space?

Such inner conflicts, particularly as they are tied to race, are beautifully played out in one of *Deep Space Nine*'s finest episodes, "Far Beyond the Stars" (S6E13). In this episode, Sisko is visited by his father (Brock Peters), in whom he confides that he is thinking about quitting Starfleet. He's experienced too many difficulties, too much death, and the long war with the Dominion is taking its toll. Perhaps as a function of his stress, or perhaps guided by the Bajoran spirits who have identified him as their prophet, Sisko collapses and begins having visions. He is now in 1950s New York, struggling to make a living as a writer for a science fiction pulp magazine. All of the major and recurring actors in *DS9* play roles in this hallucinatory drama, as though Sisko is experiencing a kind of Oz dream. Tensions escalate when Sisko, called Benny in the dream, is given an image of Deep Space Nine and told by his editor to write a story about it. Benny creates a narrative based on Sisko's experiences—a strong Black captain with a strong female first officer. While Benny's colleagues and even his editor think it's a remarkable story, the editor won't publish it; no one wants to read about "Negroes in space." Benny's wife thinks he should give up writing science fiction and focus on their dream of opening up a restaurant, but Benny persists, writing several sequels to his story. A street preacher (played by the same actor playing Sisko's father) encourages him to stay the course and write his stories. Ultimately, the editor agrees to publish one of Benny's stories—provided that the narrative is shifted so readers understand that the plot of the story is just a dream, the dream of a young Negro boy. Feeling victorious, even with this concession, Benny wants to celebrate, but tragedy occurs when a young Black man in the neighborhood (played by the same actor who plays Sisko's son, Cirroc

Lofton) is shot and killed by police, ostensibly while trying to break into a car. Benny then learns that the magazine's publisher is not going to print his story and actually orders his firing. Benny breaks down, sobbing and yelling in anger that he, too, is a man, a human being, and that he might be dismissed as a Black man but his idea—his idea of a better future—cannot be destroyed. On Deep Space Nine, Sisko wakes up, recommitted to his purpose of serving Starfleet. *Deep Space Nine* thus reimagines peaceful space exploration as a commitment to social justice and a better future, even if the series lapses into the problematics of liberalism.

The power of the episode lies in its frank engagement with the histories and legacies of racism and its willingness to note the impact of racism on the history of science fiction storytelling. Sisko is reminded of his own race's struggle for equity and justice, not to mention acknowledgment and recognition. But that reminder does not result in a happy ending for Benny, and Sisko is not promised any resolution of the various crises that beset his station or the larger Federation. The force of the hallucination, a kind of Blochian daydream, perhaps, lies in its exhortation to continue fighting—and hoping—for a better future, even if such isn't imminently realizable. "Far Beyond the Stars" originally aired a decade after the end of the Cold War, a time that saw renewed calls for racial and economic justice, and it turns viewers' attention both to the histories and the ongoing struggles within a liberal humanist framework. The steady expansion of enfranchisement, rights, and protection is difficult work—so difficult that Sisko questions its value, even if he ultimately recommits to it.

In significant ways, the next Star Trek series, *Voyager* (1995–2001), which overlaps with the production and airing of *Deep Space Nine*, intensifies the interrogation of the values of the Federation. At the same time, *Voyager* marks something of a "retreat" in the Star Trek canon—both metaphorically and literally. The basic premise of the series is that a ship, *Voyager*, sent to track down members of the Maquis, a resistance group, is unexpectedly transported by an alien device across the galaxy to the far side of the Delta Quadrant. Stranded, with no way to communicate with Starfleet, the crew of *Voyager* face the daunting prospect of traveling back to the Alpha Quadrant, a journey that will last about seventy-five years and take them through hostile territory held by the Borg. This narrative arc allows the crew to encounter a host of aliens and alien cultures in the now-familiar episodic format of other Star Trek series, pitting the Starfleet characters against new challenges. In a further twist, some members of the stranded crew are Maquis, a renegade group of Federation colonists who fought the Cardassians after a treaty between the Federation and the Cardassian Union redrew the boundary between the two powers and left them within Cardassian territory. The Federation considers them outlaws, even terrorists. The crew of the *Voyager* finds themselves thrown into the Delta Quadrant with the very Maquis they had been tracking, and the two groups must find a way to work together to get home. The Maquis, led by Chakotay (Robert Beltran), agree to Captain Kathryn Janeway's (Kate Mulgrew) proposal that the groups abide by Starfleet regulations, with Chakotay becoming her first officer. Several episodes and story arcs deal with the tensions between the two crews, intensifying the challenge to the Starfleet and Federation values that sit at the heart of this series.

While *Voyager* certainly offers numerous episodes of discovery and exploration—which remain key components of Starfleet's mission—the overriding mission of the series concerns getting home, returning to safety, in effect reversing the previous Star Trek series' mandate. To boldly go becomes a desperate wish to return. This aspect of the series might parallel contemporaneous real-world American (and largely Western) moves to decolonize—perhaps less as a retreat from colonialist values (economic and otherwise) but from the end of the Cold War and a sense that America had less of a call to "police" the spread of socialism. While *Voyager* might seem to value "home," then, numerous episodes, like those of *Deep Space Nine*, nonetheless offer some of the deepest interrogations yet of Federation values and liberal humanism—as though the end of Cold War hostilities and the putative "end of history" allowed room for more intense self-reflection.

Some of those values are clearly forwarded and upheld, even developed and defended, throughout *Voyager*. As Robin Roberts notes, "*Voyager* finally realizes Gene Roddenberry's vision of a female space captain. In its inclusion of a Native American, an Asian American, and a woman who is half-Klingon, half-human, as well as a Vulcan played by an African American actor, the series contains a more complicated racial mixture." *Voyager* maintains and extends Star Trek's overall commitment to diversity, augmenting it not just with a diverse cast but by addressing the diversity of the actual characters, as much as and perhaps even more so than in *Deep Space Nine*. Roberts even argues that what is important about *Voyager* is that it "departs from [earlier iterations of Star Trek] in its depiction of female scientists," specifically in presenting "a version of science that embraces feminist ideas about how women can alter the practice of science."[11] We frequently see Janeway balancing pragmatic needs to survive in the Delta Quadrant with the values of the Federation against cultural interference. Such conflicts and dramas even extend to her own personal life: she, like many of the crew, finds solace on the holodeck, interacting with highly sophisticated artificial intelligences that become, sometimes, more than entertaining diversions but instead often friends, even lovers. Janeway finds herself giving up her authority to control and manipulate some of these intelligences so that they can have their own full and independent existences—a feminist valuing of consent.

In many ways, *Voyager* is not just about getting home but about the home that the crew constructs to survive together. They become—and sometimes even refer to themselves—as less a crew and more a family. Mutual care and understanding are paramount. Lisa Yaszek has previously coined the phrase "galactic suburbia" to refer to the kind of mid-twentieth-century science fiction, often written by women, that dealt with domestic issues, gender, family structure, and other issues of "home," which were being radically transformed by scientific, technological, and political changes and advances. We might use "galactic suburbia" to describe the overall story arc of *Voyager*—a narrative about the complexities of forging and maintaining a survivable home, one that can accommodate numerous internal differences as well as numerous external threats.

Some of *Voyager*'s best episodes probe those external threats and how they test the Federation's commitment to liberal humanism. In "Remember" (S3E6), the *Voyager* crew receives help from the humanoid Enarans, a race that can telepathically transfer knowledge. They seem a peaceful, honest, and forthright species, glad to assist the crew with technology and other aid. At the same time, B'Elanna Torres (Roxann Dawson), the ship's half-Klingon/half-human chief engineer, starts to have strange and vivid dreams in which she is the daughter of a high-ranking Enaran who advocates for "expansion and colonization" through terraforming; to complicate matters, though, she's in love with someone of whom her father disapproves, Dathan (Charles Esten), a member of a faction, the Regressives, that radically rejects most advanced technologies. The Regressives are being relocated, often forcibly, and we learn that they are frequently being killed, some by being burned alive. By the end of the episode, we discover that B'Elanna's dreams are actually the memories of one of the Enarans, an elderly woman sharing her memories without mutual consent. She wants to reveal the truth of what has happened to the Regressives, a truth long denied by the Enarans and kept from their descendants. She herself had ultimately turned against the Regressives and is trying to alleviate her guilt by forcing her people to confront their hidden past. As with *Deep Space Nine*'s "Far Beyond the Stars," this episode substantively approaches the lingering legacies of discrimination and intolerance. But it also directly questions the value of ongoing technological advancement. Having *Voyager*'s chief engineer receive the memories of the repression of the Regressives, with B'Elanna becoming a defender of their memory, suggests at the very least some ambivalence about technological progress as an unassailable good—and in the process, one of the cornerstones of Star Trek's mythos is held up for interrogation and critique. While the original series seems to assume that once we have great tech, we'll have postscarcity, and then all our social problems will melt away, this episode asks viewers to consider the very real possibility that ethical and social progress will somehow run parallel to technological progress—and not necessarily mirror each other.

A similar kind of metacritique of Star Trek occurs in the episode "Nemesis" (S4E4, originally aired September 24, 1997), in which Chakotay is stranded on a jungle planet and captured by the humanoid Vori, a species at war with the Kradin, whom they constantly refer to as their "nemesis." Out of touch with his ship, Chakotay tries to find a way to get word to his crew, depending on the Vori for assistance. As he learns of their war, Chakotay tries to be neutral, offering the soldiers with whom he talks other ways to think about difference: perhaps the "nemesis" is frightened as well, and perhaps the war is a misunderstanding. Chakotay argues that people on his planet, Earth, try to negotiate and seek peaceful solutions—a stance certainly forwarded by the Federation but still odd coming out of the mouth of a Maquis commander, as well as a character clearly marked as a Native American, one whose people have been brutally slaughtered by colonizing whites. Chakotay, as he mouths the liberal humanism of the Federation, seems to be suffering from multiple forms of cultural amnesia.

Over time, though, as Chakotay learns of the Vori's fight and sees how the Kradin desecrate the bodies of the Vori, he begins to side with them, ultimately fighting alongside them. He remembers his own fight against the Cardassians and comes to empathize with their struggle. In a strange twist, Chakotay is then captured by the Kradin, who have been working with the *Voyager* crew to find Chakotay, and we learn that the Kradin refer to the Vori as *their* "nemesis." While Chakotay has come to believe that the Kradin are vile beasts, it turns out that the Vori have actually been brainwashing Chakotay in a training simulation to help them fight their war. The Vori are every bit as savage, brutal, deceitful, and vicious as they say their enemies are.

"Nemesis" is ultimately about the education of hostility, the training of people to fear difference, to the point where an outsider, like Chakotay, begins to fear and become violent toward an "other." Certainly, as with other episodes discussed, "Nemesis" dramatically treats the legacies of intolerance and racial violence, with Chakotay poignantly saying about his own newfound prejudice against the Kradin, "I wish it were as easy to stop hating as it is to start." At the same time, though, intolerance and even racism are figured in this episode as pure social constructs, fully denaturalized, and the implication is that if they are cultivated, they can be unlearned and changed. However, read in the larger context of the Star Trek narrative, this "unlearning" must be understood as an ongoing process. We see Chakotay struggle with the fear and hatred he has so quickly learned, which suggests that the rationalized optimism characteristic of early Star Trek is still subject to regression, even after Federation citizens are supposedly "enlightened." The episode shows the importance of the ongoing need to educate desire toward valuing difference, as well as the ease with which utopianism can slip into the backward-looking fearful nostalgia that Bloch warns against. In a way, we are at the furthest reaches of the series'—and of Star Trek's—interrogation of difference and the possibilities of the reeducation of intolerance.

The fact that so many episodes deal with hallucinations of various kinds (Sisko's dream, B'Elanna's implanted memories, Chakotay's simulation experience) suggests the need to think differently, to open up new vistas and alternative visions of both history and the present, not to mention the future. The emphasis on the hallucinatory in many of these episodes across the series is suggestive of the Blochian daydream, a desire to continue to imagine possibilities.

The utopian impulse completely changes with *Enterprise*, which aired from 2001 to 2005, its production beginning before the 9/11 terrorist attack but quickly becoming marked, if not dominated, by it in the series' development of plots and character arcs. In terms of the history and chronology of the Star Trek universe, *Enterprise* takes viewers back to before the founding of the Federation. Starfleet has been established, and humans are taking their first tentative steps into exploring the galaxy after the invention of the warp drive, but the Federation is not yet imagined. The Vulcans, the first aliens to make contact with humanity, are assisting humans, acting as guides and mentors, in a relationship that is often resented by many humans, including the captain of the new warp-capable ship, *Enterprise*, Jonathan Archer (Scott Bakula). His primary science officer is the Vulcan T'Pol (Jolene Blalock), with whom Archer has an often tempestuous relationship as she tries to caution humans from not venturing too hastily into contact with other alien species. But the crew of the *Enterprise* is intent on exploring, and the first two seasons of the series present some of humanity's first steps into the Alpha Quadrant as they learn to navigate not just the stars but also interstellar relations. All of the guidelines of the Federation, such as the Prime Directive, have yet to be invented, so conflicts around what constitutes appropriate intervention (if it is ever appropriate) form a significant part of the plot arcs of the first two seasons. In reading *Enterprise* from our contemporary vantage point in the early 2020s, it is hard for us not to see this series as somewhat "retrograde," the human resentment of Vulcan superiority paralleling growing American resentment about its global leadership steadily coming under scrutiny, if not actually also deteriorating.

The drama significantly intensifies in the third season, developed in the aftermath of the 9/11 terror attacks and airing in 2003–2004. An alien species, the Xindi, have launched a surprise and seemingly unprovoked attack on Earth, using a weapon of mass destruction to carve a channel between Florida and Venezuela, resulting in the death of seven million humans. The *Enterprise* and its crew are sent to find out why this attack has occurred, and their mission constitutes the bulk of the series' third

FIGURE 1.4 A scene of torture from *Star Trek: Enterprise*:
"Anomaly," season 3, episode 2.

season. Archer discovers that the Xindi, intent on destroying Earth, are
in the process of creating an even more powerful weapon. The Xindi, we
learn, are actually being manipulated by another species, which has convinced the Xindi that the future Federation will kill them, so they should
be destroyed now to prevent its founding. In actuality, this species, called
the Sphere Builders, are themselves at danger of being destroyed by the
future Federation as they are interdimensional beings trying to gain a
foothold in and colonize the galaxy. A complex Temporal War serves as
the backdrop for such conflicts, adding an *X-Files*-type air of background
conspiracy to *Enterprise*.

When the third season aired, the Xindi terror attack and their war on
Earth, as well as the *Enterprise*'s search for the even more devastating
weapon of mass destruction, certainly seemed timely, paralleling the
events of the early twenty-first century (not just the 9/11 attacks but the
subsequent wars in Afghanistan and Iraq and the search for WMDs). Even
more complexly, we can read the initial Xindi attack as reminiscent of
many American strategies of preemptively interfering in other nations,
such as the invasion of Iraq in search of WMDs. Despite such possible
complexities, the series offers the military response of Starfleet as admittedly difficult but necessary. The members of the *Enterprise*'s crew, particularly Archer, face tough decisions about how to proceed, and some
significant plotlines consider the viability and justification of torture
in gaining information. In a set of shocking scenes, Archer actually
authorizes torture, something that would later be in stark contrast to

Federation policy, but he wagers that the ends justify the means in this dire case.

Eventually, the Xindi are repelled, notably with the aid of a Xindi scientist who is convinced that his people are being manipulated. Earth proceeds in developing relations with other species, and we see the beginnings of an alliance form. Indeed, the Xindi conflict forces humans to partner not just with Vulcans but also Andorians, the traditional enemies of the Vulcans, just to survive. In the process, Earth presents itself as not just able to form alliances but also to broker peace among former enemies—a position that the United States has attempted to hold, this time projected onto the entire planet. The series' final season, particularly its penultimate two-part episode, dramatizes the emergence of Earth in interstellar politics curiously set against a background of ethnonationalists trying to stop it from happening.

The first part, "Demons" (S4E20, originally aired May 6, 2005), shows us Earth's minister, Nathan Samuels (Harry Groener), leading a conference of aliens just starting to form an alliance, both for mutual economic benefit and to help protect one another from mutual threats. A major obstacle to this alliance, however, is Terra Prime, an Earth-based resistance group that does not want humans to form any alliances with aliens or even for aliens to be on Earth and—an important point—possibly interbreeding with humans. Their prerogative represented the contemporaneous hostile feeling of some Americans about immigration in the immediate aftermath of the 9/11 attacks, including the presence not just of foreigners but especially Muslims in the United States. Terra Prime's radicality has perversely led the group to clone a human/Vulcan child—the very first such offspring of the two species—from two *Enterprise* crew members' DNA; Terra Prime presents such a child as an "abomination," using it to stir up resentment, fear, and animosity toward aliens and the threat of making the human race "impure." Terra Prime then takes over an array on Mars used to divert comets and uses it as a weapon to threaten vessels in the system unless all aliens leave.

While the members of the crew of the *Enterprise* are ultimately successful in defeating Terra Prime, these scenes—and the episode in its entirety—suggest that military decisions are fully independent of civilian control. "Demons" actually begins with the crew of the *Enterprise* expressing concern that their role in the creation of alliances between

Earth and other species was being diminished, with civilian leaders taking center stage; at the end of "Terra Prime" (S4E21), it is not Samuels who speaks forcefully about the importance of alliances and mutual aid but Archer, the captain, a military leader.

With such gestures, and in an interesting deployment of "retcon" (the retroactive creation of narrative continuity within a larger story arc), *Enterprise* makes clear that the origin of the future Federation is primarily *military*. The Federation, in this telling of the Star Trek mythos, emerges in response to the Xindi terror attack. Its origin is not an impulse for peaceful exploration but rather military defense. Even more, while previous episodes in the other series often showed Federation citizens grappling with the consequences of history and conflicts in values as a set of *internal* debates about how to be in the galaxy, *Enterprise* fully externalizes threats to humanity and, by extension, the future Federation. The introspection and critical reflection that was beginning to characterize *Deep Space Nine* and *Voyager* are replaced with jingoistic military posturing. What is only suggested in the original *Star Trek*'s adoption of military ranks for its boldly going crew is literalized in *Enterprise*'s narration of the beginnings of the Federation. If *Voyager* is a retreat from liberal humanist values, then *Enterprise* is a regression.

STAR TREK IN THE STREAMING ERA

The two most recent Star Trek series, *Discovery* and *Picard* (2020–), have emerged under the streaming era's markedly different conditions, as discussed in the introduction. In some ways, there was less industry change in the roughly twenty years between the end of the original *Star Trek* and *The Next Generation* than there was in the twelve years that separates the conclusion of *Enterprise* from the emergence of *Discovery*. *Discovery* was not simply produced in the streaming era but was also launched as a flagship series to drive subscription to the newly released CBS All Access service. CBS has become the home of all new Star Trek.[12] What's more, the longevity of Star Trek overall is predicated on its early adoption of what would now be called a transmedia franchise. Thus, as we analyze the differences between *Discovery* and earlier Star Trek series, we

need to keep in mind that these differences reflect not merely new ideological contexts to which the series speaks but also the shifting political
economies of the television industry.[13]

Within this framework, *Discovery* walks a careful line between being
enough like the familiar Star Trek beloved to fans to drive subscribers to
the new service while at the same time expressing the darker, post-9/11
political imaginary that we saw emerge with *Enterprise*. It continues the
trend of seeking to diversify the cast and takes the novel step of making
its focal character not the Federation leader but instead a more junior officer and one who—at least at first—is a criminal within the Federation
because she disobeyed orders and thus started a war. Michael Burnham
(Sonequa Martin-Green) eventually finds her way back into the familiar
Federation ethos in her idealistic speech in the season 1 finale regarding
how the Federation will not be moved from its values, no matter the tactics of its enemy. Yet this comes after a season in which we see the Federation at war, not pursuing diplomatic or scientific missions, and we
eventually learn that Captain Lorca (Jason Isaacs), who has overseen a cultural transformation of their science vessel into a military flagship,
proves to be a Terran from the "evil" Mirror Universe.[14] *Discovery* pulls
back from being the jingoistic "anti–Star Trek" that caused so many fans
to reject *Enterprise*, but it also insists that the world remains a darker place
than that envisioned by the 1960s-era optimism that inspired the original series. In addition to the revelation of Lorca's true identity, this series
relies heavily on storylines about the secret agency within the Federation,
Section 31, to which the Terran version of Captain Philippa Georgiou
(Michelle Yeoh; the Federation version dies in the pilot)—a genocidal
empress in her reality—is recruited.

Discovery reads less as a movement away from the liberal humanist values that informed Roddenberry's vision and more as a critique of the
inherent contradictions that have always haunted its utopianism: the military ranks and procedures that define the Federation, the default uni-
versalism of heteronormative whiteness that undermines attempts to be
more diverse, and honorable officers who leave no room for stories about
baser human motivations and frailties.[15] As noted earlier, successive Star
Trek series have often continued to push this point of the possible limitations of the Federation, from Picard's struggles against bureaucratic myopia to *DS9*'s reinvention of the Mirror Universe as a space in which our

familiar characters appear as revolutionaries against an unjust order rather than as "evil" opposites of their "honorable" Federation selves.[16] As Michael notes, on either side of the Mirror people start out with "the same drives, the same needs," and it is only historical contingency that differentiates the good from the bad iteration (S1E12). *Discovery* finally offers an openly gay couple, Stamets (Anthony Rapp) and Hugh (Wilson Cruz), something long demanded by franchise fans,[17] and although they briefly fall into the dreaded territory of the inevitable death of one partner, a narrative about another dimension enables the couple to be reunited in a storyline that insists on the complexity of finding their way back to each other after one has endured a transformative, traumatic experience. Season 2 features a version of Spock (Ethan Peck) revealed to be dyslexic, and the resolution of its puzzle narrative relies on the style of thinking his disability enables, a relationship to disability pointedly different from the corrective default typical for a character such as Geordi (this failure to critique the normative also informs Data's obsession with passing as human). Relationships take center stage in much of the series' narrative, reminiscent of the dynamics of *Voyager*, but here the personal too is portrayed with the same darker tone that characterizes the political narratives.

Overwhelmingly, *Discovery* conveys a desire to endorse the ideals that make the Federation so beloved by its fans alongside a pointed recognition that this goal cannot be achieved by erasing cultural specificity, often present in earlier series merely as the superficial difference that is celebrated in liberal multiculturalism. There is less ethnocentrism than in the original *Star Trek* and *Enterprise*, to be sure, but here the Klingons are not straw-figure adversaries but instead individuals worried about the loss of their culture—and with good reason. Ash Tyler (Shazad Latif) stands out as a particularly innovative character: Ash was a Federation individual, but he died in the war against the Klingons; his mind is overlaid on a Klingon warrior, Voq, whose body is transformed to pass as human. The resultant person is never fully human or fully Klingon: his memories of each individual past are not segregated into two neatly differentiated personalities but instead produce a single, troubled individual who, for example, remembers his Klingon lover's touch as violation, experiencing memories of his transformative operation as if he were a human tortured by Klingons.[18] Yet there are familiar Trek narratives here as well:

struggles with the Prime Directive and stories of cultures transformed toward more just societies, such as the Kelpians, who learn that the putatively natural hierarchy among sentient species on their planet is ideological rather than biological, prompting a revolution that transforms their world (S2E6).

Season 2 tries to link more tightly with established Trek characters and offers an extended storyline for Christopher Pike (Anson Mount), the original captain who was replaced by Kirk following network notes on an unaired pilot (Pike's denouement in the original *Star Trek* is skillfully woven into several episodes here). Yet even as *Discovery* nods to the past, it also opens its first episode with a voiceover not about going "where no man has gone before" but instead about an African myth of how "we have always looked to the stars to discover who we are" (S2E1). Despite ongoing interspecies tensions, the main adversary is an AI seeking to supersede humans, and the final climactic battle requires even the Klingons to briefly ally with the Federation, anticipating their later inclusion in the Federation by the time of *The Next Generation*. Ultimately, it proves too difficult to negotiate between homage to canon and the desire to tell new kinds of stories for a generation no longer at ease with the default whiteness of liberal humanism or the colonial underpinnings of space exploration, and thus at the end of season 2 the series launches forward almost a thousand years, beyond any extant Star Trek timeline, into a future where the Federation has collapsed.

The future that Michael and the crew of the *Discovery* find themselves in is politically fractured—akin to the present that many U.S. viewers have found themselves in during and as a consequence of the Trump presidency. About 120 years before their arrival, a disaster called the Burn occurred in which most dilithium (the primary substance used to enable warp engines) exploded, killing countless millions on ships and disabling most faster-than-light travel. Because of the scarcity of dilithium, the Federation fractures, reduced from several hundred planets to under forty. Earth is no longer the home of the Federation, and even the Vulcans have withdrawn to deal primarily with their reunification with the Romulans. Competing political entities arise, most notably the Emerald Chain, formed by several non-Terran species; it is primarily a mercantile network whose leader, Osyraa (Janet Kidder), names "capitalism" (S3E12): it is also

FIGURE 1.5 Star Trek's first openly gay couple, in *Discovery*.

brutal and savage, reliant on slavery and other forms of terror to maintain a semblance of order.

Michael and the crew undertake a series of adventures, both to discover
how the Burn occurred and to help the remaining fragments of the Federation rebuild. Episodes often center on the ideals of the Federation or
on its people as opposed to its colonial holdings. American viewers are
likely to understand the Federation in this third season of *Discovery* as a
stand-in for the contemporary decline of American hegemony and its
inability to uphold consistently its own proclaimed ideals of equality and
peace, while the Emerald Chain seems to represent the worst excesses of
capitalism. In the closing episodes of the season, with a new source of dilithium about to be made available or the possibility for *Discovery*'s spore
drive to become replicable, thus restoring quicker interstellar travel,
Osyraa and the Emerald Chain propose unification with the Federation,
including a willingness to abolish slavery and adopt Federation principles
such as the Prime Directive. The Federation's Admiral Vance (Oded Fehr),
a white man, considers the possibilities but only if Osyraa will stand trial

for the many crimes she has committed, including the imposition of slavery. She refuses, but all is not lost, as the Federation is victorious in the season's final battle with the Emerald Chain.

In many ways, this third season of *Discovery* plays to nostalgia for the older ideals of the Federation, while also worrying over the dominance of rampant capitalism in the contemporary era. But what is particularly interesting in this season, especially in the final episodes in which the Federation refuses to unite with the Emerald Chain, is the recognition that the past cannot simply be forgotten. Crimes must be accounted for, and criminals must be held accountable. The desire to move forward in peace, in other words, cannot turn a blind eye to the past. Vance's counterproposal to reunification is essentially a call for truth and reconciliation. It is telling that the representatives of capitalism in this season cannot quite hold themselves accountable for the atrocities committed in the name of economic expansion. It is also interesting that the creation of a narrative binary—nostalgia for the Federation versus the danger of rampant capitalism in the Emerald Chain—sidesteps holding the Federation accountable for *its* colonialist fantasies. *Discovery* longs for the cooperative collective of the Federation at its most idealistic, even if it cannot imagine a passage *through* capitalism toward such, except to vanquish the Emerald Chain in battle—a narrative solution that might feel good momentarily but does not offer a way to think through actual alternatives to contemporary problems of economic inequity, precarity, and injustice.

The more recent *Picard* faces a similar balancing act as it harks back to a beloved captain known, above all others, for his strict commitment to duty above personal gain and to the integrity of Starfleet values over his personal feelings about a situation. The storyline involves both Romulans and the Borg, two antagonists central to *The Next Generation*, but interestingly both are given more sympathetic treatment. The Borg appear not as the implacable force of assimilation but via the return of Hugh (Jonathan Del Arco), who, introduced to the idea of individuality in "I Borg" (*TNG*, S5E23), ultimately became the first lone Borg to recover his humanity, thus inspiring Picard's crew to abandon their plans to use him as a vector to introduce a genocidal virus into the Borg Collective. Seven of Nine (Jeri Ryan), from *Voyager*, also becomes a main cast member in *Picard*, a series that is about heroism outside of the Starfleet command structure: Picard has retired, and his new crew, recruited across several episodes in the first season, have also either separated from Starfleet or had never joined. By distancing the crew from Starfleet—but only to a degree—the series can both critique the limitations of the original series' liberal humanism while also celebrating the ideals that the franchise was intended to convey, always best embodied by Captain Picard (Kirk, while first, is more of a individualist renegade than an exemplar of high-minded virtue).

The first season's storyline is largely about reestablishing an idealistic vision of what the Federation could and should mean: Picard retired in pique over the Federation's refusal to rescue and relocate Romulan citizens threatened by their sun going supernova fourteen years before, and when he is questioned about these events in the pilot, he angrily insists he left because Starfleet "wasn't Starfleet anymore!" This new crew is more diverse than his previous one, not only in the inclusion of nonhuman characters and diverse casting, always a hallmark of Star Trek, but also in allowing more evidence of diverse cultures to shape the crew and their interactions, no longer all adhering to a universalized Federation default.[19] While Picard remains the archetype of high-minded Federation values, his tendency to act without consultation is frequently critiqued by his multiethnic crew, suggesting the recognition that Starfleet's stated values were always in conflict with its military structure. A more isolationist Federation has not only withdrawn from offering humanitarian assistance but has banned synthetic life following a terrorist attack on Mars, a clear allusion to the 9/11 attacks and their cultural effects. By the end of season 1, Picard has convinced the Federation to return to its earlier values and to protect a planet populated by synthetic beings from Romulan genocide— yet even the Romulans prove to have been motivated, ultimately, by a fear that the emergence of synthetic life would bring great harm to other species. The old binaries of clear good and evil no longer hold. Although the threat proves real, to an extent, Picard simultaneously proves that there is nothing inevitable about the path synthetic life will take. His new crew ultimately includes a synthetic being, but one who—unlike Data—easily passes as human, indeed believed herself to be human before the series' events, and so has no romantic ideas about humanity.

Picard is poised to reinvent Star Trek as a more complicated political allegory, renewing the optimism and idealism of the original *Star Trek* without its Western-centric myopia. It clearly makes allusions to political events of the past two decades, from the terror attack on Mars, to refugee crises, to skepticism about political leaders, a skepticism more and more common as polarization increases. It returns us to an ethos perhaps more like that of the 1990s, a willingness to doubt the intentions of government forces that characterized *The X-Files*, for example, a move away from the insistent patriotism of the immediate post-9/11 period that reflects the hardships of the 2008 economic crash and the shock of the 2016 election. Yet *Picard* does not turn to the conspiracy ethos of *The X-Files* or follow the dark narratives that dominate much twenty-first-century SF television. Instead, by reviving the principled figure of Picard, it also marks a return to a more optimistic voice, to a sense of urgency about renewing the ethos of the better future that is the hallmark of Star Trek, rather than conceding to the evident failures of the twenty-first century.

2

INVENTING SCIENCE FICTION TELEVISION
AS POLITICAL NARRATIVE

In many ways, the success of Ronald D. Moore's rebooted *Battlestar Galactica* cannot be separated from the shifts experienced in U.S. political culture in the wake of 9/11. The series directly paralleled the trauma of the surprise Cylon attack on humanity with the trauma of 9/11 in numerous examples, from saboteur sleeper Cylon agents embedded in the human community, to the use of torture, to humans as agents of terrorist attacks against a Cylon occupation, to locating the conflict in a difference of culture and especially religious belief (the Cylons are monotheists; humanity worships a Greek pantheon). The tone throughout is grim: humanity remains on a wartime footing, resources are scarce, technology must be improvised, and political differences are entrenched. Importantly, as the series continued, the narrative shifted from processing merely the distress of the 9/11 attacks to raising questions about the difficulties of living in an American society so radically changed by its response to the attacks. In the first season, humans use torture against a captured Cylon in "Flesh and Bone" (S1E8), insisting that a machine's capacity to experience pain is irrelevant; this episode also introduces the series' mythopoetic framework that "all of this has happened before, all of this will happen again," suggesting that humans and Cylons risk remaining trapped in a damaging cycle of vengeance forever. A celebrated arc in season 3, which aired in 2006 as the United States continued to occupy Iraq, puts the human characters in the position of insurgents fighting the occupation of their land by a superior military force, including the use of suicide bombers against the Cylon occupation of New Caprica, where humanity had attempted to resettle.

The series thus offers estranged perspectives on ongoing political crises related to the United States' War on Terror, which have been extensively documented in the voluminous scholarship on this influential series.[1] It also achieved something unparalleled in genre history: in 2009, the series finale was celebrated with a panel discussion at the United Nations (moderated by Whoopi Goldberg from *Star Trek: The Next Generation*) that engaged series actors and other experts in a broad discussion of the series' themes related to human rights, terrorism, children and armed conflict, and reconciliation and dialogue among civilizations and faiths.[2] Our brief discussion of the series in this chapter, followed by consideration of other SF series that followed in its wake, concentrates on the innovations in narrative that are most important for establishing a new space for political storytelling through SF television, thus creating the space into which emerged the other series we discuss in this book.

Moore began with very unlikely source material for his grim political drama: the original *BSG* series (1978–1979) aired for only a single season and was largely a campy, disco-era space opera about an exodus to find the promised land, heavily influenced by its creator Glen A. Larson's Mormonism.[3] In both series, sentient machines, the Cylons, turn on their human creators, and only a remnant of humanity escapes the genocide. The original Cylon models, Centurions, are metallic killing machines in the original, noted for their tinny voices proclaiming "by your command" as they carry out their leader's directions. This Cylon War is placed forty years in the past in the new narrative, making the attack that opens the miniseries the outcome of a generations-long conflict between species and enabling the reboot to focus on questions of misunderstanding that emerge from a cycle of violence rather than an inevitable and irresolvable conflict between entities of different ontology, human or machine. In the reboot, the Centurions are for the most part replaced by the new organic models: synthetically made from flesh, they thus can pass as human but also are able to be reincarnated into new bodies and hence immortal. There are only a set number of Cylon models, and much of the final season involves the mystery of the final five models hidden within the colonial population—who prove originally to have been the humans who made the organic Cylon technology possible and who have now been reincarnated as Cylons by the first model, Cavil (Dean Stockwell). As the intricate storyline is finally outlined in full, then, the series erodes what seems to be the absolute division between humanity and machine that anchored both the original series and the ideology that sustains the war on both sides: Cylons were made by humans, but the final five models are humans remade by Cylons, and moreover the species can interbreed. The child Hera (Alexandra Thomas/Iliana Gomez-Martinez), born to a Cylon mother and a human father, becomes the central symbol of hope for ending the conflict and enabling a shared future that is necessary for either Cylons or humans to survive. The reboot thus resituates the political drama as a kind of family conflict and reveals in the finale that Hera is the Mitochondrial Eve, the ancestor linking all people on our Earth.

Yet it is a long and difficult path toward this hopeful destination as the series works through the shock and disruption of the 9/11 attack for Americans, channeling the affect of disbelief and vulnerability that accompanied this event. The series consistently interrogates the new problems facing America in a world order that suddenly seemed insecure, contra the celebrated end of history with the apparent U.S. victory in the Cold War. How does one negotiate between civil liberties and state security? What should be the relationship between civil and military authority and leadership? What means, including torture, might be justified when the ends are deemed to be the very survival of civilization? Might there be individuals among us passing as citizens but secretly planning to destroy our way of life? How much diversity or dissension is allowable in an ongoing state of emergency? The new *BSG* explored these and related questions as it became one of the most acclaimed series of the decade, winning multiple awards, including a Peabody Award in 2005, for "pushing the limits of science fiction."[4]

Although the series does not focus on economic themes as strongly as do the others we discuss in this book, the framing of the 9/11 attacks as disrupting the seemingly bright future imagined by Western nations in the 1990s is highly relevant. As Lisa Duggan argues in *The Twilight of Equality?*, it was precisely the security that the future belonged to capitalism—conflated in Western imaginaries with democracy after the long struggle for global domination against the Soviets—that paved the way for the hegemony of neoliberalism. During the Cold War conflict, a

New Deal ethos in which capital shared some of its gains with labor and the public sphere was somewhat attentive to issues of inequality rooted in racism, misogyny, and homophobia was displaced by "a new vision of national and world order, a vision of competition, inequality, market 'discipline,' public austerity, and 'law and order' known as neoliberalism."[5] As Duggan analyzes in her critique of U.S. politics since this time, neoliberalism erased the distributive gains of 1970s political activism, creating polarization and insecurity at home. At the same time, of course, the seeds of the 9/11 attacks were planted by U.S. intervention in the Middle East, which began in part with the United States' support of insurgents fighting the Soviet invasion of Afghanistan. U.S. involvement was limited to repelling any Soviet victory and not to address underlying issues of global redistribution, enabling a reading of the family drama of the Cylon/human war as a comment on the United States' own complicity in radicalizing those who later sought what they understood as revenge in the 9/11 attacks. Duggan contends that the "overarching Liberal distinction between the economy, the state, civil society, and the family consistently shaped, and ultimately disabled progressive-left politics by separating class politics—the critique of economic inequality—from identity politics—protest against exclusions from national citizenship or civic participation, and against the hierarchies of family life."[6] We agree, and thus while *BSG* does not foreground questions of redistribution and equality, the mutual struggle for inclusion and recognition between Cylons and humanity responds to the growing inequality driven by the rise of neoliberalism as much as to the 9/11 attacks.

The most innovative aspect of the reimagined series is the focus on the joint future of humans and Cylons as symbolized by the child Hera. On the one hand, this equation of political reconciliation with family building reinforces our point that the family unit serves as a metonym of working through ideological difference in this and other series. On the other hand, the insistence on the heteronormative figure of the child as the future suggests a certain conservatism at the heart of *BSG*'s vision. In early seasons, the human/Cylon conflict seems permanent: both sides insist on the inherent inferiority of their enemy. To the humans, Cylons are mere machines, "toasters"—a term a Model Six (Tricia Helfer) explicitly deems an "ethnic slur" (S2E4)—while to the Cylons the humans are tyrants who enslaved their ancestors and repeatedly betray their callousness through their refusal to see killing Cylons as a crime. Yet even in early seasons, when the narrative is focalized exclusively through human characters, we get hints of the Cylons' point of view in experiments they run to see whether humans are capable of love, which Cylon mythology suggests is the missing key to allowing heterogeneous reproduction between couples rather than the serial production of the same model through the uploading and downloading of memories.[7]

The overarching motif that is clear through four seasons of conflict and shifting allegiances is that the future remains in doubt for both species so long as the humans and Cylons view this as a zero-sum game from which only one can emerge. Even as the characters operate via this logic, however, the narrative hints at other possibilities. For example, President Roslin (Mary McDonnell) initially orders the termination of Sharon's pregnancy, fearing what a hybrid child would mean for humanity's future, but the child is saved when it is discovered that an element in her blood can treat Roslin's terminal cancer to extend her life. When later the Cylons kidnap Hera to use her for their own ends, her health is immediately imperiled by their lack of knowledge of how to care for a child. Although the prophecies that guide their search for the homeland of Earth prove true, so long as the two sides remain in conflict finding the planet is not enough: the original Earth they find is a dead planet, destroyed by nuclear attack as were the Twelve Colonies; the new home world they find in the finale, our Earth, is not the original one.[8]

We might read the final season's narrative regarding how the progressive elements on both human and Cylon sides come together to save Hera, find a new home, and reboot civilization as something of a queer family. Although the child remains the image of futurity—precisely the endemic heteronormativity that Lee Edelman rails against—Hera's mixed heritage opens a space to think about this future in queerer terms, particularly because her mother, Sharon, is both an individual instance of the Model Eight and part of a sisterhood of Eights who understand kinship in terms of horizontal as well as vertical relations. For the most part, *BSG* shies away from such depictions, the final moments of the whole series focusing on heterosexual pairs among the survivors who will repopulate this new Earth, including Karl and this particular Sharon, also known as Athena. By this point, even Roslin and Adama have become a couple, in a storyline that seems a bit forced, and the only queer couple in the entire narrative appears only in the TV film *Razor* (2007), which provides the backstory of Admiral Cain (Michelle Forbes), commander of the USS *Pegasus*, another surviving battlestar-class ship and part of a story arc in season 3. The Cain storyline is mainly about contrasting her harsh military-led leadership with Adama's style, which has been tempered by his working alongside a civilian authority, and it includes a storyline about an imprisoned Model Six that is subjected to torture and rape on Cain's ship. In *Razor* we learn that this Six, Gina Inviere, was Cain's partner before her Cylon identity was revealed, suggesting that it is Cain's bitterness over the personal betrayal that informs her willingness to use abuse as a political tactic.[9] The series tries to distance itself from some of the extreme conservatism that can attach to heteronormative reproductive futurity—although the humans briefly ban abortion, this storyline is minor, and "The Farm" (S2E5) depicts with horror a Cylon plan to reduce human women to organic breeding machines. Yet the unrelenting focus on settling and expanding what remains of the human race means that the series never quite imagines radical queer possibilities of blended or extended families, options that might have enabled a shorter pathway toward the recognition that humans and Cylons are really one diverse family.

There are conflicts and ruptures not only between Cylons and humans but among the same species in either side of the conflict: several disputes testing the limits of civilian versus military authority are channeled through the father/son relationship between Colonel Adama (Edward

FIGURE 2.1 A scene of torture from *Battlestar Galactica*: "Flesh and Bone," season 1, episode 8.

James Olmos) and his son Lee (Jamie Bamber), who, in the context of the military logic of expediency in the fact of emergency, habitually insists on civilian oversight and due process. As the colonial fleet navigates multiple crises, from political misinformation, to an uprising of imprisoned inmates, to an attempt to steal an election, the term "family" is repeatedly used to describe the humans' choice to reunite rather than for competing factions to go their own ways. The Cylons also schism, at first only individual instances of a model, most prominently a Model Eight, Sharon (Grace Park), who falls in love with the human Karl Agathon (Tahmoh Penikett), thus saving him from execution by her comrades and enabling her to conceive the miraculous Hera. Later the entire Cylon population splits over whether they should aspire to be machines and wipe out a dangerous humanity or adopt a new policy of reconciliation with their human family. Ultimately, a hopeful future is possible only for those of either human or Cylon ontology who show a capacity for forgiveness, reconciliation, and choosing new ways of responding beyond the cycle of vengeance. [10]

This motif is most thoroughly developed through the character of Gaius Baltar, an unwitting Cylon collaborator in this version: the original willingly betrayed humanity, but this Gaius is simply greedy and power hungry, and his selfish ambition blinds him to the larger picture. Aligned with the Cylons, he begins preaching the doctrine of the "one true god" and his capacity for forgiveness, at first opportunistically and later, it seems, with sincerity. A larger supernatural force does guide the action across the seasons, drawing at times from the belief system associated with this forgiving god and at other times from the zodiac-centric pantheon of colonists. The message of forgiveness is key to the series' political vision: by the end, individuals have betrayed and done horrible things to one another, and the two species have both committed atrocities and, at the time, firmly believed themselves righteous in doing so. The only way past such mistakes and damage is to leave them in the past: the scales cannot be balanced, and only forgiveness offers a way forward. This is why a season 3 storyline following the escape from occupied New Caprica concludes with the announcement of a general amnesty, why Baltar is exonerated at his trial, and why the only crime that cannot be forgiven is that of refusing to change: the fundamentalist Cylons, led by Cavil, who insist on being and remaining machines are abandoned without resurrection technology, and two humans who attempt a coup to stop what they believe is the betrayal of humanity by collaborating with the allied Cylons are executed. The final lesson Roslin learns from the priestess who has been her guide is that "the harder it is to recognize someone's right to draw a breath, the more crucial it is" (S4E9).

Beyond this message of the need for reconciliation, however, *BSG* tends to hedge its political positionality. It raises the questions but shies away from providing clear answers, instead allowing characters to speak to both sides of complex issues. Near the end of the series, Baltar defines god not in terms of the colonial pantheon or of a creator monotheistic god; instead "god is a force of nature, beyond good and evil, not on any one side; if you want to break the cycle of birth, death, rebirth, destruction, escape, death: that's in our hands and requires a leap of faith, requires that we live in hope, not fear" (S4E20). Thus, although *BSG* positions itself as the realist and darker answer to many of the Star Trek series' naïve utopianism, it too is rooted in a concept of utopianism that echoes some of the language evoked by Bloch. The motifs of love, forgiveness, and trust point to a conviction that the future can be different from the dystopian present, that even flawed beings can create a better world. The fact that the series so effectively links its tale of familial healing to the experience of 9/11—both the trauma of the attack and the longer history of aggression and exploitation between the Muslim world and the West—exemplifies the important connection between the quotidian and the systemic that we theorize throughout this book through a unified focus on utopian thought as it has been taken up in both SF studies and queer theory.

Before moving on from this discussion, one critically neglected 1990s series deserves mention as an important precursor to *BSG*, namely, *Babylon 5* (1993–1998). It was ahead of its time in using SF as political allegory in ways that anticipate many of the central themes of *BSG*, including episodes that focus on the workers or other noncommand personnel, storylines about the tensions between civilian and military command, generations-long conflicts between species over territory and religious belief, and a larger mythopoetic framework for its space battle narrative. Space precludes a detailed discussion of the series, but its most important innovation was to tell a coherent story across five seasons of the emergence of a political crisis through to its resolution. Although it aired at a time when episodic television was more common, *Babylon 5* forged the longer-format story arcs now typical of television. Set on a space station dedicated to the project of keeping multicultural peace among previously warring species, it also offers a somewhat darker vision than Star Trek: its Interplanetary Alliance, like the Federation, is ultimately successful in bridging cultural difference and maintaining peace, but it requires an ongoing effort and is frequently threatened by political conflicts *within* member planets, including Earth, as they negotiate between authoritarian and liberal forces. Characters who appear to be the most sympathetic in early seasons make choices that reveal a darker side by the end, while those who seemed irredeemable learn to embrace forgiveness and reconciliation. It remains one of the best examples of political storytelling through SF television.

POLITICAL SCIENCE FICTION DRAMA IN THE TWENTY-FIRST CENTURY

In this second section, we briefly highlight several recent series that offer tour de force examples of using SF tropes to tell political stories in the twenty-first century: *For All Mankind*, *Watchmen*, *Counterpart*, and *Beforeigners*. These series are selected not only because of their accomplished use of the storytelling space opened up by *BSG* but also because each, in their distinct way, comments on the ongoing and entwined crises of neoliberalism and compromised democratic governance, and they thus exemplify the particular thematic we trace in this book.[11] Consistent with our vision of the end of the Cold War as setting the stage on which neoliberal austerity came to be seen as the only option, each series also imagines an alternative resolution to the Cold War as part of its world building.

We turn first to *For All Mankind*, Ronald D. Moore's most recent SF narrative. Set in an alternative past, the series begins from the premise that the Soviets rather than the Americans were the first to make it to the moon. Rather than ending the space race, this defeat prompts the United States to devote even more resources to its space program, as well as to diversity its astronaut pool, hoping that it might be the first to put a woman on a moon. Although they fail in this ambition too, and a female cosmonaut is first to the moon, the Americans are successful in establishing the first permanent base on the moon, Jamestown, and by the end of the second season also seem to have the edge on future technology, including a new nuclear shuttle capable of travel to Mars and a lithium mining operation on the moon. Shifting the Cold War from territorial battles on Earth into the space race means that the United States intervenes much less in the Vietnam conflict and that the Soviets do not invade Afghanistan; instead, U.S. and Soviet forces battle on the moon, resulting in the death of a cosmonaut shot by American marines and the brief Soviet occupation of Jamestown. The extended Cold War also seems to dampen the countercultural movement in the United States, perhaps because of the absence of the antiwar movement (although this is never discussed): what we do know is that Reagan rises to power earlier, by 1976, and that although the ERA passes, there is less credit given to an active feminist movement. The Gay Liberation Movement also is completely missing from this vision of the future. Instead, the queer characters in the show must remain closeted into the 1980s for fear of losing their jobs were they to be outed to the Republican administration.

Much like *BSG* offered a version of liberal cosmopolitanism as a way to overcome long-entrenched cultural and religious differences, the horizon of futurity in *For All Mankind* remains limited by liberal frameworks, which is why it often fails to work through the larger implications of the cultural changes it imagines by diversifying the space program. The show is very attentive to difference at the level of casting, including among its characters an African American astronaut, Dani (Krys Marshall); a Vietnamese adoptee, Kelly (Cynthy Wu); an undocumented Mexican engineer, Aleida (Coral Peña); and two queer characters: Ellen (Jodi Balfour), an astronaut and later NASA administrator, and Larry (Nate Corddry), a ground support staff member. To a degree, this diverse casting allows for some questions to be asked about decisions for the space program, such as the argument Dani has with her sister-in-law about whether the government should support space exploration when tax dollars are needed for under-resourced Black families (S2E4), or a conversation between Ellen and one of her crew members, Deke (Chris Bauer), during which he draws away in disgust when she reveals her true sexual orientation. He eventually relents somewhat, telling her she is a good astronaut and must hide her sexual identity to avoid being held back by bigoted people like him, leading to a conversation in which he insists that matters of sexual

FIGURE 2.2 Female astronauts in *For All Mankind*.

politics are beside the point of the space program, while to her the doors she and the other women have opened for the girls who follow in their wake is precisely the point (S1E10).

Similarly, while *For All Mankind* does at moments foreground the issue of gender—such as a scene in which the first woman to command an Apollo mission, Molly (Sonya Walger), crosses out "man's" to replace it with "our" on the mission logo (S1E4)—overall the series merely adds women and people of color to the same Cold War and masculinist culture that characterized the actual space race. The women in the program as much as the men want to be hotshot pilots, and it is the female Tracy Stevens (Sarah Jones) who pilots the marines to attack the Russian occupation and retake the mining site: en route, she hums Wagner's "Ride of the Valkyries," an allusion to its use in *Apocalypse Now* (1979). The territorial conquest and commercial ambitions that fuel the space race are celebrated rather than critiqued, emblematized by naming the first base Jamestown and by storylines in which the original test pilots are bored by the routine of ongoing life in space, which they refer to as "homesteading" instead of being on the "frontier" (S1E8). Similarly, it is suggested that technology in this world is far in advance of its development in our reality thanks to the engineering feats of NASA: electric cars are available by the 1980s, and the Three Mile Island meltdown never occurs. The ultimate horizon is always a colony on Mars, suggesting the series' sympathy with our contemporary space race, fueled by billionaires and their SF-infused ideas of saving "humanity" from the consequences of its environmental destruction by moving to another planet. Given the colonialist ending to *BSG*, it is perhaps not surprising that this series too remains mired in liberal frameworks that tend to conflate democracy with capitalism.

To the degree that the show engages with issues of family, it suggests that the dream of space is so enchanting as to make worldly conflicts seem petty. One of the original male astronauts, Gordo (Michael Dorman), offers this romantic perspective when he contrasts the view of Earth and the stars from space with the hate-filled perspective of the police at the 1968 Democratic National Convention in Chicago, beating protestors for what seems to him like no reason—yet, crucially, we also hear nothing from him of what the protestors are objecting to. The good the space program represents "for all" humanity, for unification and peace, is tainted by the Cold War in the view of these dreamers who resist the militarization of space, albeit without success, led in part by the unlikely figure of Werner von Braun, whose Nazi past is publicly revealed in this reality, sidelining him from future work at NASA. As the first season finale's title, "The City on the Hill," indicates, the series' utopianism is firmly located within an American worldview, a continuation of a Cold War ideology in which America was supposedly a beacon of hope and freedom to an otherwise oppressed and struggling world. The extension of the Cold War into the 1980s and beyond allows this myth to flourish without challenge for a longer period, continuing to hide, as it always did, the gap between the democratic promise of freedom and the global economic reality of the world market instantiated to benefit only some within U.S. culture. There are moments when *For All Mankind* does critique this fantasy—and the second season finale is called "The Grey," in reference to spaces of ethical ambiguity—but the series mainly reinforces rather than challenges the liberal worldview, at least in terms of its characters' choices. Even Ellen seems to think that sacrificing her personal life is worth the price of helping achieve the dream of getting to Mars, and while the Americans are the first to use weapons on the moon, the Russians nonetheless are characterized as making parochial choices as compared to the magnanimity of the United States.

What is intriguing about *For All Mankind* in the context of this chapter about the legacy of *BSG* is that it reveals the limitations of the strategy of forgiveness and mutuality that is celebrated by the earlier series' conclusion. Instead of projecting cultural differences onto Cylons versus colonial humans, *For All Mankind* estranges our perspective on the real history of U.S./Soviet difference and in this draws attention to the fact that the model of reconciliation on offer is one that requires more movement from one side to another. To the degree that some Russian characters are sympathetic in the later series, it is because they identify with American "free world" values. From this vantage, it becomes clear that something similar is at work in *BSG* in the sense that the Cylons who are sympathetic and reconciled are the ones that learn to be more like humans, that learn to love the humans. This profound shift in Cylon culture begins with two Cylons, Sharon Agathon and Caprica Six, who fall in love with human men. The humans, too, must learn to recognize the Cylons as people rather than as things, but their shift is one of inclusion within an existing framework: it is the Cylons who must adjust their framework, accepting that they are not perfectible machines but instead fallible, fleshy beings, just like the humans. This truth, combined with the limited acknowledgment of queer possibility or redistributive justice in either series, marks both *BSG*'s and *For All Mankind*'s investment in liberalism as a limitation of their political imaginary. The implication is—in terms of the analogy to the so-called War on Terror—that the more all people become like the West, the more unified and peaceful will be the future. This is precisely the triumphal ideology of the "end of history" and a new age of prosperity that supposedly arrived with the defeat of the Soviets as a rival to U.S. power. As we argue throughout this book, the economic disparities that were fueled by this supposed victory are the origin of the political and economic crises of the twenty-first century that inform the series we analyze throughout this book, including the other examples of political SF discussed in the remainder of this chapter.

The miniseries *Watchmen* offers a radical way of thinking differently about the stories we want to tell and the kinds of futures such stories enable. The series is not an adaptation of the original comic book,[12] which itself critiqued authoritarian power via an ironic depiction of superheroes, the title alluding to the question of how one guards against corruption

among the powerful.[13] Instead, the miniseries is set some thirty years after
the events of the comic and extends the critique to indict the racist culture of policing in America. As in the original, it offers an alternative
outcome to the Cold War. Here, the United States won its war in Vietnam, thanks to the power of its superheroes, although this version of
Dr. Manhattan has come to regret his role in this victory: he tried to do
the right thing in ending the war, he says, but now realizes that the violence he inflicted on the rebel Vietnamese merely fueled the radicaliza-
tion of the survivors, who become terrorists against U.S. occupation as
Vietnam is turned into another state. The series opens with a shocking
depiction of the Tulsa Massacre of 1921, during which a white mob
destroyed a prosperous Black community, lynching several residents and
burning down the neighborhood. This incident is the origin story for a
Black masked hero, Will Reeves, the Hood (Louis Gossett Jr.), whose life
story will demonstrate a line of descent from such mobs through the
KKK to the anti-Black ideology at the heart of policing.

The major crisis of the comic book—a fake attack on New York orches-
trated by the superhero Ozymandias to force people to unify against an
alien attack instead of fighting one another and risking nuclear war—
enables a long-term Democratic presidency under Robert Redford. This
shift in politics means that this future *seems* more racially just: repara-
tions have been paid to descendants of the Tulsa attack, and early depictions of the police show a diverse force whose interviewing techniques are
designed to uncover racial bias in their subjects. Rather than resort to
force in the first instance, police are required to seek additional authori-
zation to access deadly weapons, although an early episode suggests that
this puts the police themselves at risk when we see a Black officer shot by
a member of the Seventh Calvary, a white supremacist terrorist group.
The white nationalists, organized as followers of Rorschach,[14] engage in
violent assaults against Black communities and a police force they view
as having betrayed their own. Yet as the episodes unfold, we see the limitations of this liberal version of a more inclusive future: simply changing
hierarchies without revising structures is insufficient. Following White
Night (a term that evokes both Kristallnacht, referenced in the comic,
and the White Knights of the KKK), police are now masked to protect
themselves and their families from retaliatory violence: on White Night,
the homes of officers in Kansas were invaded by the Seventh Calvary,

who executed them and their families. Eventually we learn this was a false flag operation organized by Senator Joe Keene (James Wolk), a secret member of the Seventh Calvary. He uses the public outrage about imperiled police officers to push through legislation allowing the police to be masked—and propelling his own presidential bid as a law-and-order candidate.

The series thus encourages us to be suspicious of anyone wearing a mask—police officer or vigilante—suggesting that the problem lies less in whether one's violence is authorized by the state and more in the desire to control others through violence. An in-text television series, *American Heroes*, narrates the presumed story of the original Minute Men, the first masked vigilantes/heroes, and what footage we see of it emphasizes the extremes of violence associated with much of the superhero canon. The fictional Hood—a white man who is also closeted—talks about his "thirst for vengeance" (E2) as motivation for his crime fighting, but what comes through most strongly is his rage. In the imagined more-left-wing world in which this show is broadcast, the viewer advisory alerts the audience to its misogyny, racism, homophobia, and depictions of hate crimes and sexual assault—not merely that it depicts violence and sexuality, as in actual television viewing guidelines. In a later episode, when Will's descendant Angela (Regina King), one of the masked cops, takes a drug called nostalgia that enables her to vicariously live his memories, we see the real story of the Hood. Inspired by both the injustice he experienced as a victim of the Tulsa Massacre and by a film serial about Bass Reeves, the Black marshal of Oklahoma, Will joins the New York Police Department in the 1950s, inspired by the serial character Reeves's motto "trust in the law."[15]

Yet even as an officer Will is disrespected by his racist colleagues, to the point where they attack and hang him one night—although they do cut him down before he dies, stating the attack was a warning. Given the inherent corruption of the police, Will can pursue his fight for justice only as a masked hero, but here, too, the pervasiveness of racism makes his experience different from that of other superheroes. In addition to a mask, he must wear eye makeup implying that he has white skin beneath it. It means something very different for a Black man to wear a mask and establish his own moral laws than it does for a white man to do this: some violence is glamorized; other violence is criminalized. Aesthetically, *Watchmen* emphasizes the continuity between Will's experiences with his racist colleagues and his memories of the Tulsa Massacre by having the two realities visually bleed into each other as we see things from his point of view. The conceit of the nostalgia pills also prompts Angela to rethink her investment in her identity as a police officer when she does not merely learn about Will's experiences of police injustice but finds them blending with and confusing her own childhood memories. Like Will, she evokes Abel Ferrara's *Ms. 45* (1981),[16] and as she remembers her earlier life it is also clear that a female Vietnamese police officer, who helped identify the bomber who killed Angela's parents, is another inspiration. Immediately after Angela identifies the man to the police, he is executed, which gives her a sense of satisfaction. Soon though, interweaving between these memories and Will's, she begins to recognize that there is a difference between justice and vengeance and that the role of the masked crime fighter within and beyond the police offers only the latter. Moreover, linking the legislation allowing police to be masked to a white supremacist project draws a direct line between KKK violence against African Americans and that committed by the police. Will too is gay and involved in a relationship with the white hero Captain Metropolis, but despite their mutual affection, this personal connection does not enable Metropolis to understand the particularities of Will's experience. Will wants the Minute Men to fight against organized racial violence committed by Cyclops, the KKK by another name, but Metropolis sees only problems he believes are inherent to the Black community and insists that their relationship—and Will's racial identity—remain equally closeted.

FIGURE 2.3 Sister Night from *Watchmen*: "It's Summer and We Are Running Out of Ice," episode 1.

Laurie Blake (Jean Smart), the hero Silk Spectre in the comic book, is now an FBI agent who tracks and imprisons vigilantes, recognizing that masking one's identity always leads somewhere toxic. When she first meets Angela, Laurie asks, "Do you know how you can tell the difference between a masked cop and a vigilante?" When Angela says no, Laurie replies, "neither do I" (E3). She recognizes that people who wear masks are traumatized by some injustice done to them but refuses to allow the truth of these painful pasts to serve as justification for further vengeance and violence. The series portrays Will's story with careful nuance, demonstrating both that the trauma he has suffered was criminal and unjust but also that it damaged him such that he cannot remain with his family: his anger poisons his own life and makes him as toxic—if differently so—as Ozymandias. Angela and the reformed Dr. Manhattan, who we learn near the end has lived the last ten years in the body of a Black man as Angela's husband, Cal, without memory of his true identity—must find another way forward to enable true justice, not simply a revised hierarchy that perpetuates the same traumas with different targets. And in their final discussion, Will admits to Angela that while he thought he was motivated by anger, truly what he felt throughout his life was fear. He argues that given the power Cal possessed as Dr. Manhattan, he "could have done more" (E9) to redress the wrongs of history, but the series refuses to endorse this view: Cal as Dr. Manhattan stops Keene's plan for, as he puts it, "restoring balance" contra those people who "want white people to feel guilt for the alleged sins of those who died decades before we were born, sorry for the color of our skin" (E9), but Cal does this by sacrificing himself, not by sacrificing others, to achieve what he is certain he knows is right.

Ozymandias is thus the emblem of the hubris of the superhero figure: however just the cause, the decision to treat others as disposable means to one's supposedly superior ends inevitably results in more injustice, perpetuating the cycle, just as Dr. Manhattan saw with his own victory in Vietnam, which set in motion a chain of events that resulted in Angela's parents dying in a terrorist attack. Lady Trieu (Hong Chau), Ozymandias's daughter via a Vietnamese refugee who stole one of his sperm samples, suffers from the same hubris as her father, but unlike him, she comes from a background of depravation and trauma. Yet her plan too must be stopped, underscoring that the problem with Ozymandias is not (merely) that he is a privileged white man exercising power over others but rather his inability to respect other people's autonomy. Trieu invents the drug nostalgia, intended both as an Alzheimer's treatment and to free people from the "trauma of the past," but it is a failed venture: conjuring the poem that gave Ozymandias his name, and like him missing its irony, she wants people to "gaze on our mighty work . . . without despair" (E7), but the series insists that it is not so easy to move beyond the past. We need to find a way to bear the burden of the past without despair but also without amnesia, for the damage wrought by the past remains with us in the present, acknowledged or denied.

Watchmen explores ideas similar to those in BSG, then, about cyclical vengeance that prevents a better future from materializing. But it also thinks beyond the liberal horizon of BSG: the past cannot simply be transcended with some blanket statement of forgiveness. The future remains to be written, but we do not have the luxury of a clean slate on which to inscribe it. Emphasizing both economic disparities and political ideologies as the grounds that inform what possibilities people can imagine for the future, Watchmen insists that structural change in American institutions is required to enable a truly inclusive future and, most importantly, that this requires acknowledging past trauma as something that must be redressed and not simply moved past. The lineage from Will through to Angela allows the story of a single family to emblematize the larger political story of America, but unlike in BSG there is no conflation of the political community with a notion of the human family.

While Watchmen thus foregrounds political structures, the series Counterpart focuses more intensely on the familial and the personal in its story of parallel worlds that split in the late 1980s, shortly before the collapse of the Soviet empire. It too asks the audience to think about the relationship between one's circumstances and one's character in the contrasts it depicts between the same individual as he or she has diverged between the two worlds. Set in Berlin, the split is created in 1987 by a technological accident witnessed by Yanek (James Cromwell), a scientist who at the time is about to defect to the West. Yet when he finds his world and himself doubled, his desire to research the phenomenon prompts him to stay, a choice that eventually results in the death of his son, an activist against the East German state. By this time, however, subtle differences

FIGURE 2.4 The double world of *Counterpart*: "Love the Lie," season 1, episode 8.

have set the previously identical worlds on slightly different trajectories, and Yanek's son dies in only one reality; gradually this rift widens, and the Cold War ends in one world only. The version of Yanek whose son lives suggests to his counterpart that they can share in the happier reality, but the grieving Yanek becomes bitter and obsessed by a theory that the doubles all will inevitably destroy each other, that as soon as one sees an alternative life, the instinctual response is to appropriate or eliminate this other self. He does eventually kill his double, leading to strained diplomatic relations between the two worlds. In the growing atmosphere of suspicions, one side creates a virus that is lethal only to the other world (immunities, we are told, have drifted apart): putatively only a safeguard, this virus is accidentally released, resulting in stark differences between the two worlds, one devastated by a lethal plague and the other developing roughly parallel to our own reality.

All of this is backstory that we learn only in season 2; season 1 focuses on a terrorist from the plague-ravaged world, referred to as the Other Side, who seeks revenge on the more prosperous world that she—rightly as it turns out—blames for the plague. The leader of this group proves to be Mira (Christiane Paul), Yanek's daughter, in this case the daughter of the one who was killed by his counterpart; the other Mira, whom we glimpse only briefly, is unaware of the doubled world and lives a comfortable life. The spy thriller plot of the series gradually reveals the details of the revenge plan to us: a sinister school on the Other Side that recruits children and trains them to perfectly imitate their counterparts so that they can later replace them, thereby putting sleeper agents and spies within the power structures of this world, and a larger plan to create a diplomatic crisis that will force the border authority to forever close the connection between the two worlds, but only after these terrorists release their own plague in revenge. What is intriguing about this series in the context of our discussion here is the way this premise unites the legacies of the Cold War with motifs associated with the 9/11 attacks, such as colleagues and neighbors who turn out to be sleeper agents of another nation, culture, or ideology. In their most dramatic attack, these agents smuggle weapons into the embassy that processes travel between the two worlds and suddenly turn on their colleagues, killing almost everyone in the building before taking their own lives, all to prompt the border closure that Mira believes is necessary.

Pointing to the economic logics anchoring the political decisions that have shaped the post–Cold War world, the reason exchange across this border exists at all is trade: the Other Side is less technologically developed, save for some medical research related to their battle against the plague, but they have valuable information about the locations of natural resources that have been less thoroughly exploited in their world. Yet it is clear that trade gives much more advantage to the more prosperous world than it does the Other Side, mirroring the way that opening up former Third World countries to global capitalism has also tended to favor the West: the populations in the Other Side are now subjected to market discipline and austerity politics as they are integrated into the (bi)global market. In addition to the sleeper agents, who are hunted down by the FBI agent Naya Temple (Betty Gabrile) in the second season, many diplomatic personnel, couriers, and others are trapped on the wrong side of the border when the crisis erupts. These people are considered criminals for being on the wrong side of a border when political relations go wrong, even though they have done nothing wrong themselves, shifting the political palimpsest increasingly toward post-9/11 cultural formations in which a fear of difference manifests as anti-immigration rhetoric, often directed toward people of color who are not immigrants but whose ethnicity marks them as not-quite-American in right-wing popular discourse. In *Counterpart*, it is precisely the same individual who can suddenly appear as dangerous and different, inevitably and irreconcilably foreign, if something reveals that they are from the Other Side. Thus the series demonstrates that this logic of scapegoating is irrational, based entirely on projection rather than on any inherent traits.

Although such political structures are key to the world building in *Counterpart*, the series is far more interested in commenting on individual character than on political structure. The two central characters, Howard (J. K. Simmons) and Emily (Olivia Williams), are a couple who are caught up in these larger political events but not their architects: Emily on the prosperous side discovers evidence that the plague was deliberately created by her side and works with Howard on the Other Side secretly to alert the agency called "Management." The series opens as this Emily is in a coma after a hit-and-run incident, prompting Howard from the Other Side to work with the espionage branch on Emily's side, which entails meeting and switching places with his counterpart. Especially in the first season, the search to uncover the spy is overshadowed by an exploration of the personal differences between the two Emilys, the two Howards, and other counterpart pairs. The Other Side's Howard is a master agent who has prioritized his career, is estranged from his daughter, and has long since divorced Emily. He is contemptuous of his counterpart, whom he sees as something of a milquetoast; the prosperous side's Howard has never advanced in his career, and his wife, Emily, is the center of his life, although they never had children. The milder version of Howard is a kinder and more generous person, but the series frequently asks whether they are truly different because they have made different ethical choices or if, instead, the more dangerous version of Howard lies at both their cores but the milder version, because he lived in an easier and more prosperous world, was never required to draw on those capacities. Especially in the contrasts we see between other characters—such as that between Baldwin (Sara Serraiocco), a trained assassin, and her counterpart, Nadia, a concert violinist—the series frequently suggests that deprivation and suffering are what bring out the harsher aspects of anyone's character. In its focus as a character study, *Counterpart* ultimately seems to be about learning to embrace oneself more fully. As Clare (Nazanin Boniadi), the most important substituted agent, puts it in the finale, when she decides to stop the second viral attack and embrace the life she has built while pretending to be her counterpart, "the real test is about acceptance, not about eradicating this other side of ourselves" (S2E10).

The gap between the worlds thus seems ultimately to be less about different political and ideological paths and more about the fact that the plague mandated a difficult struggle for survival for those on the Other Side. Although those from the more prosperous world congratulate themselves on being better people, their luck in being born on the "right" side seems the crucial factor in their ability to make more generous choices. Clare's full story is instructive: initially one of Mira's most devoted followers, Clare does a number of horrific things, including killing her naïve, socialite counterpart with her bare hands, but Clare has also suffered greatly to become this secret substitute, not only losing her parents when she was a child but also having her legs deliberately broken to simulate her counterpart's skiing accident, to ensure their bodies will perfectly match. Clare is trained from a young age to believe that she suffers precisely because the counterpart has had an easy life, one full of everything Clare's circumstances deny her, from loving parents to economic security. Her capacity for violence toward her counterpart, then, appears less as a moral failing, and Clare's remaining capacity for love is central to why she eventually chooses to align herself with the life she has built while pretending to be her counterpart, which includes her daughter, a child, like Hera, of both worlds. Clare's redemption is mainly presented as a question of psychology, but it also suggests a provocative way of thinking about the political analogy in that it reminds us that dispossession and exclusion, not timeless cultural differences or inescapable cycles of violence, lie behind cross-border conflicts.

As in the contrast between the Howards, Clare's investment in her daughter as the anchor for her new life suggests that family is more important than career in the ethics the series promotes. Yet this focus on family remains narrowly heterosexist, and the series fails to fully consider queer possibilities that might offer more radical solutions to the problem of inequity between the two worlds. Such a possibility was suggested with the original proposal that the two Yaneks might share the single living son, allowing for more equity in the distribution of contingent luck between the two worlds. Another hint of a queer way that the worlds might relate through mutuality rather than competition is suggested in the minor storyline about Alice (Lisa Hagmeister), a defector from the Other Side who lives with her counterpart, both of them sharing their husband. The two versions of this woman support each other rather than compete, challenging the idea that the possibility for a good life is a limited resource only one of them can claim. Although most of the examples we see of counterparts meeting result in conflict rather than harmony, these hints at other outcomes demonstrate how a queer approach to utopianism enables new possibilities, ones political as much as personal.

The final example of the political power of SF narrative in the twenty-first century is the Norwegian series *Beforeigners*. Like *Counterpart*, it is a generic hybrid, in this case a police procedural enriched by a genre premise: as its title implies, the series is about the politics of immigration, but here the migrants move through time rather than across space. For reasons not made explicit, portals open in the sea and transport into the twenty-first century people from three earlier periods: the Stone Age, the Viking age, and the nineteenth century. The new arrivals require state support as they try to adjust to living in cultures radically different from their own, while their insistence on clinging to some of their own customs and lifeways is disruptive to twenty-first-century Norwegian life. The time migrants provoke a range of reactions that the SF premise of time travel refracts to provide an estranged way of thinking about these issues. For example, we glimpse graffiti that announces that Norway should be for "present-day people," and there is evidence of hate attacks; similarly,

FIGURE 2.5 A contemporary Norwegian detective and a Viking temporal immigrant detective in *Beforeigners*.

individuals are reminded not to use the term "Viking": the preferred term is "of Norse descent." Neighbors in an apartment complex are disturbed by the livestock-keeping practices of some Norse residents, and elsewhere others are even more disturbed by the raw-meat diet of Stone Age migrants. At the same time, however, we also see an educational film in which these time migrants are acclimatized to the new culture, which includes educating them on women's rights, ethnic diversity, and queer relationships as parts of contemporary culture they must accept, whatever their previous ideas.

We learn about the contours of this world as we follow police partners Lars (Nicolai Cleve Broch) and Alfhildr (Krista Kosonen) as they investigate a murder: the victim at first seems to be a Stone Age woman but later proves to be a contemporary woman who embraces the Stone Age lifestyle. Suggesting parallels with queer culture's capacity to "opt out" of normative expectations of contemporary life that merely reinforce and perpetuate the damaging legacies of colonialism, capitalism, and patriarchy, such transtemporal individuals believe that they have been born in the wrong time, that their true identity is in the practices of an earlier age whose lifeways they adopt, be this Stone Age, Norse, or nineteenth-century Christian. To be clear, we are not suggesting that this temporal opting out emerges from the same ethical paradigms as Mari Ruti's queer invocation of this term but rather that *Beforeigners* uses a temporal identity rather than gender identity to interrogate the assumed norms of twenty-first-century society, not all of which are better than those of earlier eras—but of course, not all of which are worse, either. Alfhildr, for example, as a former shield maiden, has radically different ideas about female capacity and sexual agency than her contemporary-period colleagues, and often her preferences are more enabling. The larger point is that, unquestionably, no norms can appear natural in a context in which people have been displaced through time rather than through space: although contemporary Norwegians resent the presence of these beforeigners, who take jobs and require tolerance of strange lifeways, it is difficult for them to sustain a claim that Norway more fully belongs to people who live there in the present than it does to people who lived there in previous generations.

Thus, *Beforeigners* explodes the whole paradigm of nationalist essentialism increasingly evoked by twenty-first-century right-wing authoritarianism and its blood-and-soil ethnic nationalism. This is what we find most intriguing and promising about this series. In the background to the murder investigation, much of season 1 offers glimpses of Alfhildr's past, when she was a warrior fighting in defense of the pagan world, at that time being displaced by Olaf Tryggvason, who would become King Olaf I. Olaf violently converted the Norse to Christianity as he unified the country, including torturing to death several resisting regional leaders. The increasing presence of Vikings in the Christian present reignites these old rivalries, and season 1 concludes suggesting that this battle over religion will be the major impetus for season 2. As with the question of to whom the land most rightfully belongs, this religious storyline offers intriguing parallels to real political issues associated with immigration, specifically the large number of immigrants from Muslim countries seeking entry into Europe, especially in 2015 and mainly because of the Syrian civil war. In the largely homogeneous Scandinavian countries, the influx of refugees with very different religious and cultural traditions provoked something of a culture shock. Norway, among others, revised its immigration policy in the wake of this experience, pointing to a cultural climate of uneasiness around Muslim residents. Rather than simply critiquing such cultural chauvinism, *Beforeigners* cleverly displaces the issue to one of time, reminding us that cultures, peoples, religions, and norms are continually in flux and thus that the changes visible in a twenty-first-century Norway, as a new set of people begin to live there, are not a disruption of some transhistorical local identity but merely the latest chapter in a place that has navigated massive change before. The series does not appear to offer a position on the merits of paganism versus Christianity but merely seeks to remind us that the historical Christian victory in this struggle was contingent.

Like the other series discussed in this chapter, *Beforeigners* aptly shows how powerfully SF estrangement can reframe political questions, often to make visible new choices and possible futures. Although it does not as directly comment on the Cold War reframing of global politics as do our earlier examples, the European immigrant crisis that animates its world building also has its roots in the political choices of this era. While the reasons for the unrest in the Middle East, including Syria, are complex and overdetermined, among them are the lingering legacy of the decades of Cold War policy, during which the U.S.-led West manipulated local politics not merely to prevent, as rhetoric had it, the spread of global communism but also to ensure that the emerging global markets privileged the West over its peripheries. As all of our examples have demonstrated, SF world building—as Ron Moore recognized when creating his paradigm-shifting reboot of *Battlestar Galactica*—is an ideal prism through which to see political struggles from new angles. These refracted perspectives allow novel elements to become more visible. Though the series we discuss in the remainder of this book are not all as directly structured as political allegory as the ones analyzed in this chapter, they nonetheless take up and extend the themes first made central to SF television by these influential series: fears of invasion (chapter 3), the polarized political landscape (chapter 4), the difficulty of imagining diverse community (chapter 5), and the distribution of resources fairly and inclusively (chapter 6).

3

9/11 AND ITS AFTERMATHS

Threats of Invasion

I n the twenty-first century, alien invasion narratives returned to television screens, enjoying a popularity unmatched since the 1950s. This was clearly a response to the trauma of 9/11 and the new imaginary of the geopolitical order it inaugurated.[1] As discussed in the previous two chapters, 1990s SF television tended to portray humans as part of interstellar societies (the Star Trek series) or to locate the sinister as something that emerged from our own domestic cultures (government conspiracies in *The X-Files*; our own creations in *Battlestar Galactica*). Earlier series that highlighted aliens on Earth portrayed them as open to alliances with humanity, often as refugees or exiles, such as in *Alien Nation* (1989–1990) or *Roswell* (1999–2002). In more recent series, Earth itself is imagined as a battlefield, targeted by aliens for its resources and often threatened by enemies who pass as humans, visibly an allusion to the sleeper cells feared after the 9/11 attacks. The similarity to 1950s Cold War fears of communists hiding among us is palpable, and such parallels extend, too, to the excesses of McCarthyist responses through which American culture became more oppressive than the nightmare it was projecting.[2]

This chapter looks at three television series that process the affective and ideological effects of 9/11 through narratives about alien attacks on American soil: *Threshold*, a short-lived series about an alien occupation and a government response that it attempts to keep it a secret from the populace; *Falling Skies*, a hugely popular narrative focused on militia resistance to a world-changing occupation by alien forces; and *Colony*, whose storylines focus on various strategies that humans choose in the wake of occupation, from militant resistance to willing collaboration.[3] All embody traces of the utopian desire for a better world theorized by Bloch, but in the contrast of *Falling Skies* and *Colony* especially we discern a difference between a desire that emerges from fear and an educated desire that opens a space for hope. We read these series as cultural myths that grapple with entwined anxieties both about national security and the security state as it unfolds in the twenty-first century. Like all of the texts discussed in this book, these series are centrally about the shape of America's future, emblematizing how 9/11 was largely understood as a moment of historical rupture that marks a break between America as it was before and America as it would be. All three seek to shape, in distinct ways, their audience's conceptualizations about and desires for the specific futures deemed as the correct path for the nation.

THE NEW SPACE INVADERS

In her influential essay "The Imagination of Disaster" (1965), Susan Sontag theorizes the cultural work of 1950s science fiction film, much of it about human responses to alien threats. She suggests that the power of such narratives resides in their capacity both to emblematize and distract us from the "inconceivable terror" of a contemporary age—largely bound up with the destructive capacities of the atomic bomb but also deeply shaped by the dehumanizing tendencies of technocratic modernity. At the same time, the irony of this 1950s SF is that it also works to "normalize what is psychologically unbearable" about living under such existential threat, emblematized by the fact that its logical, scientist heroes defeat the alien forces by becoming dehumanized themselves, "purged of emotions, volitionless, tranquil" in their embrace of technological solutions.[4] We suggest something similar is at work in the twenty-first-century version of alien invasion, narratives through which Americans risk being transformed into sinister versions of themselves—militaristic, xenophobic, selfish—through their efforts to repel an enemy they understand to epitomize these qualities. Following Sontag, we read the imagination of such films symptomatically, speaking as much to concerns about the growing authoritarianism of contemporary U.S. society as they do to the threat of military attack. These series provide images of how American notions of freedom have changed in the wake of 9/11, embodying the contradictions of a society more and more obsessed with the idea of the United States as the birthplace of liberal, democratic freedom even as its governance increasingly curtails civil liberties. They allegorize America's shift to the right, but our analysis also agrees with Eva Cherniavsky's contention that meaning lies in the "slippages" of allegory more than in the equivalences they map.[5]

Through images of alien invasion and apocalyptic change, these series make visible how America is now a different nation.[6] At stake in each series is the question of how much (perhaps whether?) citizens can trust their governments to protect them. *Threshold* focuses on a secret government team organized in the wake of an alien invasion, following a protocol mapped out by its leader Molly Caffrey (Carla Gugino), the head of a contingency planning think tank, who has also authored preparatory plans for viral outbreak, international monetary collapse, and cataclysmic shifts in the polar icecaps.[7] This premise works to assure viewers that, despite 9/11, America will never again be unprepared for future threats, with even alien invasion simply another entry in the national security playbook. Caffrey's assembled team includes an engineer, Lucas Pegg (Rob Benedict); a biological scientist, Nigel Fenway (Brent Spiner); and a mathematician/linguist, Arthur Ramsay (Peter Dinklage), all of whom are supervised by a Homeland Security agent, Sean Cavennaugh (Brian Van Holt). According to DVD extras, a three-season story arc was planned for the series, whose title would morph from *Threshold* through *Foothold* to *Stranglehold*, a progression that makes clear the ultimately ominous intent of these aliens, despite some scenes in this first season in which the aliens claim to be improving humanity in order to save it from a coming ecological threat. The aliens have three-stranded DNA and transform the bodies of those they infect to include this third strand, and the hybrid beings have enhanced physical strength and healing capacities. With its story of alien threat, *Threshold*'s SF narrative collapses into managerial forecasting: rather than the site of new possibilities, the future is anticipated to ensure that we are prepared to fight against change and preserve the status quo by any means necessary.[8]

FIGURE 3.1 The investigative team in *Threshold*: "Trees Made of Glass," part 1, season 1, episode 1.

Falling Skies picks up on this motif of alien/human hybrids in its story of the survivors of a catastrophic alien invasion that has left only a tiny percentage of humanity alive and destroyed all advanced technology with an EMP pulse. These aliens, the Espheni, abduct rather than kill human children, merging them with technology called a "harness" and using them as slave labor. Adults cannot be so harnessed, we are told, since only growing bodies can adapt to the required changes. But beyond the pragmatic explanation, this storyline also fuels a frequent motif about children as symbols of innocence and the future, which then turns into a more dangerous rationalization about protecting children, one that justifies violence.

Led by Tom Mason (Noah Wyle), a former professor of Revolutionary War history, survivors struggle to build new communities, fight back against this occupation, and recover children stolen by the Espheni, including one of Tom's sons, Ben (Connor Jessup). Two other sons, Hal (Drew Roy) and Matt (Maxim Knight), remain with their father, and Mason's patriarchal leadership dominates the series in significant ways. Tom repeatedly makes analogies between their struggle and the Revolutionary War, and he is positioned by the end as a modern-day George Washington moving from military success to political leadership. The series repeatedly endorses the capacity of such self-organized militia structures for governance over the corrupt remnants of whatever has survived from the previous American government and military, hinting at authoritarian strains in American culture that would become more fully visible in the coming decade. The series straightforwardly offers a fantasy of rebooting America by going back to Revolution-era values, conveniently transforming the survivors into embattled defenders of a land that is their birthright, while erasing their history as descendants of colonists who actually displaced indigenous inhabitants. It is not by accident that these survivors emerge first from Boston.[9]

Colony, the most recent of these series, depicts a West Coast under alien occupation, focused in the first season on Los Angeles. Fascinatingly, we almost never see the actual aliens in this series, getting our first glimpse of them only near the end of season 1. What we see instead is the infrastructure that sustains their occupation and control: massive walls that divide the "Los Angeles Block" from the "Santa Monica Block" and the human functionaries of the International Global Authority (IGA), who bureaucratically maintain the new structures of overtly authoritarian government that the occupation has put in place. In what is perhaps a nod to the colonialist underpinnings of all invasion narratives,[10] the aliens are referred to as Hosts by a newly disenfranchised human population, who now live only in these scattered "colonies," which might be better termed reservations but also evoke the ongoing U.S. occupation of Iraq and its own installation of local proxies for U.S. governance. The series focuses on the tribulations of a nuclear family, Will Bowman (Josh Holloway); his wife, Katie (Sarah Wayne Callies); and their children, Bram (Alex Neustaedter), Gracie (Isabella Crovetti), and Charlie (Jacob Buster), the last of whom is separated from his family, trapped in the Santa Monica Block when the walls were installed and the greater Los Angeles area was carved into isolated segments. Over three seasons, Will and Katie negotiate several ways of coping with the occupation, shifting in and out of strategic alignment; in the first season, Will is reluctantly working for the IGA to try to gain privileges that will allow him to bring Charlie home, while Katie is secretly working for the underground resistance; later Will becomes more radical and Katie more accommodating, all in an ever-shifting strategy to find the best way to protect their family.

The trauma of the 9/11 attacks clearly suffuses all three series, although it shows up in distinct ways. What is common to all is a narrative structure of suspense that easily tips over into fear: repeatedly we see scenes of people fleeing attack, hiding from infiltrators, or worrying about whom they can trust in an unstable landscape of allegiances.[11] *Threshold*, the least successful series—it was cancelled even before its limited run of thirteen episodes finished airing—perhaps makes its links to real-world threats too obvious. Like the highly successful *Battlestar Galactica* reboot, *Threshold* understood itself to be a political narrative set in a *science fiction* world. In a featurette titled "The Scary Details" on the DVD release, the series' lead actress Gugino drifts from this talking point to her own experiences of living in New York, going to bed on that day in one city and waking up the next day in a changed world in which the Twin Towers no longer existed. Repeatedly she and others interviewed in this featurette talk about a pervasive sense of threat, a new suspicion of the true intentions of those next to you on the subway.

We theorize, then, that *Threshold* failed to offer the alibi of distance or difference that Sontag identifies as a key method for SF, serving merely to heighten its audiences' anxieties rather than giving them a way to process and come to terms with this new world order. Airing in the years immediately following the Patriot Act (2001), *Threshold* reinforced the idea that civil liberties are a luxury that must be dispensed with in the interest of national security. Unlike the outsider heroes of the previous decade's *The X-Files*, in *Threshold* ubiquitous surveillance is a good thing. Alien agents are actively seeking to infiltrate our communications infrastructure, our food supply, and our social networks: we can remain safe only if the government has carte blanche to secure these spaces in advance of the aliens. The series thus seems to justify a rising right-wing hegemony while also encouraging us to believe that we need to remain continually fearful.

In contrast, *Falling Skies* offered precisely the jingoistic fable of American exceptionalism that many people desired in the wake of the attacks, providing affective release rather than intensification. Its five-season run is framed by a child's take on the shocking and unexpected alien invasion: the first episode, tellingly titled "Live and Learn," opens with a series of images of children's drawings that depict the invasion, as Tom's youngest son, Matt, provides a voiceover narration that expresses shock that the aliens did not want to "be friends"; the final battle that assures human victory in the finale, "Reborn," begins in a similar way, although now the children's drawings are accompanied by a voice singing "America the Beautiful." These visuals thus frame America as an innocent society that was compelled to take on violence only in response to unprovoked and

FIGURE 3.2 Tom, a former history professor turned freedom fighter in *Falling Skies*: "Live and Learn," season 1, episode 1.

unreasonable attack, enabling the series to offer both cathartic fantasies of violent vengeance against America's enemies (the bulk of its screen time depicts military adventures) and an alibi that once again externalizes this violence and allows Americans to identify as inherently peaceful, freedom-loving people.

Falling Skies played to the oft-repeated contention at the time of its airing that Muslim peoples and values are unassimilable with democracy (equated with America), most influentially articulated in Samuel Huntington's *The Clash of Civilizations and the Remaking of World Order*, and thus uses a typical SF technique of literalizing metaphor: the haters of freedom are actual aliens. The series lets Americans feel victorious again and emphasizes the centrality of military power, yet it also allows us to believe that peace, family, and democracy remain at the heart of a U.S. society that has in fact shifted significantly to the right and toward the suppression of the kinds of civil liberties celebrated in the country's founding mythology. Although *Threshold* had far less screen time to convey its ideas, something quite similar seems at work in its depiction of the infected hybrids, who join together in a new kind of religious community. The allegory in *Threshold* connects to ideas of ongoing immigration more than to the nation-founding ethos of *Falling Skies*; the latter series sounds more alarms about how America could be "contaminated" by the strange values of a new people with different belief systems who threaten to transform the entire nation into something unrecognizable, just as the alien "signal" in *Threshold* changes double-helical DNA into three braided strands.

Colony is fascinating precisely for the ways that it differs from *Falling Skies*. It too involves a surprise alien attack that forever changes American ways of life, but the episode that recounts this fateful day does not air until the beginning of season 2: once again, its title, "Eleven.Thirteen," makes the allusion clear. While in *Falling Skies* human survivors take to the road and form militias, all the while lamenting the values of a peaceful domesticity that has been erased, in *Colony* we see the family struggle to retain some semblance of normal life despite the barriers created by the occupation. The pilot features a typical happy family breakfast scene that quickly becomes strained, haunted by the missing son, plagued by food shortages, and made more difficult by the loss of infrastructure (no cars, electricity, medical supplies).[12] Although the series is thus another tale of America under attack, the allegory maps more clearly to people in Iraq and Afghanistan living under U.S. occupation than it does to the American experiences of the 9/11 attacks.[13] With this in mind, several other storylines in the series become more thought-provoking: the military Red Hand resistance in season 2 that uses suicide bombers; Katie's attempts to counter Gracie's indoctrination into the Host's mythos of the "Greatest Day" apotheosis by offering texts from several Earth religions, including the Qur'an and the Buddhist Tipitaka, as well as the Bible; the use of the term "total rendition" to describe the ultimate threat to the colony should resistance action become more than an irritant; and, perhaps

FIGURE 3.3 The Wall dividing Los Angeles into different "zones" in *Colony*: "Pilot," season 1, episode 1.

most significantly, the ongoing policing of the LA Block using drones (albeit ones that fly close to ground level and thus are seen by those they kill).

So while *Colony* continues to speak affectively to a U.S. populace that feels traumatized by 9/11, it also opens up a space to think differently about the ideological structures energized by this affective investment in the so-called War on Terror. *Falling Skies* confirms a sense of the United States as a blameless victim of unprovoked attacks,[14] but *Colony* focuses our attention on the complicity of humans who choose to support the alien invasion in a grab for power, as it also alludes by analogy to America's ongoing imperial occupation of parts of the Middle East. In the first two seasons, part of Los Angeles is designated a "Green Zone," an area of luxurious accommodation for those working for the IGA. With this mapping in place, the narrative focuses on class difference between these collaborators and those they exploit, but the term chosen—"Green Zone"—is that used to refer to the fortified area in the middle of U.S.-occupied Baghdad that served as the headquarters for the Coalition Provisional Authority, a transitional government of U.S.-sympathetic forces set up to maintain order following the U.S.-led invasion that deposed Saddam Hussein.

Ultimately, although all of these series use the same basic narrative structure of humans resisting an alien invasion, each of them educates its readers to imagine our present and possible futures in very different ways. We turn now in the remainder of this chapter to more specific analyses of critical differences in the education of desire in each narrative.

FIGURE 3.4 The fascist aesthetic of the occupying alien forces and their human collaborators in *Colony*: "A Brave New World," season 1, episode 2.

A MILITARIZED CITIZENRY

The relationship imagined between civilian and military authority is among the most significant sites of such differentiation. From its opening moments, *Threshold* insists that the government serves the people's best interests while simultaneously suggesting that democracy does not. "If we do our jobs right, they will never know how close they came," announces Andrea Hatten (Diane Venora), the national security advisor who puts the team together in episode 1. By episode 10, when the team loses containment of infected humans they have been indefinitely holding and, it seems, the risk of endemic infection is imminent, Molly asserts, "the public will be under strict surveillance, their civil rights curtailed, until we gain control." The series does not portray this as a dangerous erosion of civil liberties and democratic governance but rather as clearheaded and decisive leadership, precisely what is needed in this acute crisis.[15] Questions of civilian authority are not even raised, with even the president being kept out of the loop for his (and our) protection. Details of the invasion are strictly need-to-know, and experts do not have time to waste debating with politicians: in episode 6, "The Order," a senator comes to observe their containment facility, which holds the infected without charge or court proceedings, and he is only an obstacle to the team's ongoing work, failing to see how these detainees are no longer the people they purport to be but instead something else, sinister imposters. Even asking questions about extrajudicial confinement aids the enemy, or so it would seem.

Despite its bellicose tone, *Falling Skies* takes more care to debate the merits of civilian versus military authority, part of its celebration of American democracy as the guiding light of the world. As early as episode 2, "The Armory," we see a conversation about the importance of the civilian members of the "Second Mass[achussetts]" militia—women, children, and others who contribute to the war effort not by fighting but by maintaining supply chains for the soldiers through scavenging, mending, cooking, and the like. Tom is appointed as co-leader of this unit with a retired army veteran, Captain Weaver (Will Patton), explicitly to reinforce this need for the two sides, civilian and military, to work jointly, but Tom almost always functions as a military strategist—and generally frontline fighter—despite his civilian designation. Yet the series worries at this notion that America would become something like a military dictatorship and thus repeatedly offers counterexamples to reinforce the rightness of the Second Mass's organizational structure. In "The Price of Greatness" (S2E9), the group finally reaches Charleston, the headquarters, or so they have been told, of a new American president and renewed country. Here they find military authority taking its orders from the duly elected president, but the result is that these people merely hide out in the ruins of the city, not offering any resistance to the occupation. While praising what they have accomplished and the importance of democracy, Tom nonetheless condemns their president for inaction, insisting that "freedom will only come once the enemy has been driven from [the] land," a sentiment he claims to be repeating from the Revolutionary War scholarship of his mentor. Tom's rhetoric wins the day, and he is elected president, enabling the series to maintain its ideological commitment to democracy while simultaneously suggesting that "true" democratic citizens will also privilege military values.

The opposite lesson is taught by contrast in "Stalag 14th Virginia" (S5E8), about a military base run by another militia that dominates its civilians: *stalag*, of course, is a German word for prisoner-of-war camp, thus evoking the specter of Nazi governance as the malevolent counterpoint to American freedom. A notably female commander of this base, Katie Marshall (Melora Hardin), spends more time imprisoning and executing human traitors than she does fighting the enemy, something that the Second Mass must again put right—in this case through a convoluted storyline in which she is revealed to be a duplicate, made by the Espheni, of the original captain. Overtly, then, *Falling Skies* asserts that a balance between military and civilian authority is integral to democracy, but in practice it continually justifies the erosion of civil liberties in the name of the war effort. By enabling Tom rhetorically to win the day by citing Revolutionary analogies, the series offers a version of democracy that always *chooses* to capitulate to military authority.

Colony offers a more nuanced engagement with this topic, one that ultimately suggests that the central question is less how we resist the enemy and more *who we become* in the process. The series resists clear moral absolutes and asks its audience to confront the issues, largely by having the family itself divided over appropriate action and thus disrupting any easy identification among its viewers with a single point of view. In season 1, although both Will and Katie are against the occupation, they respond in opposite ways: Will tries to smuggle himself into Santa Monica to recover their missing son, and when he is caught he chooses cooperation over loss of his family, agreeing to use his skills (he is a former ranger and FBI agent) to hunt down the resistance. Katie, in turn, feeds information to the resistance but keeps this fact from Will, who later chooses to hide her actions when she might be exposed. In season 2, Will has become a fugitive, and Katie regrets her activism, a response to Will's absence and Bram's incarceration for his own illegal activities. She is on the verge of turning herself in, admitting that although she used to be shocked by how easily people gave up their freedom for some semblance of a normal life, now all she wishes for is more time with her children. The series premise shifts again near the end of this season: Will returns, and a mysterious change in the Hosts' situation requires them to flee Los Angeles entirely. By season 3, they have relocated to a different kind of colony in Seattle, which uses distraction and material rewards rather than oppression and violence to ensure its population meets the Hosts' quotas for resources. Now, the husband and wife's roles reverse again: Katie wants to believe in the shiny surface of the colony and the material comforts it offers if they refrain from asking troubling questions, while Will joins their main underground contact, Broussard (Tory Kittles), to uncover the sinister agenda behind the colony's civic structures.

In their various choices, Will and Katie serve as foils for each other, but unlike *Falling Skies'* insistence that the Second Mass and Tom Mason are always correct, here the situation is more ambiguous. Both Will and Katie make mistakes and misjudgments that cost others their lives— sometimes they are even the ones who kill people—and the weight of their decisions is palpable. They are frequently depicted arguing over what is best for their family. Although both reject the more militant Red Hand brand of activism, they both also protect its members at times, and, unknown to either of them, Bram participates in the group. What we find particularly pertinent about the Red Hand storylines, especially when reading this series together with *Falling Skies*, is the role of torture in the narrative. *Falling Skies* includes several scenes of torture, but they are almost exclusively acts committed by the Espheni against humans (the 14th Virginia soldiers who torture Ben because of their antipathy toward his hybrid status are a notable exception). In *Colony*, on the other hand, although the IGA is also putatively an arm of the alien occupation, its use of torture speaks to its status as a human tool of authoritarian control, justified by the exigency of needing information to counter future resistance attacks. Although Red Hand tactics are not endorsed, the aggressive repression of the Red Hand seems the more urgent problem, highlighting how few civil liberties remain in an increasingly authoritarian America. The red-and-black insignia of the IGA, a clearly Nazi aesthetic, only underlines this point, while in *Falling Skies* it is always the Espheni who are compared to Nazis, a typical evocation of the just war against an unambiguously evil enemy.

As *Colony* builds to its planned narrative arc—the aliens have come to Earth to recruit elite military personnel, called "outliers," for their own war against a different alien race[16]—issues of surveillance and data harvesting become much more important than issues of overt police authority. Season 2 reveals a data-harvesting center of ubiquitous surveillance, a nightmare version of what *Threshold* suggests is a prudent strategy of risk management, and season 3 of *Colony* mainly concerns an algorithm developed by a human programmer but used by the aliens to categorize people and determine their futures long before the Hosts physically arrive: some are recruited into IGA positions and the privileges of the Green Zone, outliers are hunted down and stored for future use in the war, and the remainder are a flexible pool of labor, gradually "renditioned" to "the factory" to work on other materiel necessary to the Hosts' war effort.

This shift in season 3 is particularly interesting to us. The third season of *Colony* points to one of the arguments that we make throughout this book, namely, that in SF television of the twenty-first century we can track a shift away from post-9/11 culture's focus on external enemies and national security and toward a recognition of the internal damage done to American culture by its hyperbolic response to 9/11, as well as the damage consequent to the 2008 financial crisis. *Colony* alludes to the importance of economic differences, of course, through the clear deprivation that people suffer outside of the Green Zone and season 3's storyline about Seattle as a different kind of colony in which the temptations of material comfort seduce people into ignoring the erosion of democracy. More important, however, is the fact that the IGA is headquartered in Davos, Switzerland, home of the World Economic Forum, an annual gathering of the global financial elite. Putatively intended "to demonstrate entrepreneurship in the global public interest while upholding the highest standards of governance,"[17] the WEF, like the Seattle colony, speaks in compelling terms about the collective good and better futures while ensuring that economic hierarchies and capitalist values remain the status quo.

CITIZENSHIP AND FAMILY

Such questions of governance speak to the SF world-building elements in these series, but what of their affective and familial narratives? To create empathy and identification with their viewing audiences, such series often (with some notable exceptions) foreground the lives of and connections among family members, allowing us to track evolving plot lines through the immediate and intimate impact of apocalyptic changes on individual lives. The most important observation to make here is that unlike series we discuss later in this book, the alien invasion storyline as filtered through 9/11 trauma eschews queer possibilities. There are no queer characters in any of these series, and even *Colony* orients our affective investment toward a heteronormative family.

Threshold deviates from the focus on family by not addressing questions of family in any significant way, representing all of its team members as either so dedicated to their jobs that family recedes from their lives or else willing to sacrifice time with their families for this more important work of saving the world in secrecy. Isolation is a large part of Molly's protocol for the absolute secrecy of their unit: not only do team members lie to their families, but they are forbidden even from ordering takeout food from the same restaurant too often, lest their orders leave a data trail someone might follow. In contrast, it is the aliens who are obsessed with reproduction, as we see in the creepy finale "Alienville," about a small town occupied only by the genetically transformed. They represent themselves as an "improved" species. Here the small-town community is sinister: the food they grow and sell at farmer's markets is infected with alien blood and will transform those who consume it, and they are obsessed with fostering pregnancies because breast milk from the infected will transform the babies. Yet if small-town heteronormativity is sinister, queerness fails to offer an alternative: the least family-values-oriented team member, Ramsey, is unsympathetically portrayed as a substance-abusing womanizer who is almost infected himself when he hires a prostitute. The team members form some affective bonds, but their tendency to call one another by their surnames speaks to the degree to which family-like connections are deemphasized in *Threshold*.

In contrast, *Falling Skies* seems obsessed with family, especially patriarchal heteronormativity, yet in a characteristically uneven and convoluted way. On the one hand, the Second Mass comes to describe itself frequently as a family (especially from season 3 onward), a rhetoric that emerges especially when this group aligns with other survivors and the exceptionalism of the Second Mass's leadership and bond is underlined. At the same time, however, the Masons are a strange type of biological family unit without women: the boys' mother, Rebecca (Jennifer Ferrin), is killed in the invasion before the depicted events, and Tom's new partner, Anne (Moon Bloodgood), is never fully integrated into their domestic bond, especially after the daughter whom she and Tom have during the series, Lexi (Scarlett Byrne), proves to be partly Espheni and complicit with their invasion (she finally chooses the humans at the end of season 4 and sacrifices herself).[18] As well as expressing a xenophobic fear of hybridity, this storyline reinforces the superiority of masculinity: although both Tom (season 2) and Hal (season 3) are also briefly infected by Espheni biotech, neither betrays humanity to the extent that Lexi does. Race becomes intertwined here as well: a Latina woman, Lourdes

FIGURE 3.5 A "harnessed" boy in *Falling Skies*, killed by human forces: "Live and Learn," season 1, episode 1.

(Seychelle Gabriel), is similarly infected and causes much more damage. Moreover, although Ben, a white boy, is "deharnessed" but retains the ongoing connection to the Espheni via remnant "spikes" in his spine, he steadfastly remains loyal to the human cause; Ricky (Daniyah Ysrayl), an African American boy in season 1 who is similarly deharnessed, never escapes his attachment to the Espheni over the humans and is soon killed.[19] Consistently, the Masons display superior bravery, resistance to alien influences, and martial skills in comparison to the other characters.

The exceptionalism of the Masons informs the series' uneven treatment of issues of family, which is similar to the sleight of hand by which the series affirms democracy yet somehow always allows military choices to win out. Just as with its take on the balance between civilian and military authority, *Falling Skies* offers several foils to the Mason family and Second Mass to reinforce the justness of their particular framing of the relationship between society and family. In "Sanctuary: Part 2" (S1E7), the children are sent to the countryside to stay with rural families to keep them safe as the Second Mass mounts a major offensive, but it turns out that these families have spaces of safety only because they have made a deal with the Espheni: so long as other people's children are given up, their own can remain at home. Similarly, in "The Pickett Line" (S3E7), the Masons are robbed by another isolated family who hide and hoard resources rather than contribute to the collective war effort. Of course, the heroic Masons are victorious in each encounter. Yet in "Respite" (S5E6), when an injured Tom comes across yet another family that has managed to continue a pioneer lifestyle untouched by the war, they become for Tom "a clear picture of what we're fighting for," and he advises them to maintain their isolation, since the war will soon be won. The difference here is twofold: this family is not preying upon or exploiting others to assure their own safety but instead simply living independently, an ideal of the Jeffersonian yeoman farmer; second, this ideal family is headed by a grandfather too old to fight (but with a background in military service) and a mother—that is, no able-bodied men are shirking military duty.[20] Yet beyond military service, the collective is not as central to notions of the good life.

Just as the series espouses a balance of civilian and military authority yet stacks the deck such that the two always align as needed, the Mason men are always at the front of the line, putting their bodies at risk again and again. Yet the Masons seem chosen by god, and, like a modern-day Abraham, Tom never has to go through with the sacrifice of one of his own; a substitution is always offered. Others die (frequently described as "sacrifice") for the greater good, and they are appropriately lamented, though never in a way that raises questions about inequality within the Second Mass family. Weaver is briefly reunited with a daughter, Jeanne (Laci J. Malley), from whom he was estranged before the war, but only long enough to reconcile their relationship and thus offer Weaver a redemption story arc. Jeanne is later changed by the Espheni into some kind of monstrous hybrid, retaining her humanity only enough to save her father from an assault by other such creatures, another example of a woman failing to be as strong as the Mason sons. For the Second Mass, the greater good and family collapse into one and the same thing, but it is a model of family from which one can be expelled: those who do not concede to a notion of the collective good as epitomized by Tom and his revolutionary nostalgia are deemed traitors, never truly a part of the family after all but merely imposters. A queer approach offers us a framework to read these exiles as disavowed models of alternative sociality: just as queerness rejects the strictures of heteronormativity and opens up the possibility of another kind of family, those expelled from the Second Mass hint at other models for rebuilding America, but they are ones that Mason/Revolutionary ideology cannot countenance.

The most significant such example is Pope (Colin Cunningham), initially an outsider antagonist who fights against the Second Mass early in season 1. They take him prisoner, while one of his former gang members, Maggie (Sarah Chalke), is quickly integrated into the Second Mass family and becomes Hal's romantic partner. Pope is always somewhat at a distance from the rest of the Second Mass throughout the series: he is suspect because of his criminal past, he offers cynical ripostes to their earnest evocations of patriotism, and he often suggests he is contributing to the greater good only so long as that good aligns with his own self-interest. Yet time and again he rises to the challenge and makes meaningful contributions: drawing fire to himself to help rescue Hal in season 1, returning to report on a hidden camp of nearby aliens in season 2 when the others think he has run away, nurturing an injured Tom after a plane crash in season 3, and trying to rig a draw of names for a dangerous mission in season 4 not to avoid his own name being drawn but in an attempt to ensure that Tom remains within the community that needs him. We eventually learn he also had children before the war, and he gains a romantic partner, Sara (Mira Sorvino), in season 4. But these somewhat normalizing touches do little to mitigate Pope's continual reputation for "badness"—which is necessary to produce Tom's inherent "goodness," as the series all but admits in "Compass" (S2E3), when Tom acknowledges that they need the "berserker" unit led by Pope, since that unit is willing to do things necessary to the war effort but that require levels of violence other militia members are unwilling to enact.

Pope enables Tom to have his military victory and his moral superiority, and his role as Tom's foil is particularly intriguing when we consider some of the critiques he makes of Tom's rhetoric. In the second episode of the first season, as Tom delivers one of his speeches about reigniting Revolutionary values, Pope quips, "Is that the right analogy? . . . Isn't it more like we're the Indians and they are the never-ending tide of humanity coming in from Europe? How'd that work out for the Indians?" He is right, of course, but the series wants us to see this as just part of his cynical refusal to understand what is required to support the greater good, and thus Pope must remain a villain.[21] In season 5, Pope explicitly challenges Tom's commitment to the greater good, pointing out how many have died in its service while the Mason family remains intact; his passionate assertions are fueled by grief over Sara's death, caused by Tom's decision to delay rescuing her until after a needed vehicle was first used in a military offensive. Pope's grief and sense that the social fabric privileges some, like Tom, while it discounts others, like him and Sara, is correct, but yet again, this is a truth the series refuses to admit. The final few episodes sever any familial connection between Pope and the Second Mass: he shaves his head to resemble a neo-Nazi and begins to prey aggressively on surviving settlements, kicking out anyone he deems unable to make a sufficient contribution. The series wants us to think of Pope as Tom's opposite, but he is really Tom's double, the ugly face of neoliberalism's biopolitical management of people and resources that is the hidden truth of Tom's own management style, without the fantasy of exceptionalism that protects the Mason family from difficult choices. Pope is not a queer character, then, but he offers a queer perspective on the heteronormative, conservative nation-as-family championed by Tom, an alternative that *Falling Skies* strives to disarm rather than cultivate.

BEYOND FAMILY?

Questions of the collective "common good" versus the more narrowly conceived needs of the individual family are paramount for these series. We argue that such debates are key to how these series allegorize economic crisis as much as they do national security, although not necessarily with the same degree of conscious intention. Cherniavsky argues that the neoliberal individualism famously announced by Margaret Thatcher's statement that "there is no such thing as society," just "individual men and women" and "families," has "the effect of eroding the sense of a common reality in which a national or even a local (not to mention a planetary) 'we' live in simultaneous time and convergent social and material worlds."[22] This disappearance of any basis on which to construct a common good is the key reason that the crisis of neoliberal economics is also a crisis of democratic governance. In this final section, we turn to an analysis of how our remaining series, *Colony*, works repeatedly to show us why we must, under the pressure of crisis, resist the tendency to think only in terms of small groups like ourselves and our families, even as it also shows why such solipsism is tempting.

Ideas of collectivity and family are explored in season 1 largely through the contrast between Katie and her sister, Maddie (Amanda Righetti). From the opening episode, we see Katie work to help her sister, who initially lives as part of the Bowman household. Yet contact with former colleagues from the art world enables Maddie to begin to spend time in the Green Zone and eventually to become the partner of an IGA official, Nolan (Adrian Pasdar). The more she regains her material comforts, the less she is willing to think of others beyond herself and her son, until by season 2 Maddie refuses to help secure the release of an imprisoned Bram, agreeing with Nolan that "to risk our family for someone else's would just be foolish" (S2E6). This narrow perspective is insufficient, as the series makes clear by the end of season 2, when Nolan turns on Maddie too as the price, he thinks, of securing his own continued power. Both end up renditioned to the factory by season's end, outplayed by IGA operatives even more predatory than themselves.

During the first part of season 3, an IGA official who is one of the series' main antagonists, Snyder (Peter Jacobson), briefly joins the Bowman family in exile, seeming to have changed sides but actually working as a double agent to identify a hidden resistance camp. Here, too, we see a price for the failure to think generously, when the Bowmans' son Charlie is killed in the chaos of the IGA attack on this camp: this death forces Snyder to confront the emptiness of the luxury he gains in return, knowledge he struggles to repress. The contrasting example is offered by Will's coworker Jennifer (Kathleen Rose Perkins), who briefly tries to blackmail Katie when the IGA takes a more fascist turn in season 2 and Jennifer's job is threatened. She has surveillance footage that proves Katie worked for the resistance and that Will covered it up, yet when told by her new boss that her "lack of personal attachments" (S2E4) make her a good fit to rise in their ranks, she prefers suicide to complicity: as she overdoses, she watches a live feed from the Bowman home that shows Gracie comforting a traumatized Charlie, recently returned home from a year in the Santa Monica Block where he was a thief and, it is implied, a prostitute, controlled by a gang leader. Jennifer wants to protect a world in which families matter, a small utopian trace, and although it is challenging to read any hope in suicide, it does at least confirm that not all humans will easily change into neoliberal, selfish versions of themselves under conditions of hardship.

With such moves, *Colony* asks us to think beyond the family even as it centers on the family. Will and Katie fight over the best strategy to keep their family safe, but such arguments are always framed within a wider commitment to a world they want their children to inherit. Even though the series ends with them affirming that they need to better protect their children and have to start putting their own family first, our last view of Will shows him volunteering to be one of several "outliers" given to the Hosts to save the Seattle colony; meanwhile, Katie finds herself trapped outside the protective dome as the attack begins because she went to offer assistance in a refugee camp. Unlike Tom Mason, they must face the true hurdles of commitment to a larger social collective alongside the concern for their own children. Though complex and sometimes fraught, *Colony* imagines resistance as beginning with people seeking to help one another and finding ways to survive ongoing crisis and to create a new social order, rather than as a military effort to restore and expand the old America.

The Seattle colony of season 3 and its different mode of governance become key to understanding the series' themes, which shift the invasion narrative away from nationalist concerns about security and toward the biopolitical structures of the security state. The algorithm narrative suggests that an alien point of view on humanity would reduce individuals to the status of merely another resource to be maximally exploited, and like the surveillance narrative of season 2, it asks viewers to think about the degree to which their lives and choices have *already* been captured as data to feed the algorithms that structure the contemporary economy. Similarly, a refusal of family or other human connection is crucial to success in the IGA: Snyder's superior Helena (Ally Walker) advises him that "you just have to tell yourself that what is happening is inevitable" (S2E1) when he briefly has qualms about the required instrumental attitude toward massive death, explaining that their job is merely to make the process run smoothly, not to question it. In contrast, a Red Hand broadcast in "Lost Boy" insists, "Our occupation is rooted in moral compromise: men and women who have told themselves that the only way to survive is to join the enemy, that the treasons they have committed against their own kind are justifiable, that they have no other choice." It is not only that the IGA is the human face of the Hosts' occupation but that it is a tendency *within humanity itself* that has made this dystopia possible. Curiously, in "Hospitium" we learn that the Hosts are apparently refugees themselves, fleeing some other aliens, and a confused Bram asks his mother about the war and justice: the Hosts have still killed many, even if in pursuit of their own survival. Katie responds that she wishes things were simply black and white, but the truth is that the real war has always been "against ourselves"—against the human collaborators, of course, but metaphorically against the selfish tendency to divide humanity into us/them categories, family or outsider, American or alien, precisely the themes that alien invasion narratives always address.

This episode's title, "Hospitium," is a Greek word for hospitality and reminds us of the classical era's notion of the right of the stranger to expect hospitality, the familial bond formed between guest and host. The series comes close to breaking the fourth wall here, inviting us to ponder this question less in terms of the diegetic situation and more in reference to the real-world questions the series allegorizes. Facing the vast and alienating forces of dystopic social change—climate crisis, neoliberal austerity, the rise of the fascist right—can feel overwhelming, as if the only choices available are to smash ourselves hopelessly against this inevitable future (Jennifer) or to rationalize that its inevitability means we might as well maximize our own self-interest, as any effort against this tide will be futile in any case (Helena and usually Snyder). Yet the Bowmans offer a third way, a difficult model that often involves missteps and readjustments yet is also rooted in the hope that the feared future might not be quite so inevitable, if we fight against it in solidarity with others. The fact that we almost never see the Hosts in the series is crucial here, serving to mark the fact that the forces that seem impersonal and alien, like capital, are sustained by human choices and actions, even if this is not always easily visible. We retain agency because these forces are not, in the end, truly alien.

Thus, the difference marked by the Seattle colony is vital to examine, even as it offers a vexed model for alternative social organization and one ultimately that the Bowmans must reject. It works by *seduction* rather than coercion. In contrast to the LA Block's fascist policing, we have the Seattle Refugee Management Agency (SRMA): people are enticed to this colony with promises of food, shelter, jobs, medical care, precisely the things the state once sought to provide its citizens. These refugees are processed through the algorithms and then assigned housing and jobs, or, as Katie eventually discovers, they may be assigned to the "D bus": promised relocation to the cutting-edge Portland colony to alleviate overcrowding in Seattle but really taken to be disposed of since they lack the skills Seattle needs in its workforce. In "Lazarus," when a newly suspicious Katie follows one of these buses to its destination, she views people politely and patiently queuing up to be processed, their faces shining with hope. The lesson is clear: fantasy that is hope not grounded in a material possibility, then, can be a far more effective tool of social control than overt oppression. After their period of desperate struggle on the road, the Bowmans welcome the material comforts offered by Seattle and are actively encouraged not to ask any questions that might jeopardize their own status. As with the shrinking "pie" of economic security and state resources of debt-driven neoliberalism, the fundamental question they are discouraged from posing is about how their own relative privilege requires the exclusion of many others, particularly those on the D bus that Katie follows. Indeed, the D all but overtly stands for "disposable" or "discarded," and SRMA might equally be an acronym for Seattle Resource Management Allocation.

Even when Katie and Will try to accept Seattle at face value and fit in with this community, there are subtle forms of coercion in the pressures to join the community watch or host neighborhood parties: everyone is always watching one another, and one's loyalty is attested to by one's lifestyle. This is precisely the sort of complicity between heteronormativity and capitalist exploitation that our understanding of queer theory seeks to disrupt, and so we suggest that although the series fails to offer us any queer characters, the modality of queering is central to its utopian potential.[23] By "Disposable Heroes" (S3E11), Will openly describes this colony as "just bright and shiny enough to keep us from wanting to dig any deeper," and in the next, penultimate episode, when Kynes (Wayne Brady), the coder of the algorithm, is revealed to have had a secret plan to redirect resources in preparation for a day of human resistance, he explains that "the way to control a democratic society is not through fear but through distraction"—something he now calls upon everyone to reject as they shift from underground preparation to overt resistance.

We also learn that those selected before the occupation by the algorithm to work for the IGA were those already most given over to neoliberal hegemony: Snyder, who claims to have been a provost at Stanford, was really a purchasing agent embezzling from his employer, for example. In "End of the Road," when Snyder is interrogated by a conspiracy-theorist resistance leader, he deflects accusations about his complicity with death-dealing aliens by demurring, "They are not exterminating mankind; that would imply intent. They are simply using humans as a labor force and a lot of us die." In this view, humans are figured precisely as a kind of commodity, the resource labor power. And it is especially important here to think about global supply chains in contemporary neoliberalism through which some are reduced to being seen as mere containers of labor power while others retain the capacity to be seen as fully human subjects. Just as the aliens are indifferently genocidal through their exploitation of humans as a pure source of labor power, so too are the lives of many in the Global South unnaturally shortened by the hardships of the kinds of labor they endure in global capitalism. The aliens have no concern with human consciousness and agency and instead think of humanity as simply material to be positioned and deployed for their own economic and political interests. Provocatively, this understanding of the alien's approach to humanity parallels that of many in the Global North, who have no critical consciousness regarding how the objects and increasingly services they use on a daily basis are often made and delivered through supply chains of production built on conditions of immiseration and inequity.

Thinking of the aliens and their agents as emblems of the forces of globalized economic exploitation, then, we might also take note in *Colony* of the shift from Los Angeles to Seattle in the final season. This city was the site of widespread antiglobalization protests against the G7 economic hegemony in 1999, a movement seemingly on the verge of significant social power before this perspective was drowned by the din of post-9/11 nationalism. Just as the series ends, then, with Kynes shedding his pretense of cooperation with the occupation and supporting an active resistance movement, we see perhaps a hint of this Seattle spirit returning. Into the second decade of the twenty-first century, after the 2008 crash and in the midst of rising right-wing nationalism as the most dominant response to the economic hardship fostered by global capital, it is time to think with Seattle once again. The geographic placement of the narrative signals, at the very least, a desire to think differently, perhaps even a desire to resuscitate eclipsed forms of protest and action contra a capitalist regime.

Unlike *Falling Skies*, then, which vilifies the character seeking to queer its conformist future, the end of *Colony* pushes us toward something other than the return of suburban comfort, couched in nationalistic pride. Certainly, the Seattle colony is more problematic than not, especially with its narrative of disposing of those without needed skills; the algorithm used to make judgments about who should be let in seems eerily reminiscent of real-world neoliberal policies about exclusion and inclusion, particularly at borders to the United States and Europe. But the series' conclusion, which came unexpectedly with cancellation, suggests that it is well aware of—and openly critical of—how the promises of community and jobs were managed as tools of biopolitical governance by the aliens and their IGA collaborators. Kynes more than once protests that they are using his algorithm in the "wrong" way, and *Colony* concludes with its characters on the verge of orienting these tools and techniques toward the production of a different kind of social collectivity. We might see the Seattle narrative in *Colony* as a gesture toward Blochian abstract (as opposed to concrete) utopia, one that indexes a desire for alternative and potentially more sustaining forms of social and collective organization, even if not yet depictions of what such a future might look like.

DESIRING THE INVASION

How, then, have invasion narratives post-9/11 educated our desire, and how might Bloch help us activate this Seattle spirit? It is important to keep in mind that despite their clear ideological divergences, from a Blochian perspective all of these series are utopian texts: they emerge from a dissatisfaction with given conditions and animate a fantasy of a better world. Yet not all represent the kind of forward-looking, capacity-enhancing concrete utopianism that Bloch endorses. Responding to the trauma of 9/11, each of these series expresses a desire for our families to be safe and valued in the future, yet this desire is attached to very different futures indeed.

This desire is most muted in *Threshold*, which largely serves to intensify anxiety about potential hidden threats and the risk that America may not prevail in the next attack; the concern that the wrong people will reverse engineer alien technology permeates the series. Yet although *Threshold* works predominantly through the affect of fear, the team's ongoing work to reverse the beginning of hybridizing speaks to a fantasy of a single and pure America that nationalist post-9/11 discourse sought to protect, a spirit that has transformed into a desire for a white ethnostate in more recent debates. Implicit in these fears and the fantasies that structure the series, then, is a faint acknowledgment of the true geopolitical instability of a world order premised on always privileging American hegemony. And although xenophobia remains the series' standpoint, the fact that the person who emerges as a leader of the transformed hybrids, Manning (Scott McDonald), was once a high-ranking member of the U.S. military hints at the reality that America's antagonists are created from *within* U.S. policy, not strictly in opposition to it.[24] We might suggest that this "hint" is part of the political unconscious of the series—an unconscious left undeveloped and unexplorable given the series' cancellation.

Falling Skies is always pro-American, but its obsession with the Revolutionary War acknowledges that something has gone wrong with present-day America. The solution it offers is the utopianism of a right-wing constituency grown all the more visible in the years following this series' conclusion in 2015, just before the election of Donald Trump. It wants to return America to the promise of liberty when "liberty" meant something more than market freedom, but at the same time it wants to extend the neoliberal agenda by which the world itself serves America—that is, serves the American economy. *Falling Skies* articulates this move in the language of civic freedom, of course, in a mawkish finale scene that begins with Matt reading aloud his description of the final battle that ended the war and cleared the way for a new future: "as the world's survivors emerged from the smoldering aftermath, we found we reached for each other, bonded in a way we never had before." The voiceover switches from Matt to Tom reading the narrative, explaining the need for a leader, the selection of which will now be "truly informed by the consent of the governed, just like the founding fathers of America had intended." We cut to Tom giving a speech in front of the Lincoln Memorial to a gathered international crowd of survivors. "Once upon a time there was a place called America," he proclaims to enthusiastic applause that is sustained uncomfortably long. Finally, he can finish: "But before we were countries, we were human beings," and we are on our way together to becoming "better human beings" now that we have discovered that "we are not alone."

There is much to say about this finale sequence. It asserts a unified humanity at the end, but one brought together so clearly based on *American* values, essentially a moment of world constitution building in the image of the American constitution, that its real lesson remains about uniformity. So long as the world is like America, peace is attainable. Anne joins Tom at the event, visibly pregnant with what will undoubtedly be a fully human child this time, symbol of a future that is deemed desirable, unlike the queered future that might have been possible had the hybrid Lexi remained within the family. All of the Mason men have female partners beside them, save the middle son Ben, the one who had been changed by Espheni spikes. Ben was briefly romantically involved with Maggie, his older brother Hal's partner, when a transplant of his spikes into her body was necessary to save her life. The shared spikes create an intense bond between them, but the queered and posthuman possibilities that their partnership hinted at were never developed. Maggie chooses to have her spikes removed in a conscious display of fealty to Hal and the human future he promises, and the series even conjures a new character to be the partner for the youngest son, Matt, in its last few episodes. Although Ben stands on stage alongside his family, still part of them despite his spikes, only he stands without a romantic partner, suggesting that his

non-normative embodiment must end with him; only he will not reproduce into the future this series desires.

Despite all the cheering for the new American globe, it is a prosthetic
hegemony deeply entangled with disavowal that Tom—undoubtedly about
to be proclaimed president—carries into the future. The Jeffersonian values of economic independence Tom champions, ideals shared by the vocal
critics of so-called urban elites, whom they see as a threat to a proper
America, have no hope of taking root in today's neoliberal America, and
that is before we begin to take into account that America is itself a force
of occupation today. The series seems unwilling to acknowledge the irony
that it forwards a vision of America as championing liberty for all (reminiscent of a similar narrative of American positioning as global savior in
previous alien invasion films, such as *Independence Day*) when in fact
American policy, militarism, antienvironmentalism, and capitalism are
often the source of trauma across the globe. Perhaps such ironies cannot
be acknowledged given the values and self-imagination of the middle
American viewers to which *Falling Skies* seems pitched. Those viewers are
perhaps overly wedded to a simplified version of "America" that might
return the country not only to Jeffersonian ideals of economic independence but also a supposedly simpler time rooted in agrarian and smaller
communities—and, despite the series' nods to collaboration across cultural differences, a time of fantasized cultural homogeneity. Curiously,
only a catastrophe that wipes out most of humanity makes a return to this
agrarian ideal possible, a bitter irony indeed. What is wiped out in pursuit of that ideal is precisely the kinds of global militarized and capitalist
reach that America represents—and embodies—today. So, in a further
irony, *Falling Skies* cannot help but represent some of the realities of what
hampers American democracy today, even as the series seeks to direct our
attention elsewhere, to America as planetary savior. We will return to this
motif in the next chapter.

Colony, in contrast, refuses to offer us a neat package that smoothes
over the contradictions. While *Colony* uses the same narrative structure
of the alien invasion to highlight the erosion of democracy in America, it
also offers us in accessible, narrative form a vision of the power dynamics of the present that Wendy Brown diagnoses as part of the waning of
democracy in the face of neoliberalism. Like the Seattle colony, neoliberal discourse transmutes structures of governance from civic, democratic

institutions into those of technocratic management. As Brown puts it, "'stakeholders' replace interest groups or classes, 'guidelines' replace law; 'facilitation' replaces regulation, 'standards' and 'codes of conduct' disseminated by a range of agencies and institutions replace overt policing and other forms of coercion. Together, these replacements also vanquish a vocabulary of power, and hence power's visibility, from the lives and venues that governance organizes and directs."[25] *Colony*, we suggest, through the allegory of alien occupation, makes the operations of power visible once again. And through the Kynes storyline, it suggests we might yet have a chance to reengineer the systems designed to exploit us into the resources we need to build another kind of future—even as it recognizes that the model offered is only a work in progress, not a utopian blueprint.

Ultimately, we might contrast *Threshold* and *Falling Skies* with *Colony* in terms of Bloch's understanding of hope and the kind of utopia cultivated through cultural products and aesthetic encounters. Bloch understands hope as contributing to the education of desire in that it offers a "directing act of a cognitive kind," or the sense that what is needed to move us further down the path toward utopia is something truly new and anticipatory.[26] *Threshold* and *Falling Skies* seem at many points in the unfolding of their narratives to focus on the darkness of the lived moment, where the best that can be hoped for is a return to something past, some former glory, a lost vision of America. Bloch might call this backward-looking and fear-driven desire for change a form of "negative astonishment," the opposite of hope. In contrast, Bloch maintains that we also need seeds of hope in discourse that can produce "positive astonishment." *Colony* marks a turn toward alternative social and political structures that might allow at least some humanity to rebuild on the apocalyptic ruins of a former order. Such "positive astonishment" imagines a Blochian "not yet" that turns away from nostalgic desires for the return of a supposedly glorious past and toward an unknown but necessarily different future.

4

AMERICAN CIVIL WARS

I n this chapter, we look at the transition in American SF television
from narratives that imagine the threat coming from without to those
that suggest instead that the risk comes from within a split America.
In chapter 2 we discussed series that were concerned with allegorizing
America's overall shift toward the right in the wake of the 9/11 attacks; in
this chapter, our focus turns toward four series that speak to the increased
polarization of the political landscape between right and left: *Jericho*, *Revolution*, *The Man in the High Castle*, and *Continuum*—the last, notably, a
Canadian series set in a future with a unified North American government. *Jericho* and *Revolution* are set after attacks on America that evoke
the post-9/11 concerns we focused on in the previous chapter, but in these
series what at first seems to be an external attack proves instead to have
been initiated by rogue factions within the United States intent on transforming America into a different and more bellicose republic, and both
series concern attempts to restore the "real" America by returning to the
Revolutionary values we also see celebrated in *Falling Skies*. The more
recent *High Castle* draws upon alternative history and parallel worlds to
depict a fascist America following a World War II victory by the Nazis, a
device used to critique fascist tendencies within actual American history.
Continuum is also a time-travel narrative, this time one concerned with
struggles between democratic voices and those that have capitulated to

neoliberal hegemony in a battle to ensure that the correct future materializes.

All of these series are thus concerned with the trajectory of American politics contemporary to their production, and each is concerned with both futurity and an ideal of what constitutes the "true" America—and some directly suggest that a new "civil war" will be required to decide this issue. By shifting the focus from external enemies to internal ideological divisions, these series begin to depict a sense that America's political *response to 9/11* in many ways presents a bigger risk to ideals of freedom than the risk of another external attack. This critique focuses on two main motifs: the hegemony of neoliberal economic structures that consistently privilege profit over people, confusing political liberty with the freedom of the market, to the detriment of ordinary Americans; and the ongoing consequences of systemic racism that frustrate any attempt to depict America, without complication, as the bastion of freedom—a mythology that clearly haunts this concern with defending a "true" vision of America against competing ones.

FRAGMENTED AMERICAS: *JERICHO* AND *REVOLUTION*

Jericho depicts a postapocalyptic America riven by internal divisions and conflicts. It begins as a narrative seemingly about an attack from outside the country but quickly shifts into a story about corruption and chaos born from factions within the nation. Unlike *Falling Skies*, *Jericho* seems more willing to take risks with its narrative, probing how communities are made, what sustains them, and perhaps pushing beyond (at least at first) the restoration of America and reassertion of family as the primary modes through which democratic political order can be envisioned and enacted.

Jericho ran for two seasons and is a powerful drama about an eponymous small town in Kansas trying to survive in the immediate aftermath of a nuclear attack on twenty-three major American cities, including nearby Denver. What's perhaps most interesting initially is how much narrative force comes from not knowing who the "enemy" is: Islamic terrorists? The Chinese? Homegrown traitors? Midway through the first season, the Chinese make a food drop, with notes saying "Do Not Fight"—but this seems a red herring. A subplot revolves around the character of Hawkins (Lennie James), a Black man, who seems to have been an FBI agent who relocated with his estranged family to Jericho just days before the bombs detonate. But his background and intentions are shrouded in mystery. For much of *Jericho*'s first season, we do not know what is happening, and we are also asked to identify or at least sympathize with the plight of someone who, we are led at times to believe, might actually be one of the terrorists, now trying to protect his family. It is not insignificant that Hawkins, although ultimately one of the main heroes, is at first under a cloud of suspicion, because he is one of only a few characters of color on the series. The uncertainty builds narrative interest, but it also gestures toward conspiracies and plays to a sense shared by many viewers that rarely do we have the "full picture" in a complex world of competing interests and increasing threat. The most we learn in the first season of *Jericho* comes midway through the first season: apparently "cells" set off the bombs in a coordinated attack to "change the world." But who controls these cells, and to what purpose?

The answer, we ultimately learn, is corporate interests, part of an attempt to "reboot" the American nation, a plot that is unsurprising given that *Jericho* started airing in 2006, shortly before the economic collapse and at the height of the Iraq war, which increasingly seemed run by—and for—corporations. An entire background story emerges about one of the main characters, Jake (Skeet Ulrich), who is trapped in Jericho after the bombings and who had some initially unclear connections to a Blackwater-style company named Ravenwood. This background steadily becomes important, especially in the second season, although the town has to deal with Ravenwood in season 1, as a gang of its mercenaries have gone rogue to collect and control increasingly scarce resources.

The series contrasts such "dark," multinational companies with the romance of the small town, Jericho, whose isolation is its primary saving grace, out of the way of more mercenary and predatory interests. The townsfolk use their relative safety to keep American traditions alive, such as celebrating holidays and hosting communal picnics. But those traditions keep running into economic issues. One major subplot revolves around the town's supermarket and the management and distribution of commodities. What controls such practices? What's "fair"? The fight for mayor—between the salt-mining company-owning Gray (Michael Gaston), who wants to take a hard line on crime and on regarding who's in and who's out of the community, versus the recently ousted patriarch Johnston Green (Gerald McRaney), who seems to want more "state" control over the distribution of resources but who also talks a lot about democracy—references different versions of and approaches to economic policy (not to mention immigration) in early twenty-first-century America. Gray's insistence on giving away all the available food maps onto George W. Bush's tax cuts and refunds in particular and the conservative desire to deregulate more broadly. Johnston's more city-controlled policies of food distribution hark back to Bill Clinton's fiscal management while maintaining more liberal policies of state support and social welfare. And it is significant that Jericho decides between them through an election and that both sides respect its outcome, however much the losing side might disagree. The emergency of the situation does not become an excuse to suspend democratic governance in the name of expediency. Moreover, by series end, both Gray and the Johnsons are united in their resistance to the Ravenwood-backed military coup that has been perpetuated by these attacks.

With such plots, *Jericho* invites viewers to think about how Americans might remake society when existing systems of power, communication, and commodity distribution are eradicated—a scenario that, however apocalyptically rendered in the television series, is one many Americans feel is inevitable. While many series, most prominently *The Walking Dead* (2010–), figure a social order in which violence is necessary and survival is the only goal in a dangerous world, *Jericho* depicts, for the most part, in its small-town Kansas milieu, folks genuinely trying to help one another in times of difficulty. In the first season especially, neighbors help one another and seek to share resources, and although there are some tensions—about whether crops from farmland now "belong" to the farmer or to the community and whether supplies in a local store are still commodities or now collective resources—for the most part local politics focuses on working out solutions premised on the overall survival of the community. Granted, more serious rifts begin to appear as it becomes clear that the extreme situation will continue into the foreseeable future, and the town struggles to negotiate (with nearby towns and with passing transients) the boundaries of belonging and entitlement to resources such as power and food. But a basic critique remains intact: there is a strong hint that capitalist-centered democracy has long been interested more in property than in people. This critique becomes evident in the story of one of the people marooned in Jericho by the bombs, Mimi Clark (Alicia Coppola), an IRS investigator who is there to audit a local farmer, Stanley Richmond (Brad Beyer). The generosity with which the town and the Richmond family embrace Mimi stands in stark contrast to the heartless rigidity of tax regulations that would have deprived Stanley of his livelihood without the intervention of the bombs. With such narratives, *Jericho* seems to aim to reeducate the desires of its viewers, inviting them to consider how collective care is far preferable to violence, greed, and self-interest, especially at a time of increasingly scarce resources.

At the same time, *Jericho*'s vision of small-town America—a town of "real" American values—depends on more than a bit of racial homogeneity. Most of the townsfolk are white and from the middle class. As noted, Hawkins is largely treated with great suspicion for much of the series, and indeed he and his family at one point openly confront local sheriff's officers about the implicit racism implied by their insistence on searching the Hawkins home. Yet, Hawkins *is* hiding something, even if this turns out to be his attempts to undermine the coup. The series seems to want to overcome its own racial tensions; for example, a South Asian doctor becomes an ally of the townspeople, providing them much-needed medical care. But these are token efforts at best, failing to provide a systemic critique of the structural racism that existed in America before this crisis. Perhaps more importantly, from our contemporary vantage point, the series' emphasis on small-town values versus corporate "elites," oriented at the time of broadcast toward economic inequality, is now also recognizable as sharing certain rhetorical strategies with the overt white supremacy discourse that has entered mainstream U.S. politics explicitly since 2015. While *Jericho* never reinforces such perspectives, the predominance of white characters and a conclusion that relies on civilian rights to arm themselves against unjust governments—a favored platform of right-wing groups within the United States—shows how easily this style of political rhetoric can move toward the overtly racist elements in U.S. political culture.

FIGURE 4.1 Gray, the law-and-order candidate, giving his mayoral victory speech in *Jericho*: "Vox Populi," season 1, episode 11.

Concern with articulating appropriate membership in the civic community is relevant to how *Jericho* imagines political and economic community being entwined. Many of the struggles over how to continue a civic order in the wake of the disaster have to do with access to resources needed for survival—a vision carefully calibrated to ensure that private property is not discredited, while at the same time a notion of *voluntary* collectivity in which neighbors assist and share with one another is valorized. The community remains the arbiter of membership, and access to resources is always predicated on contributing to the town's overall welfare. Nearby towns' turns to authoritarianism and appropriation stand as foils to Jericho's renewal of colonial self-reliance and democracy.

But maintaining liberal democracy is challenging in the apocalypse. In season 2, the arrival of federal military authority under the command of the new presidency in Cheyenne offers a critique of shifts in U.S. governance after 9/11 in storylines that also reveal the series' underlying libertarian ethos. Jake's experiences working with contractors in Iraq are pertinent here, and, as in the example of *Colony*, one way to read this storyline is as a comment on how we might differently perceive U.S. actions in Iraq and elsewhere if the same techniques of those military occupations were visited upon American civilians. This concern is already apparent in "Rogue River" (S1E8), when Jake and his younger brother Eric (Kenneth Mitchell) go to the eponymous nearby town in search of antibiotics Johnson needs, only to find the town empty, supposedly evacuated by FEMA: the hospital, however, shows signs of a violent struggle. Inside they find a traumatized military contractor who tells them that what he witnessed rivals his experiences in Fallujah. Homeland Security has deployed such contractors on domestic territory, and his undertrained team panicked and executed the patients deemed too old or sick to move when faced with opposition to their authority.[1] In the next episode, Jericho fights off an attempted occupation by Ravenwood, there to loot supplies, and their leader, John Goetz (D. B. Sweeney), warns Jake that this will not be their last encounter and that when the government arrives to restore order, it will be Ravenwood they send to towns such as Jericho.

A more benign entity initially shows up in "Reconstruction" (S2E1), Jennings and Rall (J&R), who arrive under the authority of the Cheyenne government and promise help with things such as restoring power, procuring supplies, and transitioning to the new currency. While much of the J&R storyline critiques the Cheyenne government that they represent, their interventions into local economic issues also implicitly critique the diversion of U.S. foreign policy toward occupations that provide the pretext for massive rebuilding by U.S.-based contractors such as Halliburton, for whom warfare thereby becomes productive of profit. In short order, J&R convinces Stanley to sign a contract that gives them a share of future profits from his farm in exchange for facilitating access to needed supplies, and the company demands that local businesses all register with it and submit to inventory and other monitoring or face closure. Later (S2E3), it denies that a viral disease has spread to the local area, and when Dale (Erik Knudsen), who knows better from his contacts in the informal economy, nonetheless procures a supply of vaccine doses, J&R confiscates them for destruction, under the pretext that unlicensed pharmaceuticals present a risk to public health (our heroes, of course, manage to retain the supply nonetheless). By "Oversight" (S2E4), the townspeople have a meeting about J&R-mandated price freezes, from which J&R exempts itself, thereby maintaining a stranglehold on supplies and destroying the autonomy of local businesses. It is little surprise to later learn that Ravenwood is a subsidiary of J&R. Jake warns of the risk of the kind of unchecked violence he witnessed in Iraq (and Rogue River), since civilian police have no authority over these contractors and the military just wants transgressions covered up. Eric demurs, "This isn't Iraq!" but Jake replies, "The rules are the same" (S2E3).

While economic exploitation is a central concern that we trace throughout this book, in *Jericho* concern about J&R is subsumed into a more urgent concern with the transformation of America into a state that erodes traditional freedoms, economic and otherwise. Among their transgressions, when J&R arrives, it takes down the town's American flag and replaces it with a new one similar in design but with the thirteen stripes running vertically, an emblem of the Allied States of America. Confronting Gray about this and changes to newly distributed history textbooks that characterize 1945 to the present as the period of "The First Republic," which fell because "the United States got weak," Eric asks, "at what point is this a country that we don't even recognize?" Near the end, we learn that a radical agent within Homeland Security, Valente (Daniel Benzali), initiated the atomic attacks in order to seize power and remake the country, in league with a former senior official within J&R who is now the Cheyenne president. A risk scenario created by J&R as part of military contingency planning was transformed into a coup, and now this Cheyenne government is poised to merge with Texas, creating a combined force that can finally destroy what remains of the old USA to the east and reunite the country under a new vision. In the series conclusion, Jake and Hawkins expose the origin of the original attacks and prevent this, with the promise that—in the coming civil war—Texas and the USA will defeat the corrupt ASA, restoring the true America.

Significantly, their victory is possible only because Beck (Esai Morales), the leader of the official military forces also working on reconstruction, is compelled by their evidence against J&R and ultimately against the government from whom he has been taking orders. He and his men shift allegiance to the USA, while Goetz is discredited as an embezzler whom even Ravenwood will no longer defend. Despite its critiques of some of the excesses of post-9/11 America, then, *Jericho* ultimately endorses a nostalgic vision of a return to a purer America, a land of the free: Jericho's self-reliance (and Second Amendment rights) have ensured they could fend off the illegitimate government, and the integrity of real military personnel—as compared to private contractors—topples the false government. The ASA flag is replaced with the Gadsden flag as the series draws to a close, yet the emphasis on eliminating specific, corrupt individuals (Goetz, Valente) prevents *Jericho* from articulating a critique of structural contradictions in U.S. ideals of freedom. Released only a few years after 9/11, it sees risk in the fractures that are taking hold in American politics but suggests these gaps can be sutured.

The turn toward restoration—recovering the United States in the face of fracturing civil war—becomes more narratively and affectively central, including an intensification of nostalgia, in a series produced just a few years after *Jericho*. *Revolution* describes a postapocalyptic America in which all human-made forms of electricity across the globe are no longer operational, suppressed by some fantastical form of technology possibly developed out of combined corporate and military greed (or so we are led to believe through a series of flashbacks). In the aftermath, as contemporary American civilization is thrown back into a literal "dark ages" with the technological sophistication of the mid-Victorian era, militias and armed bandits have taken over, dividing the country into different nations and republics, seemingly always on the verge of war. One of these new "nations," the Monroe Republic (formerly the U.S. Northeast and Midwest), is led by the series' main villain, Sebastian Monroe (David Lyons), who keeps his republic of impoverished suburbanites in check with a troop of rifle-toting psychopaths. In various flashbacks, we learn that Monroe had been a longtime friend of the series' principal protagonist, Miles Matheson (Billy Burke), who had served as Monroe's general in helping, at times brutally, to establish the new republic. Experiencing a change of heart, Miles quit the militia and seems to be in hiding, tending bar in an out-of-the-way locale. He is approached by his young-adult niece, with whom he has had minimal relation and contact, to go on a mission to help her find her brother, who has been taken prisoner by Monroe to ensure that their mother, Rachel (Elizabeth Mitchell), repairs a series of amulets that might have the ability to restore the power. Monroe, as is, is awful, but a Monroe with electrical power would be particularly dangerous, and *Revolution*'s primary drama revolves around Matheson and others trying to undermine Monroe's expanding power and emerging technological advantage.

In many ways, *Revolution* is fairly par for the course with similar, contemporaneous series depicting a moment of catastrophe and the resulting civil wars, regime changes, and further scrambles to solidify power. What makes it interesting for our purposes is its embedded narrative of family and friendship. While focusing on personal relationships in such series normally allows viewers to identify with characters as they struggle within dire circumstances, *Revolution*'s family dynamics assume the forefront in the series' understanding of sociality and politics in the face of apocalypse.

As Miles and his band arrive in Philly, confront Monroe, rescue the brother and mother, and are on their way to escaping, we encounter a long series of flashbacks that explains the earlier friendship and brotherly love between Matheson and Monroe, including a few touching homosocial scenes of their vows to remain lifelong friends—the two of them as kids sitting on the bank of a river pledging brotherhood and drawing a stylized "M" on their arms together (which becomes the "M" on the flag of Monroe's republic)—as well as the cementing of that bond when Matheson saves Monroe from a suicide attempt. It is also relevant here that the military dictatorship began with intentions of helping people by keeping order in an increasingly lawless world but that the death of Monroe's pregnant partner turned him toward a more nihilistic agenda. The flashbacks culminate in a confrontation in which Matheson tells Monroe that they can no longer be friends because Monroe is going too far (that is, killing too many people in the pursuit of power) and that Monroe now "means nothing" to his supposedly lifelong friend. None of that faceoff is necessarily unusual—until this once deep friendship is set against the context of Matheson agreeing to risk his life for a niece whom he barely knows to save a nephew he has never met. None of these family members much like one another, though they commit rather easily to sacrificing themselves for one another. Granted, Monroe has become a psychopath who must be stopped. But the counterbalancing relational tie for Matheson—the avuncular connection—seems weak in comparison to the vows of friendship that Matheson and Monroe had previously declared for each other. In contrast to his avuncular ties, the relationship between Monroe and Matheson is depicted as having had some weight and heft. This intense homosociality turns into mild homophobia as Matheson "disowns" Monroe and asserts the primacy of his family ties over the bond of male-male friendship; in the process, Monroe just seems stuck, never having grown up out of his boyhood love of Miles to take care of a "real" family. The second season attempts a slight recuperation of Monroe as he becomes an ally of Matheson's group in their combined fight against a new and even more deadly foe, the Patriots, but family connections remain paramount: characters choose with whom to form alliances based on blood ties, including several father-son dyads. Indeed, Miles, Monroe, and

FIGURE 4.2 Miles and Monroe share a moment in *Revolution*: "Nobody's Fault but Mine," season 1, episode 10.

Rachel form something of a "triangle," with Miles and Rachel ultimately pairing off, restoring a heteronormative order that runs parallel to the nostalgic desire for everything to return to the "normal" before the lights went out.[2]

Such conservatism in the series—a desire to conserve even the weakest of family ties in the face of catastrophic change—parallels the other major subplot, a set of characters bent on rebuilding and restoring the United States, much as is the case with *Falling Skies*. In the process, *Revolution* cannot quite imagine a different kind of sociality, a different set of relationships and exchanges of affection that do not play to the easy and traditional sympathies of family ties. *Revolution* thus forwards nostalgia as the appropriate antidote to apocalypse, and nothing really revolutionary in terms of political—or personal—reorientation occurs in the "two Americas" storyline in either series. Something beyond restoration is required to address the divide manifesting in SF television's representations of the country's future.

NEW AMERICAS: *THE MAN IN THE HIGH CASTLE*

Responding to intensified and sedimented divisions a decade later, *The Man in the High Castle* more boldly suggests the need for reinvention rather than restoration. Loosely adapted from Philip K. Dick's 1962 novel of the same name, *The Man in the High Castle* is set in an alternative 1960s wherein the Axis powers have won the Second World War.[3] The eastern part of North America is now a territory of the Reich, while the Pacific coast is occupied by Japanese forces; a "neutral zone" in the Midwest separates the two, characterized by the remnants of former U.S. culture—a western, frontier ethos in Colorado; visible African American citizens—but although it is home to resistance members, no official U.S. government remains. Alternative-world stories exist within this setting as well—another novel in Dick's book, film footage in the television adaptation—emphasizing the contingency of history and thus the importance of fighting for the future one desires. The adaptation shifts away from the alternative history premise in its final two seasons to depict multiple worlds that simultaneously coexist: the footage begins as a propaganda project to show a world in which the Allied powers might have been victorious, thereby to inspire ongoing resistance to fascist occupation. The implication is that there are many possible worlds, that history could have taken myriad paths, but the world in which we spend the most diegetic time is one that viewers would recognize as the "real" way history unfolded.

One of the most significant themes in *High Castle* is to interrogate how significant the difference truly is between an Axis and Allied victory, in a critique of nationalist jingoism that draws attention to the potential for fascism within U.S. culture. The central Reich protagonist is not a German occupier but rather a U.S. military man who transitioned into Reich service following the American surrender, John Smith (Rufus Sewell).[4] His "everyman" name and the degree to which his wholesome family can celebrate Reich versions of major U.S. holidays, with only minor differences, further emphasizes this point and also warns against how easily America might tip over from an "appropriate" vision of nationalism into the sinister spectacle characteristic of fascism. The more central focus on characters associated with the resistance, primarily Juliana Crane (Alexa Davalos) but also her sometimes-partner Frank Frink (Rupert Evans) and his friend Ed McCarthy (DJ Qualls), ensures that the series remains critical of *tendencies within* the American political spectrum rather than critical of America as a whole. The ethnic cleansing associated with the Nazi regime is not central to the early seasons; the only such execution we witness is a Japanese official gassing a Jewish family. But at the same time, the series refuses to let such crimes be understood as only those of Axis regimes. In a story arc in which Juliana feigns defecting to the Reich and is preparing for her citizenship test, one of the questions she is asked is about "American exterminations before the Reich" (S2E4). In portions of the narrative set in the Japanese-occupied Pacific, references are frequently made to internment camps such as Manzanar.

Joe Blake (Luke Kleintank), another sometimes-partner of Juliana, first appears to be a regular American trapped in the Reich, complaining that he "wants [his] country back," but by the end of the pilot we learn that he is working undercover for the Nazis and thus functions to emblematize perspectives associated with Fox News in the viewers' world, namely, aggrieved white people who fear that demographic change is producing an America they no longer recognize. Indeed, the pilot's visions of a bright and functional, albeit suspiciously monochrome America resemble nothing so much as Reagan's 1984 "Morning in America" advertising campaign, which promised conservative voters a bright future, denying and sidelining the substantial critiques of U.S. democracy mounted by social activists during the volatile 1960s. In *High Castle*'s alternative 1960s, the counterculture never emerges, and thus the series subtly suggests that the extreme right's vision for a better American future is discomfortingly close to a vision of America had it become part of the Reich—which was itself enamored of colonizing the future in its proclamation of a coming thousand-year reign. These parallels are evident in "Three Monkeys" (S1E6),[5] in which Juliana uncovers a massive surveillance operation in the Japanese territory, while at the Smith family home in the Reich a VA Day celebration closely mirrors a typical Fourth of July, complete with fireworks and apple pie. A visiting German guest who will prove to be a traitor tries to engage John in a discussion of the exterminations enacted in their pasts, but John insists "now we have a better world" and that sacrifices are necessary to achieve such ends.

We later learn that the Smiths' son, Thomas, has multiple sclerosis and will be declared defective, putting sacrifice into a different light for John, who tries to hide the truth and save his son. Thomas, however, has so fully identified with Reich ideology that he turns himself in for extermination, believing his own death justified (S2E10). By season 4, the Nazis have built a machine that allows them access to the parallel worlds, and John travels to a "real" version of 1960s Virginia, where Thomas still lives.[6] This Thomas is as committed to American patriotism as his counterpart was to Nazi ideology and wants to enlist in the Marines to fight in Vietnam.

Desperate not to lose his son another time, John rails against the "bullshit" of medals, flags, anthems, and pledges, to whatever nation. As they converse in a diner, a well-dressed Black couple enter, ask to be served, and are refused. They remain polite but insistent, and the incident resolves with the sheriff arriving and arresting them for violation of segregation laws. Smith challenges Thomas, "This is the system that you want to lay down your life to defend?" and continues, "I don't see freedom, I don't see anything worth giving my son's life for." Thomas says he is surprised that John, whom he believes to be his father from this world, did nothing to defend the couple. When Thomas leaves the family home with marine recruiters (S4E6), the scene of his walking away is framed precisely to match an earlier scene of Reich-world Thomas walking away between two medical personnel taking him for extermination.

The series thus carefully navigates between critiquing systemic racism and fascist tendencies within America as we know it while insisting that the country retains values that differentiate it from the Reich-occupied version. The footage taken from multiple worlds with distinct futures parallels the utopian function of art as theorized by Bloch, but at the same time work by the Nazi Ministry of Propaganda reminds us that the affect communicated by artistic spectacle can be oriented toward either utopian hope or backward-looking fear. When Juliana's sister Trudy (Conor Leslie) first introduces her to this footage, Trudy describes it as "a way out" (S1E1). Juliana sees these films as important tools for the resistance, evidence that Nazi defeat is possible and thus that the future in her own world remains open, a vision of the world "not as it is but as it could be," as one character describes it (S1E2). What is an artistic provocation in fictional films created by Hawthorne (Stephen Root) in early seasons becomes evidence of other possibilities actualized in later seasons, an apt illustration of how utopian longing might actualize another kind of world. For Bloch, the world and its people are always unfinished, and art is a medium of revelation rather than mimesis, a way to bring into consciousness the traces of unfulfilled hopes and dreams of previous generations: "Every great work of art thus still remains . . . impelled toward the latency of the other side, i.e., toward the contents of a future which has not yet appeared in its own time."[7] *High Castle* literalizes this idea by making the footage *material evidence* of these other worlds, symbolizing through resistance activism in the main, Axis-victory world a version of Bloch's notion that

FIGURE 4.3 Watching film reels of alternate timelines in *The Man in the High Castle*.

utopian projects can reactivate these traces of the Not-Yet and thus bring them into concrete being in the now.

This is precisely what the footage does for Juliana, transforming her from someone on the verge of despair in the first season—for example, she refuses to have children with Frank because the future seems bleak—to someone who makes a different future possible through her commitment to the world the footage symbolizes. She proselytizes with these images of the better world, increasingly describing them as a mechanism for "waking" people up to the recognition that reality "isn't preordained" (S3E7). The alternative worlds are a version of what Bloch calls the Real Possibility in the material world to which the utopian impulse must connect to produce change, of both the world and the self, an active choice to create another possibility "behind the cracked ontology of a supposedly attained, even finished There."[8] Hawthorne explains to Juliana that in all the multiple worlds, some people are the same, "rotten or kind" in one world and in the next, but in most they differ, and this depends upon their material circumstances, "whether they have food in their belly . . . whether they are safe or scared" (S2E1), thus linking the series to the economic questions that also touch on Bloch's notions of why the utopian at times fails to cultivate the new, when people indulge fear rather than hope. *High Castle* captures how propaganda stokes and directs this fearful affect, focusing especially in season 3 on the creation of Nazi symbols to replace American ones, a deliberate attempt to cut people off from the ideals of liberty embodied in specific icons and thus to prevent these artworks from activating any utopian trace that might motivate people to choose a different future. The new Fuhrer, Himmler, announces this project as Jahr Null (Year Zero), and the main state filmmaker, Nicole (Bella Heathcote), coaches her young participants by telling them that they are "erasing the past, replacing it with a better world, a world that is entirely yours" as she films them dismantling the Lincoln Memorial (S3E4). Another episode opens with a long sequence documenting the Liberty Bell being melted into slag that is then recast as a glowing swastika (S3E8). These performances culminate in the extravagant destruction of the Statue of Liberty by jet fighters, watched by the regime's elite from the deck of a boat in the harbor. As struggles over controversial symbols such as Confederate monuments demonstrate, such symbols are never merely about documenting

FIGURE 4.4 American Nazis in *The Man in the High Castle*.

the past but also always serve to keep specific ideals in circulation as real possibilities for the future, as *High Castle* well understands.

The Nazis must build a machine that artificially allows them to move into parallel worlds, exploiting an anomaly they discover within a coal mine, but those who are "awoken" to the transformative power of the Not-Yet can simply *will* themselves to another world.[9] One way that Bloch describes the utopians is as those having the power to "think oneself into what is better,"[10] but crucially he insists that this is a matter of direction of one's affect, of the education of desire toward a better world overall, not simply a better position within the world as it appears. The utopian needs to emerge from hope, not fear, and in season 4 this difference is emphasized by footage from a propaganda television series, reminiscent of *The Twilight Zone* (1959–1964), that a now-captive Hawthorne is forced to narrate: each episode we see deliberately seeks to inculcate fear in the presumptively white viewing public. The better world toward which Juliana strives is thus not on the same plane as the world of Nazi hegemony that Nicole similarly describes as "better"—Juliana's world remains open to continual change and new voices and perspectives, while Jahr Null is about both erasing *and* ending history, creating a frozen world of Nazi hegemony forever. Frank also creates an artistic symbol that appears throughout the series, a simple image of a line and a semicircle to indicate the rising sun, a new dawn. It appears both on its own and superimposed over other images that seek to bolster Japanese or Reich power, and Frank describes his work as about the need to remind people that change is possible: "they think this world is normal, but it is not" (S2E4).

Throughout *The Man in the High Castle*, we see numerous ways in which the series speaks to the education and reeducation of characters' desires—a narrativizing of such education that, in turn, can become a focus of critical analysis on the part of viewers. The battle over what is desirable and how one's desires should be educated is a central dramatic conflict throughout the series. Just in terms of plot and within the context of the narrative, the occupation of both the eastern and the western United States by Germany and Japan depends on the steady education of Americans' desires to accept the new political and cultural orders. Such education occurs primarily through propaganda, with Nazi symbols appearing everywhere in the east and with Japanese cultural traditions becoming part of the lives of many characters in the west. The Americana and antique collector Childan (Brennan Brown), for instance, is a prime example of a character who steadily adopts Japanese customs and traditions, at first to curry favor with rich Japanese to whom he wants to sell antiques but then more genuinely as he falls in love with a Japanese woman. In Nazi America, much of the education of desire is focused on children, who are taught the Nazi ideologies of racial purity and the need for eugenics programs to preserve and propagate the Aryan race. Racial segregation increasingly becomes a major narrative component—a marker of both the Nazis' attempt to maintain racial purity by promoting racism and also a source of critical resistance as Black people organize (especially in the fourth season) to counter Nazi propaganda and control.

The struggle over the education of desire in *The Man in the High Castle* occurs predominantly, at least initially, through storylines focused on families, as we have already seen in the major plot arc concerning John Smith and his son Thomas. A fellow Nazi tells Smith that there is "nothing more important than family," and Smith's commitment to the ideology of racial purity necessitates that he sacrifice his son to the cause of maintaining certain kinds of families. In a way, this narrative represents an extreme form of heteronormativity and heteropatriarchy, with a very particular notion of the family—straight, white, able bodied, and gender conforming—being the only kind worth promoting and reproducing. In contrast, Frank's Jewishness and a few other characters' homosexuality, most notably Frank's friend Ed and the Nazi journalist Nicole, put them in constant jeopardy.

Curiously, the Japanese trade minister Tagomi (Cary-Hiroyuki Tagawa) has a similar storyline in which he gets to visit with his family, from whom he is estranged in his own reality. The alternative-world films and the alternate realities themselves suggest that other possibilities are imaginable, perhaps enactable. Tagomi, though, in conversation with Smith, does not initially propose that those alternatives be enacted; he says, in season 3, "The different truths of those worlds are of great value. And of great personal comfort." The question of whether those alternate realities can become more than just comforting remains open. That is, are they just "fictional" imaginings that provide an "escape" from the harsh realities of occupied America? Or might they offer alternative ways of imagining—and desiring—a different political, and familial, order? Affectively, the films offer characters choices to hope for a better world or fear that such will never be realizable.

This difference in choosing hope or fear, abstract or concrete utopia, speaks to how people react when they discover better lives, better versions of themselves, in the USA alternative world. Both Tagomi and Juliana leave the safety and comfort of their alternative lives out of a commitment to improving the future of the Reich world from which they came. John, in contrast, is moved by the images he sees of a happy if significantly less economically prosperous family in the USA, but this does not prompt him to work toward change: rather, he plans to kidnap that world's Thomas and bring him to the Reich world. Interestingly, while Smith and Tagomi struggle with these different visions of family at a personal level, the series shows us other characters who actively attempt to enact alternatives in the original reality—often in ways that move beyond the immediate confines of the nuclear family. For these characters the films are not just comforting but actual guides to desiring and living differently. In the third and fourth seasons, we see more of a community in the Neutral Zone, specifically in Colorado, centered on the grounds of a Catholic church, where a range of outsiders, notably Jews and queers, are able to live in relative safety. Frank Fink finds refuge in this community, even becoming a bar mitzvah in one moving episode, and Ed and his boyfriend can openly embrace and touch each other. The community of resisters is run on a fairly egalitarian basis, with equity between genders and a decision-making governance structure that seems to value debate and consensus. To be sure, the community is fragile, in that Japanese and German spies, as well as bounty hunters looking for escaped and wanted resisters, constantly threaten it. But it also offers one of the series' few significant imaginings and enactments of an alternative social order—beyond that of the alternative-world footage. It is worth keeping in mind that "catholic" means universal or all-embracing—a concept and ethical orientation in stark contrast to that found in either the western or eastern occupied states. In fact, when Helen (Chelah Horsdal) flees the Nazi states, she finds refuge in the Neutral Zone, suggesting that it broadly, like the Catholic community, is a necessary alternative space, perhaps a queer counterpublic, for imagining different social, familial, and intimate desires.

As the third and fourth seasons progress, the contrasts between this kind of "catholic" community and the fascisms of the occupying forces, particularly the Nazis, only become starker. Helen returns to New York to be with John and to try to help protect her remaining daughters, but one of them has been so indoctrinated by Nazi ideology that she suggests directly to her mother that Helen go to a reeducation camp to learn how to be a better mother. She creepily tells Helen that "You can't love your family if you don't love your race." The daughter intuits that Helen remains deeply conflicted about the Nazi regime—a conflict that others, like Juliana, believe they might be able to use to their advantage if they can convince Helen to betray her husband. In fact, Juliana encourages Helen to seek out and view the alternative-world films, which do in fact start to tip Helen toward the resistance when she sees her son, Thomas, still alive. Between the films and the Neutral Zone, alternative structures and relationalities offer the possibility of cultivating different kinds of desires in some characters—or at least of prompting those characters to want something different than the reality they currently inhabit.

The strongest version of the reeducation of desire and a consequent attempt to enact different desires for social order comes in season 4 and the development of a powerful subplot around the Black Community Revolution. The BCR consists of a group of Black activists, primarily in the western states, who hope to oust the Japanese and create a community nation. Up until this point in the series, the ideology of racial purity had been the primary way race had been addressed. But now, the emergence of storylines focused on the BCR add nuance to the series' considerations of race and tie them explicitly to alternative forms of nation building. While Nazi ideology has been premised on *preserving* racial purity as a form of policing and reproducing a specific form of citizenship, the BCR promotes a collectivist politics based on radical equality. In fact, it is important to note that the BCR *does not* advocate for a return to the old United States. Characters in the BCR speak forcefully about how they were basically enslaved (even after Emancipation) in the old United States as well as by the Nazis. And significantly, we see none of these characters or their alternative lives in the USA world. Their goal is not to return to the old America but to *envision* a new nation built on the unfulfilled promises of equality offered by the old America. Throughout season 4, the BCR insurgent Bell Mallory (Frances Turner) advocates specifically for a Black nation, saying at one point, "All we wanted was a homeland. Forty acres and a mule. We got half of North America!" In one dramatic moment,

Mallory and the BCR break into the airwaves of Nazi television in the eastern states and proclaim their intent to establish a new communist nation, urging sympathizers to support them by abandoning their posts. Meanwhile, the Nazis plan to invade the western states, recently abandoned by the Japanese, and urge the white inhabitants to resist their "Negro overlords." Such conflicts map interestingly and in an eerily timely fashion onto contemporary racial conflicts in the United States, which might be understood as another form of American civil war.

As the season and series draw to a conclusion, with these visions of an alternative social order moving from fantastical film to realizable possibility, family tensions among the Smiths come to a breaking point, with the nonindoctrinated daughter confronting Helen about how complicit Helen has been in standing by while the Nazis killed Jews and Blacks. Family drama resumes center stage as Helen confronts John, saying, "How did we get here? This thing we have been a part of . . . it's a crime. . . . It has to stop." What animates and emboldens her is her desire to protect her family—but not *protect* them by ensuring that they *survive* but by ensuring that they grow up in a world not run by the Nazis. That is, she wants to enact the alternative-footage world she has seen, desiring that the imagined world become reality. Importantly, she refuses John's plan of bringing the USA-world Thomas into the Reich world and instead helps the resistance sabotage John's train, after making arrangements for the resistance to raise their daughters. She argues that the other version of Helen is the better mother and that she needs to leave Thomas in the better world rather than indulge her selfish desire to be with him.

In the concluding episode, the portal between worlds opens after Smith has been killed in a resistance attack and the planned assault on the western states has been aborted by American Nazis who are starting to rethink the choices they have made. Yet in this easy reversal and the implicit suggestion that America may soon be unified once again, the series too easily allows viewers to establish a gap between a "real" and a "Nazi" America. The finale elides serious consideration of fascistic tendencies within the United States, as though the fascism in America were an imposition from a foreign power and that, given the choice, Americans would readily distance themselves from fascistic forms of government. Nonetheless, the series attempts to end on a note of hope—and hope grounded in openness—for the future. The flow of people between worlds suggests a material enactment of what had largely, up to this point, only been imagined. Even more interestingly, the flow of people across the portal suggests a "borderless" world, one where the sharp and rigid distinctions enforced by the Nazis and the Japanese no longer exist, with no new borders erected and readily at hand. Radically, then, *The Man in the High Castle* ultimately concludes neither with the restoration of an older order, the former United States, nor with any kind of ready-made order: the future is undetermined and open. When someone at the portal asks Juliana where all of the people are coming from, she cryptically responds, "Everywhere." The implication here is that what the resisters have steadily been fighting for—have steadily been imagining and desiring—is an orientation toward the open, the uncharted, the undetermined, an orientation, that is, toward the utopian impulse.

GLOBALIZED AMERICA: *CONTINUUM*

While *The Man in the High Castle* rewrites American and European history to revive a spirit of resistance to fascism, *Continuum* is set in an alternative Vancouver that is imagined as part of a North American state, envisioning the future of America as the future of globalized capital. The series opens with a terrorist attack conducted in 2077 by a group called Liber8, thereby evoking 9/11. Just before the tower collapses in this attack, their leader, Kagame (Tony Amendola), issues a statement: "When corporations bailed out our failed governments, they sold it to us as salvation, but now we are awakened to the truth, that we have become slaves to the Corporate Congress" (S1E1). We cut to their post-trial execution, where another kind of explosion sends them and Protector Keira Cameron (Rachel Nichols) back to 2012, the year the series was released, and the premise is established—in the past, Liber8 will work to try to change history so that the dystopian future of corporate control will never arrive, while Keira, identifying with her role as a law enforcement officer, will try to apprehend them. Yet as quickly becomes clear, things are not quite that simple, and *Continuum* becomes instead something like a primer on educating desire and awakening viewers to the possibility that they might change the future implicit in their current reality. Over its four seasons, the series narrates shifting alliances and ideologies, as Keira comes to question her own role in upholding an unjust regime of economic inequality in 2077, while some Liber8 members lose their commitment to creating a better future and instead decide to maximize their own wealth in their new present. As Keira comes to see events in 2077 differently as she watches the seeds of this future be planted in events in the 2012 timeline, the series also demonstrates to viewers that their own contemporary choices similarly imply a trajectory for the future to come.

Like *Jericho*, *Continuum* is concerned about governance by and for the everyday citizen, and while it is not set in a small town, a significant season 1 storyline has to do with a family farm that is lost from the combined effects of the agribusiness transformation of agriculture (through corporations such as Monsanto and GMO seeds) and chronic indebtedness to banks. Stepbrothers Alec (Eric Knudsen) and Julian (Richard Harmon) experience the fragmentation of their family as a result: Julian becomes an anticorporate activist, destined in the future to become Theseus and write a manifesto that motivates Liber8 resistance; Alec focuses on using his genius with technology to create a new future and becomes Keira's confidant when her communications system connects with Alec's experiments (its prototype). Through many plot twists, Alec and Julian are sometimes rivals, sometimes allies, as they both work toward what each believe will be a better future but also seek to resist the worst aspects of their legacies as revealed to them by the time travelers—Alec is the architect of the dismal future of the Corporate Congress, while Julian's activism ultimately sparks the violence of Liber8 bombings. For both, the issue is not simply refusal to participate, although both adopt this strategy for a time. Instead, the narrative suggests, they must find ways to foster how the world might be improved by their talents but without indulging the self-centeredness that Bloch associates with the abstract utopia. For Alec, this means creating technologies but not a financial empire to profit from them. For Julian, this means insisting on peaceful protest as the only strategy, while he continues his message of economic justice.

Keira is the main focus of the narrative, however, and in many ways the series is the story of the education of her desire away from the narrow goal of returning to "her" future and the son she left behind and toward understanding the problems with that social order and thus her need to create a better world for her son, even if this might mean she is unable to return to him. She convinces local authorities she is an FBI consultant and begins working with the police department. Especially in the first two seasons, the episodes have a typical structure: they begin with an incident in Keira's 2077—for example, suppressing a "riot" in which she later discovers the perpetrators are raiding food stores, which have been kept from a starving public to drive up stock prices (S1E6)—that will offer her a vantage point on events in her new 2012-era present, in this case a peaceful Occupy protest. At first Keira remains committed to the law-and-order ethos in which she was trained, and she often uses excessive violence against suspects, much to the chagrin of her partner, Carlos (Victor Webster), who resists the tendencies toward militarization that he sees in the police department, especially as it is gradually infiltrated by a corporation, Piron, that provides technology a beleaguered municipality can no longer afford. Liber8 begins to take action in the 2012 era, reasoning that they can prevent the Corporate Congress from emerging by alerting people to the danger, delivering a message similar to the one we hear from a young Kagame (S1E4) about the way crushing debt enslaves people despite their putative political freedom. Yet it seems words were not enough in the first iteration of history, and Liber8 also takes criminal action, such as kidnapping a CEO—although ultimately this is to reveal that they were actually hired by the firm's head of security, the ransom demand a stunt to increase stock prices (S1E6)—or stealing a truck of chemicals, this time to reveal that a pharmaceutical corporation is developing bioweapons (S3E6).

While at first Keira believes Liber8 rhetoric to be empty rationalization, the more she learns about the origins of her social order in overt oppression, the more she is convinced that their resistance is just, even if their methods are not. Similarly, some Liber8 members come to embrace more peaceful strategies. All the while, as various events continually rewrite the future, viewers get hints of an even more dire possibility, in which chronic indebtedness has become the norm and those unable to make payments on their debt burden are stripped of citizenship for "civic debt default" (S2E9)—a storyline very like that of *Incorporated* (discussed in the introduction). This more sinister future correlates with the militarization of the police, who increasingly seem more like a privatized security force protecting property at the expense of social welfare, such that Liber8's violence starts to pale in comparison to the state's excesses.

Fearing what he will become in her future, Keira at one point tortures and threatens to kill Julian when he is imprisoned for protesting (S1E9), only to later realize that he is still only in his late teens, that perhaps her actions of terrorizing him are what radicalizes him: "what if I'm the one who creates the monster?"

Coming to see how the police serve corporations rather than citizens as she witnesses transformations in the 2012 era is key to Keira's shift from wanting to return to her future toward wanting to change it. This is especially evident in "Minute Changes" (S3E4), when a campus protest results in police violence against the students, killing one. The mainstream police culture moves even further toward military-style weapons and omnipresent surveillance, but by this point Keira and Carlos are both fully committed to creating a different trajectory for the future. *Continuum* recognizes that social and economic justice requires a broad rethinking of how fully the state capitulates to corporate interests in projects of austerity. The racial diversity of Liber8, whose members are mainly Asian, Black, and Latinx, suggests a further recognition of the historical role of police violence in perpetuating white supremacy, itself deeply rooted in property relations.

Keira's development and evolution as a character is the primary vehicle through which viewers are invited to consider this kind of broad rethinking. Much of the drama and tension created in the series revolves around how Keira is pushed and pulled from one interpretation of what is happening to another. As she learns more about the reality of exploitation, what she comes to question is her *desire* to help maintain the future she comes form. With Keira, we watch the corporate police state being born, particularly through the use of digitally collected information to surveil the lives of citizens and arrest them even for *sympathies* that are anti-corporate. Keira's reeducation occurs painfully, however, especially as she confronts her own complicity in creating her future world, reproduced by behavior such as torturing Julian. In asking viewers to identify with her, the series might play to *our* reeducation as well, or at least prompt us to question our sympathies in the War on Terror and the desirability of having corporate interests determine so many political decisions.[11] Early in the second season, one of the more brutal future terrorists, Travis (Roger Cross), asks Carlos if he is ever bothered by the injustices he sees, the way corporations manipulate the law and citizens to turn a profit. Carlos replies, "Guess I'm just used to it." Travis, whose brutality we later learn is a result of the fact that his body has been augmented by a future corporation working on supersoldiers, answers: "They need your complacency." The exchange seems pitched not just to Carlos but to viewers, sitting comfortably (for now) in front of their televisions. *Continuum* thus offers a narrative of Keira's reeducation that is complex and nuanced in its own resistance to simple binaries of good and evil.

Part of that complexity hinges on questions about the acceptable use of force and violence. Early in the second season, we see Julian, in prison, reading *The White Guard*, an early book by the Soviet-era writer Mikhail Bulgakov. Bulgakov wrote in *The White Guard* about different factions (socialist, monarchist, etc.) fighting over Kiev shortly before the 1917 October Revolution, and his own sympathies were mixed. He became a critic of Soviet policies, especially under Stalin; thus Julian, the revolutionary, reading Bulgakov might be a clue that the series' "take" on the War on Terror acknowledges contradictory or at least troubling identifications— and that such complications might be necessary. Both Keira and Julian sift through options and interpretations on their way to more just world building.

Such steady confusion of sympathies makes for heady, engaged viewing, calling to mind *The X-Files*. But while that show was willing to play with the main characters' foibles, as discussed in chapter 1, it did not risk identifications as strongly as does *Continuum*, which, at its best, invites viewers to question their loyalties to characters as a way to interrogate their own views on terrorism and violence and, perhaps more importantly, on the purposes of governance and the economic social order, that is, how far one should—and should *not*—go in defending—or challenging—an unjust status quo. *Continuum* constantly poses difficult questions: Does the repression of terrorism in the twenty-first century actually result in the corporate takeover? And might the terrorists have a point in organizing against the nascent corporate state?

The series' fourth and final season concludes on a hopeful note, as characters, despite ongoing conflicts, move toward recognizing their power—and responsibility—to shape the present to create possibilities for better futures. Julian rejects his legacy as a "terrorist" but also recognizes that his Theseus manifesto represents an important move against the corporate state; Alec, in an attempt to comfort Julian and help him

FIGURE 4.5 Reading the Theseus Manifesto in *Continuum*: "Power Hour," season 4, episode 3.

understand the importance of his manifesto, tells him, "It's actually quite beautiful." At the same time, in the final episode, Alec comes to the conclusion that, "What we do with it [the present] . . . is up to us. All of us." In a way, Alec's meditations are among the most metacritical in the series, offering a direct invitation to viewers to think about how speculative narrative—such as *Continuum*—offers a glimpse of possible futures born out of present choices as a way to reflect more robustly on those choices.

True to the complexity and nuance of its narrative, however, *Continuum* does not suggest that those choices will be easy. While Keira helps prevent the creation of the Corporate Congress, she does so at great personal cost. The present (our future) to which she returns is drastically changed, but her homecoming does not reunite her with her family and child—one of her primary motivations throughout the series. Instead, she sees her son with a different mother, but in a future seemingly much more just and equitable than the one she formerly inhabited. The reeducation of her own desires has led her to be willing to make that sacrifice, though, learning, as an elderly Alec tells her, that this is "The price of love . . . real love." In many ways, she makes a choice similar to the one Helen Smith makes in *The Man in the High Castle*, sacrificing her own needs so that her family might have a better future. Significantly, then, both series offer us visions of how characters move on from the desire to maintain and preserve their notion of family to embracing collective action that enables better futures for their children, for all children.

UTOPIA CALLING

Each of the series discussed in this chapter shows a continual discomfort with American identity expressed in twenty-first-century SF television, rooted in the conviction that the problems lie within rather than without. Each is concerned with ensuring that the "right" vision of the nation and the future is hegemonic, a concern we will also see in the series discussed in the next chapter. *The Man in the High Castle* suggests that the relevant historical frame of reference for this question is America's emergence into global dominance in the period following the Second World War (an event absent or deferred in this alternative history); both *Jericho* and *Revolution* include episodes entitled "Why We Fight," the title of Frank Capra's 1942 film made for the U.S. government and designed to convince citizens that intervention in the war was necessary and just. Capra's film posits a binary division of the world into "free" and "slave" nations; this requires the United States' intervention to ensure that freedom persists. And yet as the series discussed in this chapter have shown, America too has not always lived up to this ideal of freedom, especially in terms of racial justice. Similarly, most series discussed here suggest a binary division between "good" and "bad" futures, often emblematized as the need for a single hegemonic vision of "true" America to defeat and eradicate dangerous attempts to reconceptualize the nation. This vision that a single and correct vision of the better future is achievable limits these series' ability to engage with the complexities of utopian praxis. While *Continuum* raises questions about the appropriate role of violence in achieving this end, the others often celebrate revolutionary violence, although they condemn the unjust violence of occupying forces. *High Castle* depicts multiple acts of sabotage by the resistance, especially in the final season, with little concern for the inevitable civilian body counts their attacks on infrastructure produce. Even Helen's sacrifice at the end of *High Castle*, so that Thomas can live in a Nazi-free future, has significant collateral damage. In contrast, Keira's sacrifice in *Continuum* of her own desires to be reunited with her family largely eschews the violence of these other series. On one hand, characters such as Helen willingly sacrifice others for the sake of their families, risking confusion between their motivations and those of other, more obviously villainous characters; on the other hand, Keira's actions seem more clearly selfless in sacrificing her own desires so that not just her children but all children have the possibility for a better future. Hers seems a more utopian imagining. The call to engage in such utopian imagining is fierce right now. Both ecologically and economically, our current systems and ways of life are untenable in the long term, with apocalyptic turning points approaching fast. Our news media are rife with rhetorics of fiscal cliffs and superstorms and catastrophic climate change. We feel individually helpless against such changes, surely. And our consumer fetish for postapocalyptic media plays on our heady emotions about such issues. But what we imagine—and fail to imagine—about the future through our popular media might also give us a clue to thinking about what we might need to rethink now, what stumbling blocks we, consciously or not, put in the way of envisioning and creating a better world. The series we have analyzed in this chapter show how nostalgic attachment to older orders, often perceived as more equitable and socially just than they were, might be one significant stumbling block in imagining alternative forms of sociality and government. In the next chapter, we turn to series that are similarly interested in building a better future, but ones that struggle with the question of how to create community across difference. As they work toward the utopian across sites of difference, these series also more directly acknowledge the problem of using violent means to achieve inclusive ends.

5

DESIRING A DIFFERENT FUTURE

The 100 and *The Expanse*

In previous chapters, we have seen that concern about the political future of America is a central anxiety that propels twenty-first-century North American SF television. Invasion narratives channel anxieties not only about external threats but also about the rise of internal surveillance as a response to such threats, while narratives about a divided America fighting over which group represents its "true" legacy speak to the growing political distance between left and right and thus whose future is truly the "American" one. As we have argued in previous chapters, while such differences are often framed in terms of political struggles, a vast economic divide informs such tensions, and we find hints of this in numerous series. In this chapter, we turn to two series that more directly articulate the need to build a *different* future rather than to return to the "true" America: *The 100* and *The Expanse*.[1] We argue that these series highlight the need for new visions of the good future, understood as the challenge of constructing community across difference. Such difference is not explicitly posited as racial difference, although both series are also notable for more diverse casts than have been typical of the series discussed up to this point. At the same time, however, both series link their various political factions to distinct experiences of embodiment, which create different communities in these futures, pointing to the importance of discourses of racialization to American identity. Crucially for our arguments in this chapter, both series also make visible the bedrock of economic disparity that underlies and sustains the fractures within and among communities.

PRECARIOUS FUTURES

The 100 is set in a future in which life on Earth has been destroyed by a nuclear war. The descendants of those who happened to be in space at the time of the conflict believe themselves to be the sole remnants of humanity. The motif of the difficulties of sustaining community across difference are embodied by their home, the Arc, an assemblage of twelve stations, initially from different countries, that joined together to pool resources after they saw the destruction on Earth. In a few episodes we see glimpses of their tradition of celebrating "Unity Day" as they forge a new identity as Arc citizens, and the challenges of sustaining life in the hostile environment of space have produced a harsh ethos in which all crimes are capital crimes: those who violate the rules of the collective are no longer entitled to its resources. The exception is minors, who are imprisoned rather than "spaced." The narrative is set in motion when the leadership decides, after ninety-seven years in orbit, to send a crew of one hundred incarcerated teens to the surface to test the viability of living on the planet. They also hide their real reason for doing this: the Arc can no longer sustain the number of people who are aboard, and so they must either land or cull their population. Thus, the biopolitical framing for this series is starkly clear: the struggle to build community will always be on the contested terrain of whose lives are deemed to matter most.

In each of its seasons, *The 100*'s narrative is propelled by conflicts between (and sometimes within) this group from the Ark and other constituted populations: tribal communities who live on the planet's surface (grounders) in season 1; a transnational group of elites who survive within a shielded bunker (Mount Weather) in season 2; those who embrace a possibility of virtual upload and those who defend continued material life in season 3; internally in season 4, with some seeking to align with the grounders and others resolutely against it; prisoners who return on a mining ship after decades of cryosleep in season 5; human settlers on another planetary body, Sanctum, to which they have traveled by season 6; and finally, in season 7, the descendants of a religious cult who used a wormhole to escape the destruction of Earth. This final season narrates the "last war," which these cult leaders believe will ensure transcendence "for *all* mankind," pointing to the fact that throughout its seasons the series has explored the problem of racialization:[2] one humanity from an interplanetary point of view, yet one that experiences repeated apocalyptic events because of its inability to embrace this fact. The repetitive structure of this list might seem at first glance to belie our contention that the series is about building community across difference because it is so clear that the protagonists fail to do this: the lofty goal of saving all of humanity repetitively collapses into the sacrifice of some lives for the sake of extending others, which is the essence of the Arc's social structure. At the same time, however, the content of who precisely counts as "my people" to be saved shifts repeatedly over these seasons, suggesting that while *The 100* cannot articulate a clear vision of human solidarity as necessary to a better future, it nonetheless understands that this ideal—community across difference—is what is required.

The Expanse is set in a twenty-fourth century in which humanity has colonized the solar system, creating a socioeconomic structure that has some parallels to discourses of globalization, especially in terms of how a history of colonialism continues to shape current global inequality. The Earth is united under the global governance of the United Nations, but there are hints that U.S. hegemony undergirds this body: it remains headquartered in New York, and English is the dominant language, although Christjen Avasarala (Shohreh Aghdashloo), the central UN protagonist, is portrayed as having South Asian ancestry. The United Nations is economically and politically dominant; Mars was once an Earth colony but has since gained its independence, although it continues to divert funds from its terraforming projects to the military to ensure it remains so; and beyond these inner planets the Belters live on asteroids and spaceships, working in dangerous mining industries to harvest materials that are mainly shipped back to the imperial center of Earth. The United Nations (Earth), Mars, and the Belt each have distinct political orientations that could also be understood as ethnic identities: they grow up under different conditions of gravity (or lack thereof), creating distinct morphologies, and the greater wealth of the United Nations and Mars means that those

FIGURE 5.1 Belters in *The Expanse*: "The Seventh Man,"
season 2, episode 7.

in the Belt often suffer from a range of health conditions related to mal-
nutrition, periods of oxygen deprivation, and the like, mirroring existing
health disparities in the United States among ethnic groups that are also
frequently attributable to socioeconomic inequality.

As with *The 100*, a central motif across the series concerns how to form
community across difference. The plot is set in motion by the appearance
of a strange kind of biomatter, the "protomolecule," which proves to be a
technology created by an ancient race that rewrites the genetic code of
organisms it encounters. The intent of its creators remains mysterious but
seems linked to imperial expansion, and it is thus ultimately an existential threat to all human life that humanity finds difficult to counter because
Earth, Mars, and the Belt, whose political identity is the OPA (Outer Planets Alliance), are so entrenched in rivalry. Series drama is driven by a
combination of real conspiracy—specific individuals do seek to manipulate the situation for private gain at the expense of public good—and conspiracy theories—there are multiple cases of war almost erupting among
these three factions because of misinformation. While the ancient technology mobilized by the protomolecule is the most significant threat, this
risk exists only because the Mau Corporation conducted secret experiments with this substance, hoping to create supersoldiers that would
ensure the United Nations' continued dominance of the other factions.
In multiple narrative moments, most crucially a mutiny within the UN
ranks that rejects misinformation and thereby refuses to escalate an attack
on Mars and, later, the response to the mysterious technology generated

by the protomolecule, which can be escaped only by demonstrating that one is *not* a threat, disaster is averted only when all three political groups, the United Nations, Mars, and the OPA, can act in concert. Yet, just as frequently, as soon as they overcome one crisis, some faction refuses the alliance and reverts to insisting they must put their own people first.

The 100 and *The Expanse* are both premised on futures of scarcity and suggest that the ongoing fragmentation of community into competing factions has its origin in an economic disparity rooted in colonial logics. Those from the Ark who return to Earth in *The 100* see themselves as its rightful inheritors, but the grounders they encounter rightfully maintain that the Skaikru ("sky crew"), as they name them, are invaders. Similarly, those who persist within Mount Weather have lived a life of ease abetted by technology and view themselves as the true human descendants, while considering the grounders, who live a premodern tribal existence and speak a pidgin dialect, as little better than animals. Differences among the first hundred settlers are pegged to class, with the working-class Murphy (Richard Harmon) early on marked as an outsider (his father was "spaced" for stealing medicine), while Clarke, whose father was also "spaced" but had been a leader on the Ark before this, is frequently referred to as "princess" in this first season. Earth is destroyed twice in the series: the original nuclear war and later when several nuclear power stations fail, creating a wave of radiation across the planet. As with the return to Earth and struggle over to whom it rightfully belongs, various factions compete for control of the shielded bunker that will enable them to survive and, in the aftermath, for access to the one valley that remains fertile. In the end, no one gains access to the valley: their war over controlling it destroys the possibility of any future for life on Earth. Octavia (Marie Avgeropoulos) plays a key role: she is so insistent on emerging victorious over encroaching enemies that she rejects and destroys the researcher Monty's (Christopher Larkin) experimental algae, which can restore fertility to more of Earth over time. We will discuss the trajectory of Octavia's characterization in more detail in what follows, but here the key point is that while the series repeatedly depicts choices of prioritizing the in-group and engaging in zero-sum-game logics of future survival, it just as insistently shows that this way of thinking makes things worse, trapping the protagonists in an ongoing apocalypse from which recovery is impossible. After this sequence, their only option is travel to another inhabitable planet, restarting the destructive cycle of colonial appropriation and conflict.

It would be easy to read *The 100* as simply hypocritical, in that protagonists repeatedly rationalize their genocidal impulses as for the greater good, often described as the survival of "the human race." The main protagonist, Clarke (Eliza Taylor), for example, kills the entire population of Mount Weather by exposing them to ambient radiation they cannot survive (her people and the grounders have both evolved a higher tolerance), and she does this to prevent the leaders of Mount Weather from killing "her" people via harvesting their bone marrow, to transfer their capacity to recover from radiation exposure to Mount Weather citizens. Clarke characterizes her own actions as necessary to end a society premised on mass murder, but the gap between her choices and those of Mount Weather's leaders are not as vast as she'd like to believe. The series does not simply ignore this irony, however, but repeatedly points it out, suggesting that at least in part the series is about the conundrum of being trapped within a certain biopolitical logic in which humanity is always split between "my people" and those outside this community. Although the brief plot description offered here may make it seem as if nothing ever changes in *The 100*, in fact the protagonists do notice and grow weary of this repetition. In early seasons, they reassure one another that, faced with the choice of survival or extinction, they have "no choice" but to make the kind of harsh calls emblematized by the Ark's widespread capital punishment. They insist that there are "no good guys" or that, if there are, they occupy this position. Yet by latter seasons, such rationalizations ring less true: characters may still assert the necessity of their choices but with regret rather than as vindication, and the mantra "first we survive, then we get our humanity back" repeated several times especially in seasons 3 and 4 transforms into the call to "do better," not simply *to* survive but to *deserve* to do so.[3] In season 1, characters often argue that violent choices are not "who we are" (S1E7 especially), but competition for limited resources changes them: by the final season, Clarke reflects, "I used to think fighting was what we do. Now I worry that fighting is what we are" (S7E3).

Economic themes are more central to the conflicts in *The Expanse*, but at the same time these struggles use the language of the priority of "my people," whether this be assertions made by the corrupt UN official

Errinwright (Shawn Doyle) that Earth must come first, the Martian marine corps' dismissive attitude toward the softness of Earth culture, or the revolution rhetoric of Anderson Dawes (Jared Harris), who leads a militant OPA independence movement. The postapocalyptic setting of *The 100* articulates conflict over resources in all-or-nothing rhetoric based on the survival of the species, but the world of *The Expanse*, with its political bureaucracy, can openly name unfair distribution as the problem. We see little of Earth culture beyond its political elites and a brief sequence in season 2 when the Martian marine Bobbie Draper (Frankie Adams) travels to Earth for UN hearings and sees something of the life of the poor. In all three cultures, economic crises are central to political struggles. Earth, clearly an image of the Global North, has wealth but little need for the bulk of its population, who live on basic assistance because there are no jobs for them. Opportunity for education and employment is distributed to the few by a lottery system that is putatively inclusive but clearly manipulated by those in power, as we learn in a season 3 storyline regarding Nancy Gao (Lily Gao). The situation is better on Mars, which has developed a healthy and collective culture following their independence. There is near-universal employment, but this is largely because of compulsory military service. Yet once the protomolecule opens wormhole gates to other planets by season 4, this changes. Most of the military is demobilized because the seeming availability of new resources makes UN takeover no longer an ever-present threat, but with this shift come problems of growing unemployment and the social malaise that accompanies economic precarity.

The situation in the Belt, standing in for much of the Global South, is reversed. Here there are plenty of jobs harvesting materials that mainly go to benefit the United Nations, but the necessities of life such as water, air, and food are only barely within reach for most of the population: in the pilot we see the detective Joe Miller (Thomas Jane) confront a corrupt official on Ceres Station who refuses to replace air filters frequently enough, causing illness, and one of the most notorious incidents in Belter history is the UN military destruction of Anderson Station, which had been taken over by its Belter population, demanding the provision of more oxygen because their children were failing to grow and thrive because of "hypoxic brain injury." In addition to killing the revolutionaries—whom Earth insistently called "terrorists"—this action killed over one thousand civilians. In one of his radical speeches, Dawes argues there is a key difference between UN and Belter culture: "Earthers cannot look upon a thing but wonder who it belongs to, to make it their thing. . . . But that is not the way of the Belt; we say, the more you share, the more your bowl will be plentiful" (S2E7). He tells his people that he knows the Earthers regard them as little better than animals, sources of labor but not fellow human subjects, but counters that in their view the Earthers are the ones without a moral ethos because they are unable to share.

Cooperation among all three was necessary to the climactic moment of season 3, when the series protagonist Holden (Steven Strait) prevents the protomolecule from destroying all human life by convincing every ship to turn its power off, to demonstrate they are not a threat, an exercise that requires trust across the factions. Yet this alliance almost immediately dissolves in a pattern similar to that from *The 100*. *The Expanse*, however, draws attention more strongly to the systemic inequality that existed before the alliance as a reason why the alliance is not itself just. The protomolecule has constructed wormhole gates to inhabitable worlds, and while the political alliance avers that they must not occupy these planets, Holden rightly predicts that the proximity of new resources will prompt "another blood-soaked gold rush" (S3E12). Thus, it is Belters, many refugees from Ganymede, destroyed during a battle between UN and Martian forces, who violate the blockade at the entrance to the wormhole and occupy a planet they call New Terra, the basis of the season 4 narrative. They argue they have waited long enough for their chance to thrive and see the prohibition not as a sensible precaution against living near unknown and potentially dangerous alien technology but as just another example of the "Inners" keeping the wealth for themselves. Similarly, Nancy Gao displaces Christjen as the UN secretary general by campaigning on the promises of land, jobs, and opportunities for the idle masses on Earth who want to do more than just survive on basic income.

The economic conflicts in both series allegorize the unevenness of global capitalism, and they also point to environmental themes. The struggle over land and resources reflects how climate change is exacerbating existing inequalities and creating new ones. Places where agriculture once thrived may not retain a supportive climate, for example, a looming crisis captured in *The 100* by the fight over the last fertile valley and in *The*

Expanse by the fact that Ganymede was described as the "breadbasket" of the Belt before its destruction. Shifting temperatures, extreme weather events, and rising sea levels are making currently inhabited parts of the world soon uninhabitable, pointing to a coming crisis of migration and border conflicts, themes central to both series. A larger concern for the environment is evident in some of the visual scenes of both series as well, such as the sense of awe that the original one hundred show in the pilot episode when they land on Earth and experience greenery and sunshine for the first time. *The Expanse*, always more attentive to the physics of space travel, has a similar scene when Bobbie lands on Earth and is overwhelmed by an open sky and endless horizon, vistas impossible on Mars, even as she struggles to cope with the higher gravity. Much of the Martian resentment of Earth culture is that UN citizens have access to natural air and water yet pollute and destroy rather than nurture such essential resources.[4]

IMAGINING CONFLICT AND DIVISION FROM MULTIPLE PERSPECTIVES

Much of the narrative propulsion in both series comes from characters grappling with the consequences of such economic unevenness and the divisions it creates. Many of the characters that serve as foci for viewer identification take on the task of bridging such divides, however stacked against them the odds might be. At the same time, a narrative strength of both *The Expanse* and *The 100* is that the series present multiple points of view and approaches to the economic and resource crises the characters face. No one single ideology seems dominant, unlike in earlier series we have examined, such as *Falling Skies*. In fact, some of the options considered are fairly radical.

For instance, not *all* characters believe that they just must keep fighting. Notably in *The 100*, the character of Jasper, someone who has always been an outsider, at odds with many of the other characters, decides that he does not want to continue fighting. In the fourth season, as the various "krus" are planning to go into the bunker to avoid a radioactive "death wave," he and a few others decide that they have had enough; they will not be joining the rest of humanity and instead choose to intoxicate themselves, dance, enjoy one another's company, and await their death. Jasper poses a dilemma to other characters, particularly his lifelong friend Monty, who tries desperately to convince him to flee to the safety of the bunker. But Jasper is steadfast in his refusal. In a way, his stance is comparable to that outlined by Mari Ruti in *The Ethics of Opting Out: Queer Theory's Defiant Subjects*. On one hand, Ruti is wary of a theoretical approach, represented by some queer theorists such as Lee Edelman, that forwards a "politics of negativity devoid of any clear political or ethical vision: it wants to destroy what exists without giving us much of a sense of what should exist";[5] on the other hand, Ruti also sees in such a politics a refusal, even an ethical refusal, of the available choices. In the example from *The 100*, Jasper does not like his choices, so he chooses to "opt out." Such a decision, while not imagining an alternative for a survivable future, is nonetheless a *choice*, a way of signaling within the narrative that the rules of the existing thought experiment might need to be revisited and revised—or just rejected. Other characters start to follow Jasper's lead. In season 5, once the surviving humans have moved out of the bunker, Monty discovers a way to make infertile ground fertile, so that WonKru, still led by Octavia, will not have to battle (inevitably to the death) the humans who have settled in the last remaining patch of arable ground—settlers who neither want to give it up nor share control over it. Despite Octavia's insistence that the only way forward is to fight for the arable land, Monty refuses to fight. So too do Bellamy (Bob Morley) and Kane (Henry Ian Cusick), saying they have had enough. Such refusals do not always result in the characters' deaths, as they do in Jasper's case, but they also do not necessarily point to sustainable alternatives for communal world building. They do, however, signal that the choices on offer—such as the ceaseless fighting over limited resources—are both insufficient and undesirable. Increasingly, major characters want to "opt out" of their given situations, showing that they might be ready to start telling a radically different story than the one in which they find themselves.

The narrative of *The Expanse* is similarly driven by characters facing a seemingly unending series of bad options and choices, with decisions they make often leading to dire consequences for those around them and, in some cases, for entire planets or social systems. At one point, Naomi (Dominique Tipper) reflects to Holden that "Every shitty thing we do makes the next one that much easier, doesn't it?" As we have seen, much of the plot of the series revolves around problems related to the unequal distribution of resources, battles over limited resources, and control over access to those resources. As with the various factions and krus in *The 100*, such conflicts are played out at a group level, with the Earthers, Martians, and Belters comprising the major social, cultural, and political units that exist throughout much of the series in an ongoing state of "cold war" that is always threatening to erupt into a "hot" one. One response to the cold war manifests in the desire of some characters to maintain the political status quo, with an uneasy balance of power among the three major political units. The presence of the alien protomolecule could potentially disrupt the balance of power within the system, because whoever controls it could use it to their technological advantage. Main characters debate whether it should be destroyed, with Holden believing it should be. But other characters, notably the Belter Naomi, are far less sure. In fact, in a powerful speech at the end of season 2, she reveals that she has not destroyed the sample of protomolecule that the *Rocinante* crew had captured and has instead given it to Fred Johnson so that the Belters could also have it, thus restoring the balance of power among Earth, Mars, and the Belt. She makes an impassioned speech about technology, war, and human nature—which she does not imagine as capable of change; she believes, rather, that keeping all of the major powers in a perpetual standoff is the best option.

But there are hints that not everyone in the series sides with Naomi. The series poses at times a crucial question: is there an alternative to a politics rooted in resource allocation, colonization, and technological development? In season 2, some of the minor characters start to question their loyalty to various factions. Curiously, such questioning is most common among workers, often unnamed and thus potentially representative of the populist masses, who are enacting the desires of corporate or political bosses. They begin questioning the extent to which they are serving "unworthy" masters, and they wonder if the people in power actually care about what happens to them. So, within the political standoff involving Earth, Mars, and the Belt, an emergent class consciousness—which in some ways has always characterized the Belters as third-class citizens of the solar system—becomes a repeated refrain. Further, what largely animates Holden as a main character in the series is his desire to stand *outside* the status quo and balance of power; he does not want to have to pick a side but rather hopes to act independently, so much so that the ship he captains, the *Rocinante*, becomes a separate social sphere—a move we will discuss in greater detail later.

Moving beyond the perpetual standoff, however, is all but unimaginable for many characters in the series. Interestingly, a backstory offered in the second season of *The Expanse* highlights this point. In it we learn of Solomon Epstein, who invents the drive that allows for significantly speedier travel throughout the system. This drive greatly enhances Mars's potential to become one of the dominant forces in the system, but it also creates increasingly confrontational struggles for technological advancement, as Earth, Mars, and the Belt desperately jockey for edge. As Epstein presciently suggests, "That's the wonderful and terrible thing about technology. It changes everything." In the world of *The Expanse*, technology generally changes everything for the worse, and the same can be said for the discovery of the protomolecule, which various corporate and political units desire to weaponize for their own strategic ends and advantages. The obvious referent and counterpoint to the discovery of the Epstein drive in *The Expanse* is the discovery of warp drive in the Star Trek universe—a discovery that, in Star Trek, leads to the unification of humanity into a species driven by the desire to improve and explore. In *The Expanse*, no such unification occurs; the technological breakthrough leads not to a progressive humanism but an accelerated arms race. Moreover, unlike Star Trek, in which the warp drive leads to an encounter with an alien race (the Vulcans), a discovery that helps unite humanity (because "we are not alone in the universe"), the alien life form suggested by the protomolecule provides further grounds for even more advanced technological warfare, with a corporation developing human/alien hybrid soldiers and willing to sell them to the highest bidder among the three powers. As a space opera narrative, then, *The Expanse* offers a far bleaker vision of human "progress" into the stars than does Star Trek. It thus joins *The 100*, which turns in its last seasons to interplanetary adventure, as a darker vision of constant human struggle over limited resources and technologies of domination—struggles against which some characters can only imagine "opting out."

At the same time, we find it worthwhile to examine some of the more specific contours of how such factional struggle is rendered in the series. Doing so should allow us an opportunity to see how different characters attempt to bridge divides among groups and create alternative forms of community across difference. One impediment to such community building is the racialization of the various groups and factions depicted in the series. While both *The Expanse* and *The 100* have racially and ethnically mixed actors playing major characters, and while those races and ethnicities are not themselves remarked upon explicitly in the series, race emerges as a problematic for community building in other ways.

BIOPOLITICS AND RACIALIZATION

We can see how the biopolitical governance highlighted by both series emblematizes how racialization works as a biopolitical strategy of dispossession, one that is already becoming a central issue in contemporary political struggles about immigration. The need to find a way to articulate community across difference, then, and the ways that these SF series posit the future of their characters as the future of humanity as a whole, demonstrate how these series are examples of the political education of desire in the twenty-first century. Biopolitics refers to theories that consider the modes and aims of governance when the state takes an interest in managing the bodies of its citizenry at the biological level, that is, governing them as both political subjects and living beings. Foucault theorizes links between biopolitical governance and capitalism, especially in its neoliberal form, in his *The Birth of Biopolitics* especially. As early as *The History of Sexuality*, volume 1, Foucault notes that this interest that sovereignty develops in fostering the proper life of the body also entails a "formidable power of death . . . [which] now presents itself as the counterpart of a power that exerts a positive influence on life, that endeavors to administer, optimize, and multiply it." This entails a shift from wars waged in defense of a specific sovereign to wars "waged on behalf of the existence of everyone; entire populations are mobilized for the purpose of wholesale slaughter in the name of life necessity: massacres have become vital."[6]

We see this logic exemplified in *The 100* and its repeated insistence that their violence is necessary because their survival is equivalent to the survival of the human race. The series is careful to avoid simply equating the human race with the people originally on the Ark: along the way, some of the grounders become part of their community, while some from the Ark, such as Pike (Michael Beach), a main antagonist in season 3, are viewed as having betrayed the ideal of the community and thus are rejected. Pike lands at a different time than most of the other people from the Ark, and his group encounters a more militant grounder community, the Ice Nation, and develops rigid us-versus-them politics as a result. While Clarke and those affiliated with her negotiate that Skaikru can join the alliance of other grounder tribes led by Lexa (Alycia Debnam-Carey), Pike kills all the soldiers Lexa sends to protect the Skaikru against the Ice Nation, essentializing all grounders as alike. While some massacres are rationalized as essential—such as Clarke's destruction of Mount Weather to stop its inhabitants from conducting lethal medical experiments on "her" people—Pike is condemned because he defends not "the existence of everyone" but instead just those politically loyal to him. Octavia, who strongly identifies with the grounders and adopts their lifestyle and values, eventually executes Pike, even though the two are at the time allied against those infected by a sentient AI and advocating digital over material existence. The AI is aided by Jaha (Isaiah Washington), who was once chancellor on the Ark, another example of a split within a once-constituted group. The Ice Nation, too, is depicted as anomalous among the grounders for its resistance to alliances, but nonetheless one former member, Echo (Tasya Teles), becomes a core member of the group Clarke identifies as "my people."

FIGURE 5.2 Lexa in *The 100*: "Fog of War," season 2, episode 6.

The 100 thus repeatedly stages conflicts that fragment people into those deemed the rightful heirs of the human race and those deemed outside this community, but it attempts to counterbalance this by always suggesting that the "good guys," as characters often put it, are those whose notion of community is permeable, able to incorporate new members who come from different backgrounds. The most extreme example of this is the Blodreina storyline of season 5, when Octavia insists that representatives from Skaikru and multiple grounder tribes forge themselves into Wonkru.[7] She succeeds in ensuring that humanity survives this period of lockdown in the radiation bunker despite inadequate supplies, but only at the cost of the hundreds of those killed for the failure to respect this demand for solidarity, a clear caution against the thanatopolitical side of biopolitical governance. *The Expanse* less openly depicts this violent side of biopolitics, but it makes more evident the links to economic rationales that inform the political choices of which lives to foster and which to neglect. This is evident not only in the fact that the main protomolecule narrative is driven by the actions of the Mau Corporation, which is seeking to enrich itself despite the lethal risks posed by experimenting with this substance, but also in the way economic austerity is so central to the difficult lives of the Belters and the origin of the health problems they face as a consequence. Repeatedly decisions are made that prioritize profitable economic exchange over the longevity of Belter lives.

These conflicts among factions draw attention to the central biopolitical issue of how membership in the human community is calibrated and

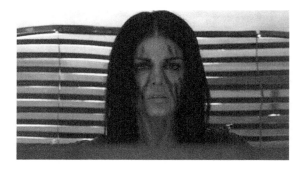

FIGURE 5.3 Blodreina watches over the fighting arena in *The 100*: "The Warriors Will," season 5, episode 10.

especially how, historically, this has not been extended to all people. Although the claim is that these wars are for the future of "the human race," membership in this future is not automatic, and this division within the definition of the human maps to a real biopolitical issue of exclusion from humanity on the basis of race understood as ethnicity. Expanding on Foucault's work, Sylvia Wynter rejects an overly narrow concept of Western bourgeois man that "overrepresents itself as if it were the human itself," offering another genealogy that outlines the history by which enslaved Africans, colonized peoples, and the indigenous have been "dysselected" as insufficiently human.[8] Although neither *The 100* nor *The Expanse* maps their exclusions to ethnicity,[9] both articulate a relationship to body morphology that draws attention to how racialization operates as a conceptual process of exclusion. In *The 100*, both the grounders and those on Sanctum (the setting for season 6 and largely season 7) restrict leadership to those who have "nightblood," an inheritable genetic modification that conveys immunity to radiation exposure. The grounder tribes have tattoos and other physical emblems of their tribal identity that mark them as different from one another and, especially, different from Skaikru initially—yet the contingency of such physical marks of tribal belonging are attested to by the fact that Octavia trains with and adopts the physical style of Trikru, the grounder tribe with whom they first ally.

When the narrative moves off Earth and to Sanctum in the sixth season, the Primes, genetically altered humans with the same implants as the Applied Lucent Intelligence Emulator's nightbloods, are a clearly separate and superior class who are practically deified by the other humans who serve and protect them. Known by their black blood, the Primes have been using the implants to transfer their consciousness from one body to another; they thus are able to live for hundreds of years, their followers willingly sacrificing themselves so that the Primes can continue their reign and cheat death. While none of these are, strictly speaking, racial divides in the sense of contemporary racial identities, they do represent embodied barriers to mutual and collective community formation. The separation into krus supports suspicion and mistrust of outsiders. We have already seen how Octavia had to deploy extreme measures in the bunker in order to unite various krus for the sake of intergroup survival. The presence of nightbloods and Primes creates a separate class of humans who are in some senses "superior" to normal humans and whom others have been acculturated to understand as "natural" leaders or even gods.

In *The Expanse* it is not only factors such as different experiences of gravity that create morphological differences among those from Earth, Mars, or the Belt but also the socioeconomic disparities among these regions: Miller notes, for example, that one of the reasons Belters have odd bony formations is that the "cheap bone density juice" they are allotted means that their bones "don't fuse right" (S1E1). Similarly, when a crew member loses a hand in a mining accident, he must make do with an inferior mechanical prosthetic replacement rather than the biogel available on Earth that would allow him to regrow the lost appendage (S1E1). Naomi, the virtuoso engineer on this vessel, reveals that her skill is necessary because it is cheaper for the company that they work for to settle lawsuits against wrongful death than it would be for them to properly repair and maintain the ship. Anderson Dawes reveals that one of the things that made him a Belter resistance leader was being forced to euthanize one of his sisters, Athena, whose fragile bones were never going to strengthen. Her weakness meant she could not survive the migration he was compelled to undertake to find new work that would enable him to continue to support his two other sisters. This became a political awakening because he recognized the problem was structural, not just a personal tragedy: "Living with this pain, I came to realize that I have millions of brothers and sisters in the belt" (S1E6).

Thus, although the different competing factions are not divided by ethnic identities, the process of racialization as a tool of biopolitical power is made evident by the link both series posit between the formation of political factions and distinct bodily morphology, traits that have arisen because of socioeconomic histories in which some were exposed to radiation and others were not or in which some experienced less than Earth-normal gravity and others did not. In *Society Must Be Defended*, Foucault argues that this exercise of the power of death in the name of fostering valued life is an expression of racialized notions of a split within a community's population. Biopolitical governance thus becomes "a way of establishing a biological-type caesura within a population that appears to be a biological domain. This will allow power to treat that population as a mixture of races, or to be more accurate, to treat the species, to subdivide the species it controls, into the subspecies known, precisely, as races."[10]

Critiquing Foucault's failure to analyze how European colonization was the first and most lethal expression of this racialized hierarchy established within humanity, Achille Mbembé theorizes what he calls necropolitics, in which a third term intervenes: it is not simply a matter of fostering some life and allowing other life to die through neglect, as Foucault suggests, but also one of actively maintaining some life in a damaged, dehumanized state, "kept alive but in *a state of injury*, in a phantom-like world of horrors and intense cruelty and profanity."[11] Jasbir Puar further argues that such biopolitical strategies are crucial to the new economic empire of neoliberal countries such as the United States, theorizing a third term, debility, between health and death, understanding it as "a product—not a by-product, but a deliberate product—of exploitative labor conditions, racist incarceration and policing practices, militarization, and other modes of community disenfranchisement." Puar calls this biopolitical strategy the "right to maim" and "a source of value extraction from populations that would otherwise be disposable."[12]

Both *The 100* and *The Expanse* demonstrate how this settler-colonial logic permeates these survival narratives but also stands as the main obstacle to achieving the peaceful and unified community protagonists in both series aspire to establish. We thus read these series as expressions of how pervasive such thinking has become in twenty-first-century modernity and how difficult it is to find a way outside of these structures. In the pilot of *The 100*, the incarcerated youth are told they are being sent to the planet "because your crimes have made you expendable" (S1E1). When the radiation wave threatens settlement on the ground and the bunker has limited space, Clarke makes another list of one hundred within their new community whose survival is deemed to most benefit the entire community—as in our own politics of debility, those with health conditions are excluded as an undue drain on limited resources. The Mount Weather leaders take this to its most extreme expression when they harvest grounder bodies to appropriate the capacity to "metabolize" radiation that has evolved among those who have survived outside the dome. They deliberately addict and thus debilitate some among their captives to serve as workers who will remove the depleted bodies of those who die after multiple extractions.

The settler-colonial origins of this way of thinking are hinted at in the fact that these people are also characterized by the love of the great artistic achievements of Western civilization—paintings by the great masters often feature in shots of their compound and are part of their claim to represent the real legacy of the best of humanity. Yet when his son Cage (Johnny Whitworth) decides to extend harvesting to include people from the Ark, who are less easily dehumanized than the grounders as they more clearly share a culture with the Mount Weather people, President Wallace (Raymond J. Barry) resists. Cage argues they are "keepers of history" and they deserve the chance to live outside, but Wallace cautions that part of the history they kept is the knowledge that they poisoned Earth with radiation (S2E5). Later, with the camera pointedly focused on the canvas of Van Gogh's *Starry Night*, Cage again tries to convince his father, claiming that the grounders are savages who will destroy everything, but Wallace points out their own destruction of human lives. Later, Jasper (Devon Bostick), one of the Ark people who most strongly rejects the rationalization of violence for survival, will also point out the irony that the art survives while the people from within Mount Weather do not, because Clarke has killed them (S3E3). Later, Clarke's mother, Abby (Paige Turco), will also resort to experimenting on outcast people in an attempt to manufacture "nightblood" and thus enable more to survive the coming radiation wave; at the last moment, Clarke will inject herself rather than the person deemed expendable (S4E8), opening the door toward another logic. The season 5 storyline, in which those in power have convinced the rest of the population that they are gods, while enacting a breeding program to ensure that this population expresses "nightblood" so that their bodies can be harvested as hosts for these leaders, further emphasizes that this logic cannot form the basis for a viable future.

The Expanse is more subtle in its representations of this right to maim, but in its restraint it better parallels ongoing settler-colonial imperialism. The Belters are regularly maimed via the economic restrictions that keep them permanently malnourished, oxygen deprived, and at risk of injury from low bone density. The production design for the series frequently contrasts well-maintained, bright spaces for the elites, including greenery, even on space stations, with the cramped, malfunctioning, and dimly lit settings of Belter life. Part of the conspiracy theory reveals that Eros Station, a Belter settlement, was deliberately infected with the protomolecule as a contained experiment to test its capacities. During early seasons, when the need to contain the protomolecule's further spread seems paramount, Holden and his crew do engage in violence: they destroy a medical ship that refuses to leave the quarantine zone, beat someone almost to death to get information, and hijack a ship, inadvertently causing the death of its pilot. Naomi, who functions as the moral center of their crew, warns them against allowing themselves the comfort of rationalizing such choices as necessary—"every shit thing we do makes the next one easier" (S2E10)—and later dedicates herself to returning and helping the remaining crew member on the hijacked ship to repair her vessel and escape the station, taking as many refugees as possible. In contrast to the violence that usually emerges in such culling in *The 100*, in this case the crowd is moved by a speech given by a Belter about their capacity for endurance, for accepting what must be done, and the crowd peacefully allows the vulnerable—not the most economically advantageous—to take the available spaces (S2E12). This is one of many examples when the series endorses the disenfranchised Belter ethos of mutuality over the dominant logic of maximizing what is deemed most important.

A FUTURE BEYOND RACIALIZATION?

In both series, repeated failures to secure community, then, are less signs of its impossibility and more promptings to recognize that until internal divisions of hierarchy are named and redressed within the putative community, any alliance can only ever be temporary. A strength of both series is how they foreground at times how various characters attempt—with admittedly varying degrees of success—to think, work, and live beyond such separations.

In *The 100*, as we have seen, Octavia's unification of the krus serves as a drastically authoritarian model of imposing community to ensure survival, and it becomes a foil for characters in subsequent seasons to consider what they are and are not willing to do ethically and morally to survive. While difficult decisions continue to be made, characters increasingly refer to the "dark year" of the bunker time as a kind of "community" building that they do *not* want to revisit and reenact. Such resolve is put to the test when the Earth humans arrive on Sanctum and have to contend not only with the Primes and their followers but also their enemies, the Children of Gabriel, who resist the Primes' self-deification and, eventually, other human factions (such as the Disciples) on other worlds. Once Clarke and others depose the Primes, they are faced with the challenge of integrating the remaining followers of the Primes (still perversely loyal to their former "gods") with their own people *and* with the Children of Gabriel. Tension and conflict persist, but many of the characters commit increasingly to building community without bloodshed.

Octavia also plays a crucial role—more so than Clarke, often seen to be the main protagonist—in the resolution of the final season. The cultists believe they must fight a final war to earn transcendence, but the term they are translating as "war" proves to be better translated as "test": a consortium of more highly evolved species will test humans to see if they can also transcend. If they cannot, they will wipe them out. Clarke responds with her usual strategies of violence to this situation, and her action almost results in the destruction of humanity. Octavia, in contrast, is able to end the violence, crucially by refusing retributive violence despite her own losses, thereby serving both to inspire others to follow her example and as evidence to the higher species that humans are capable of letting go of their cycle of violence. The species transcends, but Clarke is specifically excluded—although she too is allowed a happy ending when several of her friends choose to stay behind within embodied mortality with her.

FIGURE 5.4 The "family" of the *Roci* in *The Expanse*: "Safe," season 2, episode 1.

In *The Expanse*, the *Rocinante*'s crew is composed of Earthers, Martians, and Belters who, for various reasons, continue to make common cause with one another—often just to help one another survive. Their former "nations" see them all as traitors of one kind or another, but their mutual commitment suggests throughout the series that it *is* possible to overcome political divisions, however embodied, and work for mutual safety and benefit. In a way, then, throughout *The Expanse* the *Roci* serves as a kind of heterotopia, moving throughout a system that is otherwise deeply divided politically and culturally.

Interestingly, both series also present alien life forms or the technological remnants of alien "races" in ways that provoke and even promote unity across differences. In *The Expanse*, the protomolecule is initially used by a corporation to create new hybridized human/alien supersoldiers as part of what's called Project Caliban, referencing the part-human, part-monster character from Shakespeare's *The Tempest*. But humans across the system soon discover that they potentially have more to gain by uniting to understand the alien life forms and protect themselves and one another from a possible outside alien threat. Similarly, in *The 100*, the alien insect and plant life on Sanctum proves to be harmful to humans during the solar eclipses of the planet's two suns, forcing the humans to find a way to survive together. Such unity in the face of alien threats is a hallmark of much early twentieth-century science fiction storytelling.

Nonetheless, both series actively invite viewers to read the alien "threat" in more generative ways. For instance, the protomolecule in *The Expanse* might initially be used to create hybridized human/alien supersoldiers, but in season 2, a botanist on the farming moon of Ganymede becomes fascinated with the protomolecule because it seems to promote constant growth. As a botanist interested in cultivating and sustaining food supplies, he is interested in sustainable growth; his presence in the series, even in a minor role, signals an alternative way for humans to understand and approach the protomolecule. Similarly for *The 100*, the anomaly seems at first to be purely threatening to humans, but they soon discover that it serves as a complex wormhole network linking different planets. They can use this network potentially to find resources and safety. In this way, the "alien" in both series is not only a racialized threat but also represents possibilities for different ways of thinking about survival.

A danger here for a critical approach to these series is that political differences and conflict, which are largely based on unequal resource allocation, might be read just as "racial" problems or different responses to "alien" threats. In a way, the critique of political economy hinted at by these series might be eclipsed by a threat or issue deemed more ontological—such as the presence of alien life. A more productive approach might see the racial divisions within the series as intertwined with economic inequalities (especially in *The Expanse*) and would see the alien "threat" as a need to reassess and potentially reimagine human relationality to rapidly changing environments. That is, we could read the emergence of the alien in both series as allegorical for our own present planet's climatic and ecological "alienation" from us and our need to reevaluate our use of the planet and its limited resources. In many ways, though, these considerations are only hinted at in both series. The environmental devastation of Earth in *The 100* is largely treated as an irremediable given. And in *The Expanse*, early Martian efforts to terraform their planet start to fall by the wayside, trumped by other political conflicts and concerns.

What remains of interest to us in both series, however, is how all of the varied racialized dimensions of *The Expanse* and *The 100* forefront *bodies* and *embodiment* as significant reference points in the narratives of the series. One's body signals kru or planetary affiliation or, in the case of the nightbloods, special ability. Alien "races" represent both threats that must be faced as well as other unforeseen potentials. Most dramatically, in *The Expanse*, with its hybridized human/alien soldiers, as well as other scenes in which the protomolecule's unchecked growth radically alters human bodies, the relationship between bodies and the worlds around them becomes a significant focus of dramatic tension. It can also be a focus of *ethical* attention. That is, the alien entities in both *The Expanse* and *The 100* force humans to consider critically their relationship both to the aliens and to one another. A focus on bodies leads to our final section in this chapter, in which we consider how the characters in both series understand and grapple with the protection and reproduction of bodies. What social forms and structures maintain bodies, and which threaten them? And how might the focus on micro social forms, such as the family and its relation to the body, serve as a leverage point for critique of the larger body politic?

A FUTURE BEYOND THE FAMILY?

As with other series we have discussed in this book, both *The Expanse* and *The 100* feature family dramas that in some ways mirror larger social and political conflicts. Changes in familial relationships often suggest imaginative alternatives to larger forms of social organizing and political participation. Most provocatively, familial shifts show the breakdown of more traditional, even conservative ways of organizing the body politic and then make manifest some possibilities for revisioning it. In this way, the family tensions and dramas often serve in a metonymic relationship with larger political concerns.

In some ways, changes in family structures, both in terms of the reproduction of children and the organization of sexual relations, mark the fictional future time of the series as different from the contemporary time of those viewing the shows in the early twenty-first-century West. For instance, in *The 100*, Clarke's lesbian relationships are basically taken for granted; they are not cause for particular comment, suggesting that future time is characterized by greater openness to queer sexualities, even in the context of apocalyptic scenarios. In a way, such unremarked sexuality parallels the unmarked racial and ethical makeup of the characters, signaling that, whatever problems these future societies face, they are relatively unconcerned with identity politics as constructed in the contemporary United States and Canada. Such differences signal to viewers that "progress" has been made on some fronts, even if other forms of political disaster—such as the collapse of democracy, the rise of totalitarian forms of governance, and ecological disaster—remain impending.

Such "progress" is also marked by other radically open attitudes about sexuality. In *The Expanse*, for instance, Amos solicits information from a male prostitute who initially approaches him as a potential customer. Amos is unfazed by both the solicitation and the presence of prostitution. Again, queer sexualities remain unremarkable, but additionally prostitution seems fully legal and even normative (S1E6). In fact, Amos suggests that it is "honest work," unlike much of the political backstabbing and chicanery that characterizes interplanetary strife in the system. Even more provocatively, we learn that Holden, whose name resonates with "held" or "hero," is actually the product of eight parents—a family structure that is not necessarily common in the world of *The Expanse* but that is nonetheless not considered too extraordinary either. His unusual parenting, more communally based than traditionally dyadic, parallels the ways he has formed a collective aboard the *Roci*, a "family"—which is the word used by the shipmates—composed of a hodgepodge of Earthers, Martians, and Belters. Such a "family" alone, as we have noted, suggests an alternative social arrangement that transcends the more "national" kinds of alliances and socialites in this future solar system; it represents a "queering" of social structures that is held up as ultimately more workable and sustainable.

In fact, in season 3 of *The Expanse*, when a variety of human ships are confronted by the alien ring that might serve as some kind of transport system to other parts of the galaxy—a ring that appears suddenly and could threaten life within the system—most of the humans representing the Earthers, Martians, and Belters want to destroy it, deploying a version of shoot first and ask questions later. They are thus momentarily united by the perceived alien "threat." The crew of the *Roci*, however, urges the others to refrain from attacking so that they can approach the ring without hostile intent, showing that they are not threatening it. Curiously, a pastor who is part of a multifaction delegation sent to monitor and potentially explore the ring also urges a nonhostile approach, suggesting that it is time for people to let go of a fear-driven response and open themselves to understanding this alien presence. While the pastor offers a compelling rhetoric of an open-handed approach, it is only the crew of the *Roci* that is able to put it into practice, modeling a significant shift in what relationality across differences might look like in the system. In this way, then, the alien "threat" serves as an opportunity to demonstrate how one group—the multifaction "family" of the *Roci*—reeducates its own desires to be open to the unknown and the other, as opposed to being automatically fearful and mistrustful of radical difference.

In tension with this expanded understanding of family—and a family that models a reeducation of its own desires—is the need to protect and even reproduce the species. *The Expanse* features, especially in season 1, episode 5, several grizzly scenes from backstories of Belter miners and their families protesting their working and living conditions and then being killed for their efforts. Children floating dead in the cold of space serve as stark reminders of the price of protest in a system so socially and class stratified. The miner/protestors are labeled as "terrorists" by the status quo, although from the miner's perspective, they were only trying to secure a better future for their offspring; as one of them puts it, "We wanted to be heard for the sake of our children." Such scenes and narratives within *The Expanse* serve as reminders of the power of familial bonds and the commitment that different groups have to the reproduction of their ways of life. They are in interesting tension with the kind of "family" structure represented by the *Roci*, with its risky openness to bonding and desiring differently.

The 100 plays out similar dynamics between family and politics even more compellingly, especially in the season 6 narrative of the Primes on Sanctum. As discussed earlier, the Primes keep their power by having cultivated among their followers a sense of their "divinity" and immortality, their followers willingly sacrificing themselves at times to have the consciousness of the Primes uploaded into their bodies and thus extending the Primes' lifespans across hundreds of years. The Primes are literally reproducing themselves by inhabiting other people's bodies—a literalization of forms of social and ideological reproduction. Their commitment to their own reproduction is extreme. Russell (JR Bourne), the leader of the Primes, thinks nothing of sacrificing other humans to protect his family and make sure that they continue. Abby, Clarke's mother, is one of those whose mind is overwritten so that Russell's wife can inhabit a new body and extend her life. Clarke too faces such overwriting so that Russell's daughter can return to the family. With such measures, the Primes represent a completed and unquestioned commitment to familial reproduction, a commitment to the social structure of the family that not only centralizes but divinizes it; nothing is more important than the maintenance and reproduction of family. Even the sacrifice of others is hardly too high a price to pay. As Russell's daughter, Josephine (Sara Thompson), says in defense of the Prime's ideological manipulation of others to serve their familial interests, "It's not murder if they go willingly."

Of course, much rides on what is "willingly" done. Clarke's and others' attempts to battle the Primes involves not just ousting them from power but also essentially deprogramming their followers from believing that the Primes are, in fact, divine. Engaging in such consciousness raising is not easy but will become a necessary part of both the followers' demystification as well as a reeducation of their own desires about what social structures are worth supporting and maintaining. We are not surprised that Clarke is at the center of such a storyline; she has already been signaled, via her lesbian relationships in the series, as "progressive." But even more importantly, Clarke has adopted a young woman, Madi (Lola Flanery), whom she has protected and raised in the aftermath of the "death wave." As with Holden and the crew of the *Roci*, Clarke is often adept at finding her own family, forging bonds with others that seem to mimic familial relations but demonstrate that such relations can—and perhaps should—be extended beyond ties of blood. Such relations model forms of intimacy and sociality that transcend not just heteronormative relationality; they are also often put in conflict with toxic forms of familial and social reproduction such as the Primes. Such alternative relations show themselves as not just necessary but even desirable.

Throughout *The 100* and *The Expanse*, then, we see staged again and again the drastic choices that characters face in the push for survival, as well as in the maintenance of social and political status quos. In the process, some characters seek ways to form alliances and even affinities across identity boundaries—identities that are often tied to group affiliation or citizenship and that in some ways mimic and rewrite contemporary racial barriers and divides. In the face of such division, these characters and their storylines push beyond fear responses to the threat of the "other," even the alien other, and attempt to form connections that not only sustain them but reimagine sociality beyond dominant and normative political divisions. Throughout both series, the specter of limited resources motivates both the fear response *and* the need to think beyond the status quo, with some characters modeling different kinds of desires in the pursuit of alternatives to sustainable life.

THE LIMITS OF ALTERNATIVES

Both *The 100* and *The Expanse* series have difficulty imagining how to resolve such dilemmas in collectivist or cooperative ways. The seventh and last season of *The 100* shows Clarke and her friends battling the Shepherd, a mysterious figure planning for a "last battle" that will determine the fate of humanity. He and his followers hope to "transcend" their physical forms. Working through a convoluted series of plot twists, the narrative reveals that an alien race is testing humanity to see if it can overcome its ceaseless division into fighting factions and thus be worthy of transcendence. In a final battle between the Shepherd's religio-fascist forces and the remaining krus, Octavia intervenes to assert that "we are mankind. We are one Kru.... Our fight is over.... The only way to win is not to fight" (S7E13). Hers is apparently the right answer, and most of humanity transcends—except for Clarke, who has made too many compromised choices, which she rationalized as necessary to save herself and others. Curiously, some of her closest friends decide to untranscend so they can live with her on Earth, completing their days without the possibility of reproducing. When they die, humanity as they know it will die as well.

The fifth (but not last) season of *The Expanse* comes closer to offering a way to understand what it might take to overcome factional divides. As the Belter terrorist Marco sabotages Earth's defenses and hurls asteroids at the planet, killing millions while making it seem as though the attack is from Mars, the UN debates a proportional strike against innocent Mars, which would involve killing civilians. Avasarala, who has been something of a pragmatic hardliner throughout the series, argues *against* a proportional strike, even though she has personal reason to argue *for* it, given that her husband has been killed in the asteroid attack. In a twist for her character, she speaks movingly about needing to overcome her own grief and desire for revenge and move toward peace (S5E8). Her character thus models a reeducation of her own desire, which might extend to larger

FIGURE 5.5 Avasarala in *The Expanse*: "Salvage," season 1, episode 8.

political entities that are otherwise invested in prolonging (and benefiting from) ceaseless factionalism and division. She is momentarily successful—but for how long? The series seems to hold out a bit of hope, but further conflict is brewing in the background.

At the same time, the characters Clarissa (Nadine Nicole) and Amos (Wes Chatham), both of whom stand outside the main community, also model the kind of mutual reliance that can assist people during difficult times. They speak of themselves as a "tribe," but theirs is not necessarily a tribe designed to promulgate division; in episode 9, they talk about the desirability of adding new people to the tribe—not so much because they can contribute but because they need help. That is, membership should not depend on contribution as a measure of worth—a contrast to the test of transcendence posed by the aliens in *The 100*. Amos's understanding of tribes, which has animated his association with the crew of the *Rocinante* from the beginning, is more open, capacious, and even generous. As with Avasarala's change of heart, it is uncertain how long such a gesture of inclusivity will last or how scalable it will prove to the resolution of larger-scale political conflicts. But Avasarala and Amos nonetheless suggest alternatives—and alternatives grounded in reimagining what is personally and politically desirable.

In the next chapter, we turn to the near-future series *Mr. Robot* to show how such a reeducation of desire can be braided even more closely with a critique of political economies, particularly as *Mr. Robot* centers its narrative and characters on the effects and affects of contemporary neoliberal policies, practices, and politics.

6

REBOOTING DEMOCRACY AND *MR. ROBOT*

This chapter, the last to offer a reading of a contemporary work of speculative television, takes as its paradigmatic text the near-future series *Mr. Robot*. *Mr. Robot* is set in a reality that closely resembles our contemporary one but that is even more devastated by forces of neoliberal, global capitalism and disenfranchisement than ours. The world of *Mr. Robot* is as much a dystopia as any of the other SF texts of the future we have examined in this book. The series articulates a powerful desire for revolution and for another kind of world but also shows us how much our imagination of the future is colonized by narratives of capital's inevitable triumph, so much so that even Elliot's, its main character's, revolutionary hack enables only a pyrrhic victory, if victory it is. Even more compellingly, *Mr. Robot* shows us the tight braid of family structure and economic oppression, particularly through Elliot's family trauma and mental illness. At the same time, however, the affect of resistance that saturates the series and the density of its examination of family dynamics provide viewers some of contemporary speculative television's most powerful opportunities to think *and feel* critically about contemporary political economies. *Mr. Robot*, in the process, also models for viewers the reeducation of their desires from despair in the face of overwhelming and seemingly insurmountable obstacles and *toward* hope.

NEOLIBERAL POLITICS,
NEOLIBERAL PERSONHOOD

Mr. Robot fully pursues an overt critique of neoliberal governance that was only implicit in series discussed earlier in this volume. Whereas other series focused on threats of invasion or battles over scarce resources in postapocalyptic futures, *Mr. Robot* is set in a contemporary New York that increasingly comes to feel like an estranged world, once the operations of neoliberal disenfranchisement are laid bare. We understand this series as part of an SF tradition, following a number of scholars who increasingly see SF as a mode of perception rather than as a genre defined by specific features.[1] The hacker perspective embodied by its protagonist Elliot sees the contemporary world in terms of the disastrous future projected by debt-driven financialized capital—and it sees people through the secret vices many hide. We might understand this more sinister vision of reality as a break with the promises inherent in the notion of a liberal, democratic society. That is, we would see an apocalypse of sorts embedded within neoliberal business as usual, if only we could perceive the real forces structuring our lives. *Mr. Robot* thus directly imagines a rebellion against an unjust economic order, although not for merely monetary reasons: the series grasps and conveys Wendy Brown's insight that "neoliberalism assaults the principles, practices, cultures, subjects, and institutions of democracy understood as rule by the people," and thus "democracy is being replaced by plutocracy—rule by and for the rich."[2]

The plot is difficult to summarize because of the series' formal complexity, which includes several puzzle narrative revelations that require us to rethink previously viewed scenes in light of new information, as well as multiple dream sequences. The series aired over five years, but the narrative takes place from March 1, 2015, through the holiday season that year, with later seasons often returning to "earlier" diegetic times with a different perspective. We cannot do justice to the full intricacy of the narrative in this chapter, but the basic facts of the plot are these. Elliot is a white-hat hacker by night, computer security specialist by day, who plans a major attack on E Corp, in which, to collapse their power, he will destroy their records of debts owed. In season 1 he is introduced to this plot by another hacker, Mr. Robot (Christian Slater), who leads a group, Fsociety, that includes Darlene (Carly Chaikin); by season's end, we learn that Elliot has multiple personality disorder (MPD) and that Mr. Robot is a militant personality, or alter, of his, based in appearance on Elliot's father, who died from cancer caused by E Corp pollution, as did the mother of his best friend and coworker, Angela (Portia Doubleday). By series' end, we learn that the Elliot we have followed throughout is himself merely a personality, a more cynical version of the "real" Elliot, who might find chances for connection and hope in the world instead of only despair like the hacker version;[3] moreover, the source of his MPD proves to be that Elliot was sexually abused by his father, and Mr. Robot embodied the loving father Elliot needed but did not have. Elliot is our unreliable narrator of the action we see, and he frequently glosses E Corp—one of whose slogans is "Because the Future Is Now"—as EvilCorp, hinting a connection to cyberpunk SF and its tales of hacker heroes and corporate rule.[4]

The trope of Elliot's MPD tightly links the series' social critique with its themes related to affect and the family. The split in Elliot mirrors a split in the United States overall, not only the kinds of ideological splits we analyzed in chapter 4 when we discussed series that imagined coming civil wars but also the sort of schizophrenic perspective that comes from trying to reconcile the American mythology that sees a necessary link between democracy and capitalism with the reality of emerging plutocracy. The abusive father thematically speaks to the fact that promises of political liberty and upward mobility bound up in the American dream have become hollow, that what the country offers to most instead

FIGURE 6.1 Elliot after he turns in a child pornographer in *Mr. Robot*: "eps1.0_hellofriend.mov," season 1, episode 1.

is the perennial indebtedness that is the hallmark of both the shift to financialization—in which debt itself has become a mode of profit for the wealthy in instruments such as the collateralized debt obligation bonds that sparked the 2008 financial crash—and the rise of austerity politics, through which cuts to social services have transferred the burden for many provisions from the state to the private family, who must often go further into debt as a result.[5] The nation that was to have protected and nurtured us instead subjects us to ongoing exploitation at the hands of corporations.

Yet while Elliot's real father serves as an image of the abusive quality of neoliberalism's relationship to the citizenry, the more sympathetic figure of Mr. Robot gives voice to the outrage that Elliot experiences but acts on in only minor rather than structural ways. Thus this "good father" also nurtures a desire for structural change that moves beyond the more limited politics of punishing individual bad actors that is typical of Elliot alone. In the pilot, Elliot confronts someone who runs a child pornography site; the pornographer expects Elliot will demand a ransom in exchange for returning control of his software, but Elliot turns him over to the police instead, announcing, "I don't give a shit about money." This opening segment sets the tone for the series: Elliot's desire to make the world better for others drives the narrative, and those who are motivated by profit alone or who seek merely their own individual betterment can contribute only evil. Elliot's hacks, however, are not enough: the economic problems plaguing most Americans are structural and related to the massive increase in personal indebtedness that has accompanied neoliberal regulation since the 1980s.[6] Such costs to individuals are embedded in the series diegesis: we first see Mr. Robot, before he speaks to Elliot, as a homeless person on the subway and elsewhere, asking for change; as Elliot moves through the city, multiple advertisements about debt restructuring or similar financial services are visible; and we see Angela examine overdue bills for both her student loans and her father's mortgage. Fsociety is designed to address this problem at its root, first by wiping out debt records, later by more radically stealing dark-pool hedge funds, converting them to cryptocurrency, and enacting what Darlene calls "the greatest redistribution in history," continuing, "this is exactly what justice looks like" (S4E10).

FIGURE 6.2 FSociety's mask in *Mr. Robot*: "eps1.3_da3mons.mp4," season 1, episode 4.

Fsociety is clearly modeled on Anonymous, a hacktivist collective aligned with the Occupy movement that targets both corporate and government abuses of power: Anonymous uses the Guy Fawkes mask made famous by Alan Moore and David Lloyd's *V for Vendetta* (1982), while Fsociety uses a mask that resembles the millionaire icon of the board game Monopoly.[7] Although throughout the first season we are not aware that Elliot and Mr. Robot are the same person, Elliot's voiceover monologues explore themes similar to the polemical rhetoric of Fsociety's videos. The series opens with one of Elliot's voiceovers, about "a powerful group of people out there that are secretly ruling the world"; as he says this, the camera pulls back from a view of ongoing high-rise construction and into a boardroom filled with men in suits, whom Elliot names "the top 1 percent of the top 1 percent." We return to this image several times throughout the series, which eventually culminates in Fsociety identifying that there is indeed such a conspiracy, a dark-pool fund named the DEUS Group,[8] who manipulate politics and markets to ensure their continued returns. The final hack involves stealing their equity pool to redistribute it to the masses via cryptocurrency. From one point of view, the existence of an actual conspiracy would seem to undermine the more structural critique the series offers, once again making the issue a case of corrupt individuals who might be stopped, but from another point of view the DEUS Group is better understood as an aesthetic shorthand to capture the larger structural forces of financialized capital that create an economic context that operates *as if it were* a conspiracy. What we are suggesting is that the conspiracy captures and conveys something of the psychological experience of sociality as it has been reshaped by neoliberalism and surveillance capitalism, especially the tendencies of both to infuse all of daily life and interaction with market-based rubrics of value.[9] Although the shadowy group inhabiting their high-rise boardroom appears in the pilot, they do so by way of a figuration, making visible the difficult-to-represent forces of financialized capital that Elliot also explains to us in his voiceovers.

The paucity of a social world in which you cannot rely on overt statements because they are largely there to mask an underlying reality of exploitation—that is, the environment of neoliberalism in which advertising presents corporations as there to help us, masking their interest in us as flows of debt repayment—is conveyed as well by Elliot's MPD and especially by how his illness intersects with the series' aesthetic. In *Mr. Robot* you cannot trust anyone, even yourself, as evidenced by ongoing storylines in which Mr. Robot and Elliot fight for control. Elliot is our clearly unreliable narrator, not only unable to recognize at times that Mr. Robot is an element of himself but also addicted to opiates and prone to surrealistic daydreams. The viewer's disorientation mirrors the disorientation within the social world that Fredric Jameson diagnosed as a central problem for the utopian imagination in the late twentieth century: we cannot map the totality of the world as structured by financial capital.[10] The theme is also conveyed by the ironic relationship that frequently exists between what Elliot says in voiceover and the social interactions in which he is engaged, further emblematizing the hollowness of a social world so thoroughly saturated by capital.[11] The DEUS Group as actual conspiratorial entity is revealed only in the final season, while earlier seasons focus on E Corp and the ways business as usual in corporate America consistently distributes wealth upward.

Elliot's earliest voiceover harangue in the pilot focuses on consumerism, vacuous social media indicative of surveillance capitalism, and an overall desire to "be sedated" rather than face the reality of lives that are increasingly economically precarious and without agency. He admits, "Sometimes I dream of saving the world," a refrain we will hear frequently, generally accompanied by a visual montage that emphasizes indebtedness. Elliot mentions "the invisible hand" as the entity controlling people's options, often without our knowing it, an allusion to the ways that what Shoshana Zuboff has dubbed "surveillance capitalism" subtly directs our purchases and other choices. From this perspective, Elliot's isolation and debilitating loneliness—which ultimately proves even more extreme when the absence of the "real" Elliot is revealed—appear as the human cost of trying to protect oneself from the circuits of surveillance capitalism.

Fsociety seeks to level this unequal playing field. The first time Mr. Robot and Elliot speak, Mr. Robot emphasizes "everyone steals, that's how it works": no one is getting paid what they are worth, "someone in the chain always gets bamboozled" (S1E1). Later, Mr. Robot will hint at "something wrong with the world . . . that controls you and everyone you care about," namely, money, "the operating system of our world." He proposes the hack of erasing all E Corp debt records,[12] thereby destroying the world's economy as we know it and especially the way debt imprisons people. The series frequently cuts between diegetic scenes and real-world footage of financial news, Occupy protests, or similar contextual events, reinforcing that Mr. Robot's critique speaks to the viewers' reality as much as to Elliot's. Yet when this hack is successful, the activists and audience simultaneously learn corporate hegemony is not so easily displaced: Season 2 is dominated by images of growing homelessness and other signs of economic precarity for most, as electronic systems of payment have been disrupted, while the elite continue to enjoy luxuries in gated spaces, operating on a cash economy (while also restricting the supply of cash to themselves). Erasing the debt records has merely given E Corp license to freeze accounts—all records are now suspect—and to declare even paid-off mortgages as still under review (S2E1). Boasting of E Corp's centrality and status as an entity "too big to fail" (S3E7)—a line delivered during a meeting at Mar-a-Lago—various E Corp officers express their contempt for the irrelevant dregs of what remains of democracy. Meeting with White House staff and seeking a second bailout, CEO Price (Michael Cristofer) refuses their demand that he resign, insisting that the government's job is to tell the public a convincing story to ensure their confidence, not to reveal the truth: "the American dream, family values . . . it doesn't matter, so as long as the con works and people buy and sell whatever it is we want them to" (S2E2).

The corporation also takes the opportunity of the hack-caused financial crash to release its cryptocurrency, Ecoin, promoting this corporate

FIGURE 6.3 A protest scene in *Mr. Robot*: "eps1.9_zero-daY.avi," season 1, episode 10.

tender as a replacement for the U.S. dollar on the floating currency exchange. CEOs regularly flaunt their ability to use lawyers to ensure their actions attain legal status, even if they must break laws to gain market advantage, a strategy that Katharina Pistor argues reflects the true history of how a class of property holders used—and continues to use—the law to appropriate the commons and displace state sovereignty with their own.[13] Angela's long struggle with E Corp over her mother's wrongful death ends with them first exhausting her limited financial recourse for a lawsuit[14] and then convincing her to work from within E Corp, a decision that changes Angela from an empathetic and engaged young woman into an automaton who repeats positive affirmations to herself in the mirror as she tries to put into practice Price's advice that she "remove emotion" from all decisions (S2E2). In a flashback of Darlene recruiting a young Muslim woman, Trenton (Sunita Mani), to Fsociety, Trenton explains her willingness to participate as emerging from a betrayal of the American dream. Her parents emigrated from Iran to find freedom, yet even though "they can't shut up about how great America is," still "they are going to die in debt doing things they don't want to do" to pay their bills (S1E7). The sympathetic version of Elliot's father—a realistic portrayal, we believe, through most of the series—also links the resistance to debt to dynamics of family loss. Like Angela, Elliot has lost a parent to E Corp carcinogens: his father was first fired for taking too many sick days, and it briefly owned his own computer repair shop (Mr. Robot) before he was forced into bankruptcy by the dominance of stores such as Best Buy. Elliot thus sees E Corp's financial predation as doubly responsible for his father's death, a reality stunningly captured in a time-lapse sequence (S1E9) in which we see the Mr. Robot shopfront go from vibrant to dilapidated, replaced by a series of changing and also temporary business names, until the former location becomes a branch of the Bank of E.

The series' formal innovation also often works to draw our attention to narrative convention as a way of shaping our affect, including the narratives we tell ourselves as we narrate our "real" lives through social media. An extended parody of an early-nineties sitcom (S2E6) insistently makes the point that too much of our culture is about distraction and obfuscation, that "when the truth is painful, as it often is, a lie is the only remedy," but despite all the attempts to paper over the violence and destruction that are cartoonishly represented in this spoof, what is repressed always returns.

The hard truths of our economic exploitation are one reality the series encourages us to face, but equally concerning is the critique of how democracy has become compromised by a fetish for market values. The series regularly raises questions of means and ends: in one pointed scene, Angela asks the E Corp executive Colby (Bruce Altman) whether his decision to cover up toxic waste ever gave him pause, and he shrugs off his role in the resultant deaths from illness—"You go home, have dinner, forget about it" (S1E7). Faced with this absence of empathy, Mr. Robot easily justifies the chaos that their hack produces and is even willing to injure workers

FIGURE 6.4 The sitcom episode in *Mr. Robot*: "eps2.4_m4ster-s1ave.aes," season 2, episode 6.

in the physical destruction of a backup facility, but Elliot insists this is a line they cannot cross. He is willing to cross other lines, however, not only accepting the financial crisis prompted by the hack as a necessary evil but also exploiting people's vulnerabilities to gain access to the information he needs, including readdicting a woman to opioids and thereby risking her custody of her child (S4E6). We have seen these discussions of such tactics' ethics in other series, of course, but *Mr. Robot* links them directly to the violence enacted by corporate finance by comparing Fsociety's tactics to those of their adversary.[15]

Much of the Fsociety platform mirrors insights of recent political theorists such as Wendy Brown, and from season 3 the narrative focuses strongly on the FBI investigation of the hack, providing insight into abuses made possible by the Patriot Act as much as it interrogates E Corp malfeasance. When she is interrogated by the police after a militant Chinese faction, the Dark Army (who support Fsociety but with their own agenda), kills her boyfriend, Darlene attempts to evoke her right against self-incrimination but is told that the Patriot Act makes her an "enemy combatant" without rights (S2E11). Among the things Fsociety condemns in their activist videos is widespread domestic surveillance (as revealed by Snowden; S2E7), and it is later revealed that the Dark Army funded a Russian hack of the DNC (S3E10). But the truth of the damage done by economically motivated actors is even more sinister than the actions of nation-states. Speaking of the DEUS Group's ability to manipulate political events to ensure desired market movements, Price gloats that such spycraft was not even necessary, given the seductions of surveillance capitalism and people's willingness to generate data for corporate harvest: "we staged the biggest coup in human civilization and the whole world opted in to take part" (S4E2).

The failure of the first hack speaks loudly to how a financial elite has successfully insulated itself from the problems of ordinary people. Repeatedly, we see that those who suffer are those already victimized by the inequality built into a financial system that sees shareholder value as the only valid metric. While E Corp executives and DEUS Group one-percenters continue as before, members of Fsociety must leave their families and go into hiding, and Gideon (Michel Gill), Elliot's generous and community-oriented boss at the IT security company, is shot by a vigilante in a bar who shouts, "This is for our country!" (S2E1). By season 3, the background scenes show growing homelessness amid an improvised economy and an increased presence of armed security guards at traditional businesses. Season 3 repeatedly hints that the original hack was possible only because the DEUS Group saw a way to use the resultant financial collapse to extend its own power; that is, even protest can become commodified and sold back to us. Yet Elliot's dreams and visions continue to contain images of an unalienated life. These fuel his desire, sustain him, and prompt him to innovate, develop additional phases of the hack, and continue until they are finally successful at redistribution, at making the one percent feel the loss they so regularly cause others. In one such dream, of all his friends and family dining together in plenitude (even people we know to have been killed), we see the towers of the financial district crumble in the background, suggesting that this unalienated sociality is possible only in a world organized along different economic principles—and notably, this dream sequence ends the episode in which we learn the origin of the Fsociety mask in the diegetic *Careful Massacre of the Bourgeoisie*: in Buñuel's *Discreet Charm of the Bourgeoisie*, they try to gather to dine, but this meal never happens (S2E4).

Elliot's psychological illness, addiction, and isolation, then, all signify the violence enacted by economic policies of austerity and the prioritization of shareholder value. It speaks not only to the political split in U.S. culture, in which the right tends to privilege market values and criminalize poverty and social programs, but also to another kind of split even

FIGURE 6.5 Elliot dreams of everyone reunited as skyscrapers in the financial district fall in *Mr. Robot*: "eps2.2_init_1.asec," season 2, episode 4.

among those who seek economic reform toward models of wealth redistribution. Given how thoroughly capitalism has colonized social life and political structures—and how dependent we have all become on its continued operation, from our reliance on wage labor to the fact that pensions are now contingent on market performance—those seeking reform are faced with the paradox emblematized by the failure of the first hack: should we choose stability, even while recognizing that it is based in and perpetuates inequality, or do we take the risk of destroying this system in advance of trying to invent something more equitable to take its place? The complicity of the middle classes in enabling systems that largely benefit elites comes from this fear of losing what little security is possible, but of course one of the consequences of the erosion of a middle class, as employment becomes ever more contingent and temporary, is that more and more people have less to lose if the system fails, preparing the ground for more radical change.

FAMILY ROMANCES AND QUEER RELATIONS

One of the most salient characterological features of this series is its focus on Elliot's "split" personality—an internal "split" that metonymically traces larger structural, economic, and political splits, most notably that between the haves and the have-nots. The series' pivoting runs the risk at many junctures of tempting viewers to read Elliot's split personality as simply a function of damaged family dynamics and early childhood abuse, but *Mr. Robot* consistently troubles such a reading, all but insisting on seeing the family dynamics as fully enmeshed with, reflective of, and perhaps even an outgrowth of a schizoid culture. In much serial television, including some of the series we have analyzed, such as *Falling Skies*, any structural issues held up for analysis and critique are often backgrounded by the immediacy of personal conflict and family dynamics, which readily invite viewer identification. *Mr. Robot*, however, is perhaps among the most ambitious of such series in that it consistently troubles the typical narrative divide between a consideration of structures that condition ideology and affect and the personal dynamics and stories through which such are depicted, almost as though *Mr. Robot* is engaging in a public pedagogy of critical consciousness raising. For instance, viewers can read Elliot's persistently flat affect and exhaustion as the mark of the combination of ceaseless labor with increasingly futile—and self-damaging—attempts to console himself.[16] Elliot's drug addiction is an even more extreme version of how we all escape into addictive social media rather than think about how corporations are capitalizing our sociality. But given that *Mr. Robot* is often narratively propelled *through* dreams and hallucinations, we want to read at least this aspect of the series with Bloch in mind. These dreams often seem situated between nightmares and possibilities, gesturing simultaneously—if at times contradictorily—to both.[17]

A deeper dive into the content and presentation of the hallucinations *specifically* around family and childhood trauma reveals the nuanced contours of how Elliot's interiority and structural inequalities intermesh. While Bloch may have rejected Freud, *Mr. Robot* mobilizes a depth psychology that is held in constant tension with the economic critiques it mounts. For instance, Elliot's isolation and antisociality are not just products of capitalist culture but also of the inability of family structures to protect him from such isolation—which should not be surprising if we understand the emergence of the nuclear family itself as a "product" designed to promote the maintenance of labor forces and consumption. The contradiction inherent in the family structure is that it is supposed to provide a sense of "home" and security—Blochian *Heimat*—but is just as often the locus not just of the education of desire in capitalist culture but of the experience of abuse as well. Viewers see flashbacks of Elliot abused by his mother, calling him "nothing" and "worthless"; he is frequently alienated from his sister, Darlene, whom he really doesn't know intimately throughout much of the series despite how closely they have been working together on various hacks; and his father, the phantasmatic Mr. Robot, haunts nearly his every step, appearing as a creepy paternal force driving him to pursue his schemes of resistance and sabotage. Indeed, the splitting of Elliot's personality seems structured on his relationship with his father, who occupies the contradictory role of fatherly solace and torturing taskmaster.

The nature of that relationship becomes central to the series—not just as it structures Elliot's split personality but as we slowly learn in the fourth season about the abusive relationship between the two. The series' constant evocation of the family romance invites a hermeneutics of suspicion, bolstered by frequent scenes of Elliot in therapy with Krista, attempting to plumb the depths of Elliot's early childhood and uncover the secrets that have led to his isolation, antisociality, and split personality. By the fourth season, the series' last, the psychoanalytic dive into Elliot's split personality reaches its peak (or nadir) as we learn of his father's sexual abuse of Elliot—the damaged family that must, at least to some extent, have created some of the isolation, pain, and disabling contradiction that characterizes Elliot's life. We recognize that the opening scenes of the entire series, Elliot's confrontation of a man who collects child pornography, represent a move not just to protect children but to protect a particular *child*—Elliot himself. Securing other children's futures, which we can read as one of the goals (if not *the* primary goal) of the hack to take down E Corp and the global elite running the world, stems in part from Elliot's early childhood sexual abuse at the hands of his father.

There are many ways to read this deep intertwining of personal trauma, family dysfunction, and resistance to and assault on large-scale structures of social inequity. In many ways, the scenes of young Elliot continually jumping out of his bedroom window, clearly a primal moment for him, register as the ongoing legacy of personal trauma, a replaying over and over again of a scene of self-harm and self-sabotage as a way to avoid confronting—or even disappointing—his father, of identifying the damage at the heart of the very structure that is supposed to protect him. At the same time, we can read such scenes metonymically—both as emblematic of larger inabilities of governments to protect us and of our potential complicity in often failing to call such governments to account for the dereliction of their duties.

The scenes in which Elliot finally learns the truth of his past childhood trauma—which is more of a revelation to himself of what he has known all along but has not been able to face—are played out in a remarkable episode, the seventh of the fourth season. Structured as a five-act drama, the episode largely unfolds as a therapy session, but one hijacked by the drug dealer Vera, who manipulates and threatens Krista, Elliot's therapist, into forcing Elliot to confront his childhood abuse. But Vera, whose name is suggestive of "truth," has only part of the story; his course of action represents the anger that turns inward and attempts to drown itself in drugs, opting out of the fight instead of fighting to change the system. As Krista, under threat from Vera, forces Elliot to confront the reality of his childhood abuse—with Mr. Robot dramatically exiting the scene at one point and saying that he can no longer "protect" Elliot—we hear thunder clapping in the background, and the sheer staginess of the scene becomes increasingly evident. The highly self-conscious and "meta" nature of the episode is significant for several reasons. If the revelation of sexual abuse were rendered as a purely therapeutic moment, it might have the effect of undercutting the larger structural critiques that have been permeating much of the series. The major danger here is that all of the earlier structural critique and rhetoric of resistance with which the series began might be surpassed narratively by a family drama, a case of childhood sexual abuse. But the *form* of the episode, its very staginess as a five-act drama, strongly suggests that we have left the realm of psychological realism and entered an allegorical world—with thunderclaps in the distance—a world of Shakespearean proportions, where the smallest personal dramas are connected in a great chain of being to the highest levels of power and where a disturbance in one realm (the personal) signals a disturbance or corruption in a larger realm (often the political).

The drama of the episode centers Elliot's confrontation of his personal truth with a recognition that it can anchor, however painfully, his fight *against* a larger system that, like his family, has failed. Vera is correct in insisting that Elliot should not forget, but Vera's path of enticing others to forget through drugs is revealed as just another ruse to keep the status quo in place. Setting that option aside, the personal drama of Elliot's sexual abuse can become a metonym for understanding—and possibly confronting—the structural abuses that immobilize and immiserate the populace. The series' dramatization of this key therapeutic moment situates the deeply personal in the spread of social and economic structures as they interpenetrate subjectivities; put another way, we are witnessing in this episode the breaking down and potential reassembling of a psyche, Elliot's, that might have a clearer sense of its own motivations and potential agency within a dynamic sociopolitical system.

Along these lines, it is important that Vera, the orchestrator of the therapeutic scene in this case, is also a criminal. While criminality can sometimes work to maintain the status quo, it is often just as frequently a sign that something is wrong or amiss, a loophole or flaw in the system.

Hacking occupies a similar kind of criminal space in the series. And so too do the many queernesses throughout *Mr. Robot*. We should not ultimately be surprised that, at the heart of Elliot's personal damage, is a sexual trauma. Sex is often metaphorized as reproduction, not just personal reproduction but, by extension, the making over and over again of the system into which new humans are born. The perversion of father-son sexual abuse can signal an aberration within that system, and it can also simultaneously figure the reproduction of a damaged system, as traumatic relationships are passed on from one generation to the next. Christopher Chitty reads the long history of capitalism and antisodomy laws as a history of the regulation of different forms of social and economic reproduction. In the process, he suggests that we might consider how different queernesses have attempted to interrupt such reproduction and "ask instead about the transformative and emancipatory possibilities of love and intimacy outside the institutions of family, state, and the couple form. These creative possibilities could be universal, given certain conditions, and not strictly limited to same-sex object choice."[18] To be clear, we are not suggesting that Elliot's sexual abuse is a form of queerness; quite the contrary: it metonymizes the reproduction of larger structures of not just inequity but outright abuse of the less powerful and disenfranchised, the very people whom governments are supposed to protect. Despite this limitation, *Mr. Robot* offers several examples of queered sexuality that might, as Chitty suggests, point to creative possibilities outside the received systems and conditions—although, as we will see, those queernesses are not without their own ideologically fraught baggage.

At first glance, queernesses abound in *Mr. Robot*. Darlene has an on-again, off-again sexual relationship with Dom (Grace Gummer), the FBI agent, who is often depicted as lonely and even lovelorn. But when the psychopath hired by the Dark Army, Janice (Ashlie Atkinson), orders Dom to kill Darlene or her family will die, Dom cannot do so, however much she is threatened (S4E6). The queer choice, choosing Darlene over her biological family, seems to reinforce the move of the plot with regard to Elliot and his family; however important and impactful family is, characters can *and do* make other choices to value other kinds of relationality. If Elliot's relationship with Mr. Robot reveals the extent to which the traditional family has abrogated its responsibilities (paralleling such dereliction in the larger nation-state), then Dom's choice signals a potential opening up of other forms of relationality and intimacy that can be privileged.

The sexual scenes involving E Corp's employee Tyrell (Martin Wallström) further deepen and complicate the series' gestures toward queer critique and possibility. We see him engaging in non-normative sexual practices at several points throughout the series. Early in season 1, we see Tyrell, the would-be CTO of E Corp, being denied his promotion and then paying someone he picks up so that he, Tyrell, can beat him up. The message is glaringly clear: the rich dole out cash to the bottom 99 percent *as a form of abuse*—a direct allusion to *American Psycho* (2000). At this point in the series, before we understand Tyrell's connection to Mr. Robot, he simply seems the face of corporate evil, at times alluding clearly to Patrick Bateman (Christian Bale), the sociopathic protagonist of Bret Eaton Ellis's *American Psycho* with his fine suits and propensity for sexual violence. Along these lines, we also see Tyrell in a BDSM relationship with Joanna (Stephanie Corneliussen), a depiction that might serve further to link corporations to forms of sexualized violence, if not even the internalization of such violence as perverse forms of pleasure; Tyrell and Joanna's sadomasochistic play figures how people like them reflect and absorb the pain they inflict on others as members of the corporate ruling class by recasting it as pleasure. Walter Benn Michaels, in "50 Shades of Libertarian Love," reads the "contract porn" of *Fifty Shades of Grey*, in which a woman contracts with her boss to be his slave, as emblematic of contemporary economic relations.[19] For Michaels, someone long attuned to the forms of economic relationality as they are reflected in the forms of narrative, the increasing popularity of such contract porn runs parallel to the contract neoliberalization of contemporary (for example, gig) employment, in which more and more folks enter (with little choice) into short-term contracts that trade the comforts of long-term security for quicker, dirtier, and often more painful forms of servitude. Michaels catchily calls this arrangement "neoliberal masochism." By including similar kinds of BDSM scenes, *Mr. Robot* not only references a popular kind of sexual play more and more seen on television but also, as Michaels's argument suggests, creates a homology between sadomasochistic sex and the contractual predations of capitalism. BDSM in this guise signals how many viewers are often forced to consent to kinds of relationality that they really do not otherwise have the capacity to escape; in the process, one of their few courses of action is to recast such relationality as a form of pleasure. Tyrell's various BDSM scenes might thus invite a critical awareness of how affects of pleasure are cultivated to mask the real pain of capitalist forms of sociality.

What ultimately troubles—or *queers*—this homology, however, is that BDSM sexual practices are *supposed* to be fully consensual, and they often have "safe words" or other mechanisms for partners to signal a desire either to stop or alter the script that is mutually in play. With this understanding of BDSM in mind, we might view *Mr. Robot*'s mobilization of such queernesses as suggestive—suggestive of alternative ways of thinking sociality or, at least, of questioning contemporary economic relations—but perhaps not quite critical enough. The character of Whiterose (BD Wong) is perhaps the most significant and complex version of this kind of queerness, a queerness that is suggestive in its abstract desire for a different world but falls just short of offering viable concrete alternatives.

The final season of *Mr. Robot* offers viewers the full backstory not just to Elliot's traumatic childhood but to Whiterose's history—a history that goes some way to helping us understand what has motivated this complex and enigmatic character. We almost want to say that Whiterose is represented throughout the series as "inscrutable," the racist epithet characterizing the inability of Westerners to understand or appreciate Asian cultural forms and manners. *Mr. Robot* plays with such stereotypes, running an edgy risk of them being either misunderstood or, perhaps, understood all too well. In Whiterose's case, the dangerous line that *Mr. Robot* walks is in making this character not just Asian but also trans.

The third episode of the final season is almost entirely devoted to Whiterose's backstory and takes place predominantly in 1982. We learn of Whiterose's negotiation of a deal with IBM to open a facility, the company's first in Asia; he also reveals to his lover that he is actually a woman.[20] Fortunately, *Mr. Robot*'s characterization of Whiterose is more complex. We learn that she and her lover are plotting to leave China to pursue a more open relationship, but Whiterose's rise in the Chinese political organization (we see "him" become minister of state security) complicates their plans to leave, as well as makes nearly impossible their ability to be open about their relationship or Whiterose's true identity. Whiterose promises her lover that they will find a way to make their world a better place, one in which they can both live and love freely, but the lover despairs and kills himself, believing the world will never be good enough to make room for them. In the face of transphobia and homophobia, resulting in her lover's death, Whiterose turns toward villainy.

On one hand, Whiterose's backstory humanizes this character as we are invited as viewers to empathize with her and her lover's plight. On the other, however, its contrast to Elliot's story of sexual abuse runs the risk of making Whiterose's queerness seem problematic. Both Whiterose and Elliot are victims of sexualized trauma—Elliot's childhood sexual abuse and Whiterose's loss of her lover because of anti-queer and anti-trans discrimination. In fact, in the eleventh episode, as Elliot and Whiterose confront each other, Elliot even admits to her in a moment of empathic identification that "society deserves to be hated . . . for what we've all been through." But while the two characters might share a similar kind of pain, their choices are ultimately very different. Whiterose asserts that she was not born who she was supposed to be and, in losing her one true love, decides to take action to alter the world and the pain it causes: "All I ever wanted was to bring an end" to "dysfunction"—and "make a better world." Elliot, however, counters that what Whiterose really wants is to destroy the world because she hates the pain that has been inflicted on her. Whiterose rants, "On the contrary, it is my love for people that drives me." But Elliot insists that it is actually pain and hate that drive her, and the overarching narrative—confirming Whiterose as the villain and Elliot as the hero, however damaged—confirms his viewpoint. Elliot speaks movingly about love, about people who persist in loving, despite how much we hurt one another. We break but we keep going. Or, as he puts it, "So no. I will not give up on this world."

From a queer perspective, as Eve Kosofsky Sedgwick might remind us, the secret—especially the sexual secret—lurks at the heart of these characters' major motivations and conflicts.[21] *Pace* Sedgwick, these secrets do not stem from a Freudian unconscious and the repression of id energy as much as they are secrets that have largely been closeted because of social pressure (especially in Whiterose's case) or an inability to confront them because of shame, stigma, and the potential dissolution of selfhood in the face of traumatic reality. Further, we can understand these secrets and their consequences as the failure of existing intimate socialites to protect and nurture. If family is *supposed* to provide at least a space of solace to help us face another day of capitalism, then Elliot's family surely fails, and Whiterose never had much of a chance to develop such a family. Both then turn against the system that has failed them—but with a stark difference. Elliot becomes a hacker, bringing child abusers to vigilante justice (since the system isn't sufficiently protecting children as is), and then throws digital wrenches and quite literal bombs into the corporate system to take it down. In contrast, Whiterose cannot quite envision a path outside the party or capital accumulation, and she instead seems intent on *controlling* the system completely as a way to minimize the harm it can do to her. The sexual secret lies at the root of these characters' motivations, but their relationships to the economic systems that have hurt them develop in very different ways, with the series' sympathies ultimately and clearly siding with Elliot's path.

In this narrative context, Whiterose serves as a cautionary tale. Her anger, which is justifiable, ultimately prevents her from seeing *beyond* or *outside* the system. She can only imagine controlling it. At the same time, however, the moments in the eleventh episode in which she is applying her lipstick as we hear gunfire in the background, all of her plans crashing down around her, seem transphobic. Her defiant queerness contrasts in such instances sharply with Elliot's sexual abuse; Whiterose's cultivation of her queer anger comes to seem a perverse choice directed *toward* evil, whereas Elliot's childhood trauma is something thrust upon him and that he must come to deal with. He is a victim; she ultimately seems less so—an unfortunately transphobic gesture coming at a time of greater viewer awareness of trans lives and gender variance.

Mr. Robot's intertwining of sexual and economic complexities powerfully figures the intertwining of personal subjectivities and intimate relations with larger financial structural forces. The corruption of the latter decidedly maps onto the former. And the series invites us to consider critically how *both* need to be addressed and changed in order to begin revisioning a world of greater social and economic justice. Most importantly, the two characters Whiterose and Elliot demonstrate the significance of affect and of the conscious need to work with the powerful affects of fear and anger as a response to injustice. The arc of both characters, though ultimately divergent, nonetheless centers the characters' *desires* for a different world as key to their political actions.

METATELEVISION AND THE
EDUCATION OF DESIRE

The opposition of Elliot and Whiterose is perhaps *Mr. Robot*'s most insistent invitation to consider the functioning of a dialectic of desire for a different world. That such a dialectic emerges through risking gender stereotypes and some possible transphobia is not to the series' credit, but it might also signal some of the necessary risks in both stitching together the need for dual personal and structural change *as well as* the need to sketch broadly pedagogic types that model approaches—affectively and politically—to the current economic, ecological, and political crises facing our world. One such pedagogic type occurs through one of the series' numerous references to other pop cultural narratives, for instance, in a scene in which Elliot imagines a more "normal" type of existence in the first season: "I'm gonna be more normal now. Maybe Shayla could even be my girlfriend. I'll go see those stupid Marvel movies with her. I'll join a gym. I'll heart things on Instagram. I'll drink vanilla lattes. I'm gonna lead a bug-free life from now on. Anything to protect my perfect maze" (S1E3). Elliot, himself something of a mutant, snarkily disparages the Marvel universe, even as he and Whiterose ultimately come to occupy dialectical poles that are homologous to Xavier and Magneto. But theirs is a homology with a difference. The racial dimensions of the original X-Men story are superseded by an economic narrative that asserts that structural change must occur—but will that change be motivated through hate or love?[22] The original binary is recast as an economic problem, but one that retains a fundamental affective difference in what to do with anger at injustice. *Mr. Robot*, then, is a very contemporary kind of superhero story—a superhero story for our times in which corporate oligarchies and villainous organizations are taken on by a damaged hero.

Mr. Robot is also very "meta"—and self-consciously so. This complex play with the genealogies of the mutant and damaged superhero is only one of many instances in which the series calls attention to its own narrative histories, inspirations, and evolutions. In doing so, *Mr. Robot* constantly calls attention to itself as story while also inviting viewers to consider—critically and affectively—what they are being shown. From the very beginning, with Elliot ostensibly addressing the viewer—"Hello, friend"—we are invited in to see the world as he sees it and to witness with him his own coming to terms with the complexities that have shaped his reality. Such play with breaking the fourth wall and with other genre forms (e.g., theater, episodic television) encourages a self-reflective viewing, prompting us to see major narrative dimensions of this series—such as the conspiracy plot and Elliot's abuse—as *both* real *and* emblematic of economic themes in the real world. These meta-moves also extend to clever tricks, such as ending a scene with a voiceover announcing that we are now about to receive a "message from our corporate overlords" as we cut to real commercials. With such moves, *Mr. Robot* is asking us to think about television as more than entertainment while also not letting us forget the ways in which it still is *profitable* entertainment. That tension perhaps explains why what is most interesting to us about *Mr. Robot* is how the series risks critique of an economic system upon which its production is dependent. It invites interrogation of its own means of production.

One significant consequence of *Mr. Robot*'s metanarration and invitation to reflection is that the series actually makes demands on the *viewer*. Part of that demand comes from the narrative ploy of having Elliot address viewers directly. But another dimension of that demand stems from shifts in the production of television series. Once released weekly, one episode at a time, previous series had to build audience interest and intimacy over time; *Mr. Robot* aired weekly in its original run yet was clearly written one *season* at a time, and it thus encourages "binge" viewing, which can accommodate more complex narration, since viewers do not have to remember plot details from week to week. Indeed, the changing nature of the medium and of the way we are able to watch television series allows producers and writers to tackle more complicated topics, in a more densely visual and narratively complex way. And since viewers can binge watch, they are able to pay more *focused* attention, as opposed to having their attention distributed week to week. Watching television series such as *Mr. Robot* becomes something of a commitment, a tuning in of our attention to a dense story. The series' complexity, even its *difficulty*, seems to aim beyond pacification; it actively invites analysis. Put another way, *Mr. Robot* models for us not just an identification with the plight of its characters but also a *desire for analysis*. In this way, the series comes to seem not just entertainment but a public pedagogy about the reeducation of viewers' desires.

Mr. Robot's education of viewer desires might be its most fundamentally challenging—and useful—dimension. The series' engagement with Blochian ideas is fruitful because the series shows the temptations of indulging selfishly oriented and escapist fantasies *and* the difficult work required of us if we wish to translate our longing for an unalienated world into a political project of activating more expansive possibilities in this one. More than any other series we have discussed, *Mr. Robot* makes the active practice of *educating* desire part of the narrative as well as one of the effects the series has on its viewers. The Not-Yet Consciousness must be social and political, not merely personal: thus, the "genuine future" cannot be accessed by mere contemplation but requires the education of this desire toward enacting change in the world. Recall that for Bloch hope is what he calls "a directing act of a cognitive kind."[23] The cognitive element of this formulation is crucial, and *Mr. Robot* offers versions of how this utopian energy might be siphoned off and redirected toward sustaining the status quo as well, which serve as illustrations of the fact that the mere existence of desire is not sufficient.

We see the regressive side most strongly in a period of Angela's storyline during which, defeated in her attempts to win redress from E Corp through legal means and exhausted by their strategy of depleting her resources, she instead agrees to work for them and indulges the fantasy narrative that she can produce change from within. Her desire remains the same, but immersion in the corporate world quickly results in a shift in her orientation toward the world. In the immediate aftermath of the initial hack, she accompanies an E Corp executive to a television interview in which he is meant to reassure the public in the face of this catastrophic loss of value—instead, he admits that life savings and pensions have been destroyed, then commits suicide on camera, splattering the traumatized Angela's shoes with blood. Price gives Angela the option of going home or attending to a later event, where she might "pick up some invaluable lessons," and gives her some cash to replace her shoes. We next see her shoe shopping. The clerk expresses alarm that she could be so cold as to simply replace her shoes and continue to work for such a "despicable" company. At first Angela is flustered and agrees with his sentiments, but as he shifts into condemning her more directly, she demurs, "I just needed a job," continuing more harshly, "I don't know who you think you are talking to, but I'll try the Pradas next" (S1E10). In the absence of a path toward the good life other than through economic security and obtaining the luxury goods we have been taught by advertising to accept as emblems of success, Angela begins to orient her desire toward success within the system rather than changing it. Through much of season 2, we see only an uncanny version of Angela, fully identified with this corporate world, who robotically repeats self-affirmations into her mirror in a desperate attempt to form new neural pathways: "I am confident . . . My confidence is powerful . . . I recognize myself as exceptional . . . I will follow my dreams no matter what" (S2E1).

The education of desire is most obvious in the strange relationship to temporality that Whiterose introduces into the narrative via her "project," whose function is only clearly revealed very late in the series. During phase 2 of the hack in season 3, Whiterose and the Dark Army offer support for a plan to blow up the buildings containing the paper records that might allow E Corp to reconstruct its database, and Mr. Robot and Elliot fight within their shared body for control: they have different levels of commitment to this plan because of the risk it presents to people within the buildings. On a formal level, we often see this through gaps in the linear narrative—as the screen cuts to black and then "jumps" to another time and place—we follow only Elliot, whose experience is disrupted by chunks of lost time during which Mr. Robot has taken over. Whiterose is able to convert Angela to her side after inducing Angela to play a strange and anachronistic video game on a Commodore 64, whose primitive aesthetics evoke a much earlier ethos of online "dungeons" and text-based role playing. Angela works secretly with Mr. Robot (betraying Elliot) to ensure the success of the plan to bomb the buildings, although she is aware that lives might be lost. She has become convinced that in the bigger picture this will not matter, because the success of Whiterose's project means that all the inadequacies of the past will be corrected, that all that was lost will be restored—"We are going to look back and see that these consequences were necessary . . . [people] are going to be fine, including your father and my mother," she insists to Elliot (S3E6). Yet later, when the casualties from the attacks are revealed and Whiterose's lies are exposed, Angela is devastated: in one very poignant scene in the following episode, she repeatedly watches footage of a collapsing building in reverse, trying to convince herself and others that this representation of time and loss reversed will become a material possibility.

For Whiterose, all of this was about a UN vote that allowed China to annex the Congo (whose citizens, in another strange temporal logic, are described in S2E9 as "soon-to-be-corpses" and hence irrelevant), where Whiterose plans to relocate her machine and culminate her project—time travel. Converted to this plan, Angela believes that "when we succeed, a whole new world will be born" (S3E1). This desire, of course, sounds disturbingly similar to Blochian ideas about world transformation through activating the inherent utopian impulse present in daily life and art. There is a crucial difference, however, which has everything to do with the education of desire, the needed cognition to direct it toward a new (and better) world in the future, rather than nostalgically and fearfully looking toward the past, searching for a fantasized lost wholeness. In this storyline, *Mr. Robot* seems to be working specifically to educate us into differentiating between material life and the kinds of escapist fantasies often afforded by our media—the rewinding of video footage that obsesses Angela, the restore option to reboot a computer system to a previous state (Elliot tries to undo the phase 2 hack), the respawning into another life that is ubiquitous to video games. By playing with the temporality of the narrative (especially in S3E6), the series prevents viewers from simply being fully immersed in the narrative as a kind of realism and instead draws attention to how experience is structured *into* narrative, thereby educating the viewers' desire as well, reminding us that the thematic stakes explored here are relevant not only to the diegetic world but to the viewer's.

Thus, in many ways, the final contrast between Elliot's desire and Whiterose's comes down to this question of cognitive direction and the relevance for thinking about the better world beyond one's personal and familial situation. What we are being educated to appreciate is the need to create the better world from the real, material conditions of this one: indeed, Whiterose tries but fails to compromise Elliot by promising him the fantasy that Angela (who was killed at the beginning of season 4) can still live. Similarly, we cannot indulge a fantasy of returning to a better time, the fantasy of postwar American prosperity, which was largely available only to white, male workers in the first place, the fantasy of capitalism in its welfare-state form, before outsourced globalization. The time-reversal fantasy is backward looking and incapable of producing the new, the utopian, an example of fear rather than hope, in Bloch's terms. Instead of trying to reverse the disaster, we need to find a way to live with consequences that have inevitably happened, to chart a different path that refuses to repeat these mistakes, a lesson that is reinforced twice in the series finale. First, Elliot too plays a version of Whiterose's anachronistic computer game, an exercise he continually loses, finding no way to escape the in-game explosion until he realizes that the only correct action to take is to "stay with [his] friend" in the dystopian place, rather than seeking his individual escape: when he chooses this option, a new possibility for action emerges. Later, in the final moments of the series, the "real" Elliot finally awakens, freed from all the multiple personalities who have shielded him from trauma. He tells us, the "friend" he has directly addressed through the "fourth wall" throughout the series: "What if changing the world is just about being here, by showing up no matter how many times we get told you don't belong. . . . And if we all held onto that, if we refused to budge and fall in line, if we stood our ground just for long enough, just maybe, the world can't help but change around us" (S4E13).

As we leave the series, the Mastermind (that is, the Elliot we have followed throughout) addresses us directly one last time: "this only works if you let go too," before we follow him into a movie theater, where he sits to join all the other versions of Elliot's MPD, as they look out into a screen we do not see. A projector lights up the back of the screen as the camera slowly pulls in on the Mastermind's face, then tilts upward to pull into the light itself. We have left the projection to return to the world of action, signified as the circle of light becomes the real Elliot's eye, as he wakes up. The series thus asks us similarly to wake up to new ways of perceiving and acting in the world we see around us, to recognize "our democracy has been hacked," as a series tagline puts it, but at the same time to do more than immerse ourselves in this narrative as a way of escaping this painful knowledge. We, too, have to let Elliot go and return to the world beyond the screen.

CONCLUSION

Democracy in Crisis

What do we want our future to look like? Will we, as we did after 9/11, sacrifice civil liberties and human rights? Will we, as we did in response to the financial crisis of 2008, create even greater wealth inequality? Will we, in other words, choose solutions that exacerbate the root problems? . . . Or will we commit ourselves to reinvention?

—MASHA GESSEN, *SURVIVING AUTOCRACY*

As we began work on this project to theorize how SF television intersects with the American political imaginary, it was clear to us that the national trauma of 9/11 marked a distinctive break in the genre as well as in the larger American culture. Our initial discussions were guided by the conviction that the 2008 economic crash had become a far more urgent issue to address, the conditions leading to it obscured by an overdeveloped concern with national security, borders, and defense. We were intrigued by the way that SF television that overtly focused on questions of the political seemed inevitably to entwine them with economic questions of social inclusion and material distribution, of centers of profit and regions of dispossession, a tendency that accelerated in the wake of the crash. When we began this project, we had no idea that we would be finishing it during another moment of momentous crisis and coming change in America, marked not only by the economic strain caused by the COVID-19 health crisis and its unprecedented disruption to global capitalism but also by the end of one of the most damaging presidencies in American history, whose entire tenure was haunted by the threat that democracy could be displaced by authoritarianism.

Indeed, as we write, we are living through a situation that challenges comprehension and almost seems to suggest that we have fused with the SF narratives about which we write: the results of a democratic election continue to be challenged by an ousted incumbent, three weeks after the election. Attempts to shift the results using court challenges have failed, and now the campaign has turned to efforts to manipulate the certification of state results, to count as "legal" only those ballots that favor their own victory. More alarmingly, such strategies on behalf of an administration that has lied with regularity and impunity, while it floats the idea of "alternative facts," appeal to a voter base that has willingly followed their leader into a post-truth world of manufactured reality, believing with intense sincerity—and without evidence—that the election was somehow tainted. The sense that democracy is in crisis has never been more palpable, and it increasingly seems that Americans inhabit two separate realities, two worlds of meaning that have few—perhaps no—points of intersection. Fantasized visions of coming apocalypse or salvaged utopia are an indispensable element of this new political reality, and thus the education of desire has never been more important. We end this project on the cusp of a transition that will mark another shift as significant as was 9/11, although what will emerge into the next decade is not yet visible.

One central element in the rising power of authoritarianism worldwide is its link to white supremacist organizations and, through them, to domestic terrorism. In *Hate in the Homeland*, Cynthia Miller-Idriss reports that hate group membership, hate crimes, and violence related to them have increased in the past four years. In 2018, she reports, white nationalist groups experienced a 50 percent increase, and "right-wing extremists killed at least fifty people in the United States, outnumbering all other terrorist- and extremist-related deaths."[1] She suggests that the ongoing framework of 9/11, which means that American intelligence agencies prioritize Islamic rather than domestic extremism, hampers American efforts to recognize and counter this threat to the nation's democratic future. As our analyses show, the SF television produced in the wake of 9/11 originally shared this preoccupation but soon shifted storylines to address the related problem of how America was changed by its response to 9/11—instead of narratives about foreign invaders, we have narratives about polarized visions of the country's future, about collaborators or enemies within. And we are hopeful that American SF television of the next decade will similarly play a role in educating desire and awareness in ways that enable us to come to terms with the related threats of white supremacy and authoritarianism. We have already seen hints of this in *The Man in the High Castle*, as we argued in chapter 4, and more recent programs such as HBO's *Lovecraft Country* (2020) demonstrate that genre tropes ably capture how a racist past continues to shape the nation's future, even as the series also insists on our need to change this dynamic. As Miller-Idriss notes in her analysis of the recruitment strategies of white supremacist groups, the role of apocalyptic fantasy—understood as coming reality—is foundational to their rhetoric. In the face of such political cultures, the work of creating different and inclusive imaginaries of our possible futures is vital.

Masha Gessen, one of the most perceptive critics of the risk that autocracy will displace democracy, suggests that under the Trump administration Americans live in two realities. Describing how Democratic and Republican politicians responded differently to Trump's subversions of the norms of governance and law, she notes that their different realities collided in the impeachment hearings: "His lawyer claimed absolute immunity and impunity; the White House ordered administration employees not to testify. Washington split into two camps, one that inhabited a representative democracy and one that lived in an autocracy."[2] This fictionality and multiplicity of "reality" speaks to the importance of imagination and affect in the most consequential elements of our lives, as we have argued throughout this book. And while Trump clearly marks a nadir point of the crisis, he is not so much a break with the American past as evidence of a greater emphasis put on its worst aspects, as Gessen argues. She points out that Trump "was building on a four-hundred-year history of white supremacy, and he was building on a fifteen-year-long mobilization of American society against Muslims, immigrants, and the Other. A future historian of the twenty-first century might point to September 11, 2001, as the Reichstag Fire of the United States."[3] The risk to democracy crystallized by Trump and, more importantly, by the authoritarian forces for which he stands as metonym is just the latest chapter in the ongoing struggle about the essence of the American nation, a battle whose contours, we have argued here, are visible in the narratives of SF television.

In the light of 2020, the crash of 2008 may not loom as large in our imaginations as before, yet we maintain that the neoliberal economic policies we have critiqued here are deeply relevant to both the rise of authoritarianism and to how America will negotiate the economic crisis of COVID-19 and its aftermath. Wendy Brown argues that it is the ways that neoliberalism has put futurity into doubt for hegemonic groups, who could once take for granted their continued prosperity, that encourages their investment in apocalyptic fantasies in the first place. Channeling what would seem to drive this viewpoint, she suggests, "If white men cannot own democracy, there will be no democracy. If white men cannot rule the planet, there will be no planet."[4] The historian Jill Lepore also sees conflicts over race *as they are entwined with economic entitlements* as crucial to understanding the struggle between what she refers to as the "good nationalism" of civic ideals and the liberal state and the "bad" or "illiberal nationalism" of "nativism, racism, and recourse to aggression."[5] America is neither one nor the other but always both, she insists, and the rise of illiberal nationalism in the United States began with "white farmers and wage laborers left behind in the Gilded Age's economy [who] looked for explanations for their suffering, and searched for enemies."[6] These histories and their ongoing effects are why we have focused on economic disenfranchisement throughout this book, but this emphasis on economic matters should not be taken to minimize the omnipresent importance of racism to the American imaginary and to our contemporary struggle. Capitalism is always already racial capitalism, and thus the relevant histories of dispossession include the multigenerational economic disparities cultivated in the nation from slavery through Jim Crow and into the present.

In *Programming the Future*, we have sought to show how SF television narratives stage these political conflicts over values and futures, with a particular focus on the importance of the future as a site of affective investment. As we demonstrated in our first chapter on pre-9/11 texts, utopian strains are visible even in the most dystopian seeming of texts, such as *The X-Files*. At the same time, a careful reading of a utopian series such as several of the earlier Star Treks can reveal blind spots in any static vision of the good future. The remainder of our chapters moved from texts that most directly referenced 9/11 as the founding moment of a twenty-first-century political imaginary in chapter 2 to our discussion of *Mr. Robot* and its focus on debt culture and austerity crisis in chapter 6. A number of patterns become visible when we look at this trajectory as a whole, including the shift from external to internal enemies, the dangerous forms that patriotism sometimes takes, the strain of imagining a single American future in an increasingly polarized country, and the fact that the central challenge for American futures is imagining diverse and inclusive communities. The clear vision of a desirable and victorious future that was conceivable for a series such as *Falling Skies*, discussed in chapter 3, gives way to the endless conflicts over "my" people versus the Other in a series such as *The 100*, discussed in chapter 5. Throughout, we have focused on how the affective bonds of family—and especially queer ideas about family and futurity, which disrupt the reproduction of the same—map onto the larger notions of community, tribe, or nation. By taking up at once the twin discourses that have drawn extensively on Blochian theory, speculative fiction, and queer theory, we have sought to show the necessity of desiring differently, of conceptualizing futurity and belonging differently, beginning with the familial and the affective but insisting on the extension into the structures of political community.

Just as the return of authoritarianism has its roots in a longer American history of economic disparity, so too are there reasons to understand the extreme right's anxiety about traditional family values and heteronormative reproduction through an economic lens. As Melinda Cooper argues in *Family Values*, the alliance of neoconservative economic forces with fundamentalist Christians in the new right has produced a version of the Republican Party that seeks the same ends but for different reasons. While fundamentalist Christians attack abortion and support homophobic legislation as a defense of religious freedom, neoliberal forces align for reasons that are rooted in logic of human capital.[7] With less need for a public workforce, conservative politicians have less motivation to invest—dollars or their followers' affect—in structures of the public good but instead seek to place all responsibility for well-being (financial and otherwise) on the family unit. As we discussed in the introduction, this shift toward self-reliance in place of the welfare state became dominant at a time when consumer credit also became more readily available, encouraging families to "deficit fund" their own social reproduction.

From Cooper's point of view, this is a renewed version of "the poor-law imperative of family responsibility,"[8] and this alliance of neoliberal and neoconservative forces in the new right is one of the central reasons we end our analysis with *Mr. Robot*'s imperative to undo the damage of debt culture.

We conclude this book while we are still in the midst of the pandemic, with politicians portraying our responses as a debate between protecting health through lockdowns versus protecting the economy, exemplifying the biopolitical logic we discuss in chapter 4. It is clear that a significant economic crisis is coming, even as vaccines and antivirals promise that the health crisis will eventually be controlled. How governments will respond to this new economic crisis is as yet very unclear. As our epigraph states, reinvention is required if the next decade is not to repeat the errors of the last two, decades that have increased both inequality and polarization. The framing of debates over topics such as school closures in terms of families *or* economies warns us that issues of human capital and social reproduction will be central to the unfolding of this coming economic crisis, again reinforcing the centrality of thinking the affective and the structural jointly. We anticipate that women especially may be further marginalized as they are shifted from the workforce into childcare, and this added emphasis on the nuclear, heteronormative family may also spell further marginalization for queer subjects—who are already under attack by the patriarchal values so central to authoritarianism and white supremacy.

Eva Cherniavsky argued a decade ago, in response to the increasing replacement of civic values with market values, that the state no longer has an economic interest in cultivating a single national "people" who are all equally regarded as participants in the collective project of the nation. As with the fragmentation of realities prompted by authoritarian post-truth politics, this economic disinvestment in the political has "the effect of eroding the sense of a common reality in which a national or even a local (not to mention a planetary) 'we' live in simultaneous time and convergent social and material worlds."[9] She thus argues that neoliberalism must be understood as a political ethos, not just an economic system, and our analysis follows a similar trajectory. We focus on the role of imagination, projected images of the future, and affective investment to the creation of this ethos. The rising threat of authoritarianism and white supremacy is similarly both a political ethos and an imaginative culture with a distinct mode of future making. As we conclude, therefore, we want to spend some time thinking about the role of political fantasy in creating what Cherniavsky aptly characterized as the "unreal" of our neoliberal present and its rising threat of authoritarianism, to reflect on how the Blochian education of desire might offer both a counterdiscursive ethos and an alternative future.

The conservative critic Anne Applebaum contrasts the "Big Lie" of twentieth-century totalitarian regimes that are critiqued in SF texts such as George Orwell's *Nineteen Eighty-Four*—states that insist on absolute capitulation to state ideology and require people to "proclaim that black is white, that war is peace"—with the "Medium-Size Lie" of twenty-first-century authoritarianisms: the latter, she argues, "encourage their followers to engage, at least part of the time, with an alternative reality."[10] These alternative realities tend to be backward looking, indulging precisely the kind of fearful "negative astonishment" that Bloch argues is the opposite of hope and its cognitive directing of affect toward the truly new. Fear looks to the past for models, is invested in restoring a fantasized time of plenitude that mythically existed in the past, as it seeks to restore this illusion as a ground for the future. We can see the widespread interest in this kind of nostalgic regression in the rhetoric of white supremacist groups and, in less overtly racialized tones, in the slogan "make America great again." Yet Bloch would argue that these kinds of alternative realities are not properly utopian; they do not partake of a dialectic between desire and manifest possibility within the material world. Most importantly, they see the world as closed and finished (if out of sync with the fantasized time of greatness) and are thus not open to Bloch's vision that the world is "unfinished" and thus to the new emerging. Fear, he suggests, leads only to "lament" and not to change, and the utopian requires hope.[11]

The centrality of alternative realities to right-extremist politics today cannot be ignored in terms of their affective force, yet it remains crucial that we continue to differentiate them from the world-changing utopian imaginaries of the Blochian tradition. Strategies other than the dystopian exaggeration of *Nineteen Eighty-Four* are needed to counter this new threat, strategies that can account for the affective lure of certain narratives even as these new kinds of SF point to the danger they embody. Several of the series we have discussed in this book—especially those that show the need for diverse cultures to work together without hierarchy, such as *The Man in the High Castle*, *The Expanse*, and *The 100*—suggest ways that speculative fiction can continue to educate our desire, to insist on the need for the new. And although we have argued throughout this book for the importance of the affective identifications these series prompt, equally important is the fact that they maintain a gap between text and world: they are presented as *alternatives* precisely so that we can see our material world more clearly in its difference from them. The ending of *Mr. Robot*, most explicitly, demands that we turn from the screen and back to the world, once we understand how all the pieces fit together. Authoritarian fantasies, in contrast, blur truth and fiction, imagined world and reality, and thus work to distort rather than to enhance their adherents' capacity to see. This is not a new strategy—writing in the aftermath of World War II, Hannah Arendt identified the ideal totalitarian subject as "people for whom the distinction between fact and fiction . . . and the distinctions between true and false . . . no longer exist."[12] Yet although it is not new, it is the perhaps the most important factor to consider today as political alliances on both right and left reinvent and newly imagine themselves to confront the twenty-first century.

Speculative texts, then, offer a counter to the right's nostalgic immersion in alternative reality precisely because they insistently recall this distinction between fact and fiction, between the world of the text and the material world it refers to but never displaces. In her prescient work on the political imaginary of nostalgia, Svetlana Boym argues that nostalgia has a utopian dimension in language that is reminiscent of Bloch in the sense that the nostalgic longing proceeds, like the utopian impulse, from a dissatisfaction with the present. Her analysis reveals how important the education of desire is to this project of public affect, to differentiating forward-looking utopian hope from backward-looking nostalgic fear. We must take responsibility for our nostalgic dreams, Boym argues, because "fantasies of the past determined by needs of the present have a direct impact on realities of the future."[13] For Boym, nostalgic longing that constructs a mythical version of the past "is an abdication of personal responsibility, a guilt-free homecoming, an ethical and aesthetic failure."[14] Evidence of such ethical and aesthetic failure is everywhere visible in the alternative realities conjured by the extreme right, both in their fictional narratives about the past greatness of fantasized homogenous cultures of white men and in the political attempts to manipulate reality on the part of the Trump campaign in 2020, which echo the rise of so many other authoritarians. The longed-for past is always the so-called traditional past, and thus patriarchal suppression of queer peoples and cultures is also a central element in this authoritarian displacement of reality with fantasy. Gessen starkly points out that "countries that have grown less democratic in recent years have drawn a battle line on the issue of LGBT rights."[15] Against such historical distortion and erasure stands the speculative imagination and its assertion of the never-foreclosed possibility for change.

The crisis of the aftermath of the 2020 election further points to the fact that the ongoing struggle between liberal democracy and extreme right fundamentalism is as much a battle of affective identification as it is one of electoral strategy. As we write, it is clear that none of the frivolous lawsuits will succeed, and it seems unlikely that state certification boards or Electoral College voters will be compromised. Yet the point of the challenge to election results seems to be less an expectation that its outcome may be changed and more an invitation for more Americans to join the extreme right in their fantasized reality: a reality in which the election was illegitimate and where the nation continues to live in the never-ending Trump regime, a reality where the debts of colonial and other racialized violence will never have to be paid and white men can continue to hold a monopoly on social, economic, and political power. We should hasten to add that we are aware of the risk of overstating the present in this focus on Trump, and thus we repeat once more that he is not the origin of these tendencies in American culture, just their most recent and flagrant manifestation. We dwell on this example not because of its singular importance but because it is exemplary of the next stage of the crisis of American democracy, the polarization of the country into two political realities.

This polarization is something Cherniavsky anticipated in her critique of the unreal of contemporary politics long before Trump became a candidate:

> We are reminded of what we should probably not have lost sight: that the "real world" is not a transhistorical given, but an invention specific to (and decisive for) modern, horizontal sociality and the incorporative aims of a hegemonic power—specific to and decisive for the political life

of the masses. Insofar as the state is reimagined, no longer the proxy of a sovereign national people, but a managerial power dedicated to the concentration of capital among an ever-smaller fraction of elites, there is scant political value to the ideological production of an inclusive reality and of the relatively fixed, relatively durable reference points that sustain it.[16]

Cherniavsky's focus is on economic stratification, the hollowing-out of democracy and the public sphere by neoliberal state policies that replace civic values with market values. This argument is similar to Wendy Brown's claims in *Undoing the Demos*, claims Brown later modifies as she takes account of right-wing extremist ideologies in her later book *In the Ruins of Neoliberalism*. Yet although Cherniavsky makes her point in references to economic fragmentation, her larger point that power no longer works through ideological appeals that convince "the masses" that they are best served by the hegemonic interests of the dominant class still stands. In place of such traditional political tactics, Cherniavsky sees a power that operates by "rescinding our reference points and scattering us to the winds of fear, loathing, delirium, and despair."[17] This seems as good a description as any of the affects cultivated and exploited by the extreme right's attempts to install authoritarian power in America and to continue the dominance of its white supremacist foundations.

In the face of such a transformed public sphere, new strategies of political resistance are also required. As we hope to have demonstrated here, we believe that the Blochian education of desire is just one such political strategy adequate to the crises of the present. The importance of affective identification, visions of a future that can inspire hope and security rather than fear and despair, is paramount. Through the intimacy of television as a medium fused with the world-building capacity of SF, the futures projected in SF television are a space for working through the political imaginary today. The displacement into another world that they provide gives viewers a way to engage with questions—such as community and belonging, what constitutes the essence of America, and how economic issues of resource distribution should be managed justly—without immediately falling into the default answers and affects so common in the polarized world of social media today. To be clear, we do not argue that these SF texts necessarily embody visions that align with left-wing resistance to authoritarianism, but we do suggest that by displacing these conflicts into future worlds or onto alien subjects they make concepts available for debate in a public sphere that is increasingly lacking substantive exchange.

Moreover, this appeal to affective investment is a strategy already well developed in right-wing extremist culture, as Miller-Idriss demonstrates in her work. Young people especially long for a sense of belonging or desire to engage in heroic and meaningful action, and Miller-Idriss credits the success of their apocalyptic fantasies of the destruction of the white race with their careful fusion of "both negative and positive emotions—not only anger and resentment but also the desire for belonging, meaning, and purpose."[18] The nostalgic fantasies of restoring past greatness can serve this function, but we suggest that other imaginaries, such as those found in several of the texts we have analyzed here, can also serve as points of affective identification that can mobilize new understandings and changed behaviors, and we think this is especially true for series that show their protagonists struggling with their own political investments, sometimes shifting allegiances once they learn more and understand their social world in a different way. *Colony*, for example, not only sustains narrative tension by having its protagonists shift between supporting the resistance or capitulating to occupation but demonstrates the possibility of moving beyond a static political position. *The 100*, similarly, mainly uses its repeated confrontations with new external enemies to offer speculative battle scenes, but it also allows its characters to change—both for the better and for the worse—under the weight of never-ending conflict, suggesting that its conclusion, focused on peaceful transcendence, is not a sudden reversal but arrived at out of the experience we share with protagonists across its seasons. Other series, such as *Continuum* or *The Expanse*, put characters with multiple viewpoints into dialogue, not clearly identifying any with righteousness, as we learn alongside the characters how economic context is central to shaping one's political viewpoint. These series offer fantasized stories, to be sure, but of a distinctly different texture than the alternative realities inhabited by right-wing extremists, precisely because of this emphasis on multiplicity, exchange of viewpoints, and change.

We should not underestimate the power of fantasized stories to provoke alternative political imaginaries—either on the right or the left. The alt-right may be fulminating in conspiracy theories and antidemocratic plans for the overthrow of governments and the establishment of auto-cratic, theocratic, patriarchal, and white supremacist regimes akin to that glimpsed in Hulu's televisual adaptation of *The Handmaid's Tale*. But other thinkers and activists mine the archive of speculative narrative to imag-ine much more equitable futures. Kara Keeling's *Queer Times, Black Futures* looks to the textual work of the Black writers Samuel Delany and Nnedi Okorafor, among many others, for inspiration on how to imagine a futurity that will not continue to damage Black and queer people. For Keeling, Sun Ra's 1972 film *Space Is the Place* offers a powerful early exam-ple of an Afrofuturism that does not naively or sentimentally deny the ongoing realities of racial oppression while still holding out the possibil-ity for imagining a future for Black people that thinks and feels beyond the contemporary corporate commodification of Black culture. Similarly, adrienne maree brown turns to the work of Octavia E. Butler for inspira-tion in *Emergent Strategy* and *Pleasure Activism: The Politics of Feeling Good* to consider how an anticonsumerist ethic of collaboratively and col-lectively pursuing pleasure might form the basis for more socially just and equitable forms of world building. These authors are only two of many possible examples of writers and thinkers, academics and activists, who are cultivating other ways of using speculative narrative to keep the future *open*, so that more people than ever before can experiment with and experience freedom and resist the safe-feeling foreclosures of autocratic worlds.

Television is starting to follow suit, with series such as *Lovecraft Coun-try* and *Utopia Falls* (2020). In the former, African Americans encounter the horrifying monsters of racial injustice in America, the Lovecraftian images no longer cosmic terrors but the all-too-real tragedies of white supremacy. The latter, a Canadian television series, imagines a future "per-fect society" riddled with its own class divisions and a troupe of young kids who discover an archive of hip hop, which inspires them to critique and agitate against the injustices in their own world, despite that world's constant claims of exceptionality. As with all of the series we have exam-ined in this book, these two most recent examples are responding to the specific historical moments in which they are produced. But they are also, in Blochian fashion, gesturing to the unfinished work of building the future. They offer hope for a different kind of tomorrow.

We cannot expect television or even speculative narrative to save democracy from the authoritarian and fascist impulses that are, if nothing else, a fearful response to a world of pandemics, economic disparity, climate change, mystifying technological advances, and general anxiety amid widespread global upheaval. Yes, stories comfort. They can also offer hope, even if not blueprints. It is up to us to determine the next concrete steps that will build on the abstract desire offered by such narratives for a different, possibly better future. The question facing all of us invested in more just and equitable futures is what kinds of stories of that future we want to cultivate. In our analysis of contemporary speculative television in this book, we have tended to side with those narratives that do not foreclose on the future, that keep a vision of it open, a never-ending story of making the world better for more people.

NOTES

INTRODUCTION

1. Eva Cherniavsky, *Neocitizenship: Political Culture After Democracy* (New York: New York University Press, 2017), 5, 134, 135.
2. Henry A. Giroux, *On Critical Pedagogy* (New York: Continuum, 2011), 134.
3. Stuart Hall, "Notes on Deconstructing 'The Popular'" (1981), in *Essential Essays*, vol. 1: *Foundations of Cultural Studies*, ed. David Morley (Durham, NC: Duke University Press, 2018), 348.
4. Stuart Hall, *Cultural Studies 1983: A Theoretical History*, repr. ed., ed. Jennifer Daryl Slack and Lawrence Grossberg (Durham, NC: Duke University Press, 2016), 205.
5. Catherine Chaput, *Market Affect and the Rhetoric of Political Economic Debates* (Columbia: University of South Carolina Press, 2019), 138. Early in his career, Hall argued how "in the analysis of culture, the interconnection between social structures and processes and formal or symbolic structures is absolutely pivotal." We take his theorization here as axiomatic in arguing that critical engagement with symbolic structures is intimately tied to critical understanding and potentially agency with regard to "social structures and processes." Stuart Hall, "Encoding and Decoding in the Television Discourse" (1973), in *Essential Essays*, ed. David Morley (Durham, NC: Duke University Press, 2018), 1:257.
6. Hall, *Cultural Studies 1983*, 197.
7. Wendy Brown, *Undoing the Demos: Neoliberalism's Stealth Revolution* (London: Zone, 2017), 9.
8. David Harvey, *A Brief History of Neoliberalism* (Oxford: Oxford University Press, 2005), 2.
9. This much-cited statement was made during an interview in 1987. It was reprinted in the *Guardian* on April 8, 2013, as part of an obituary made from her public statements.

See "Margaret Thatcher: A Life in Quotes," *Guardian*, April 8, 2013, https://www
.theguardian.com/politics/2013/apr/08/margaret-thatcher-quotes.

10. Melinda Cooper, *Family Values: Between Neoliberalism and the New Social Conservatism* (New York: Zone, 2017), 63.

11. Wendy Brown, *In the Ruins of Neoliberalism: The Rise of Antidemocratic Politics in the
West* (New York: Columbia University Press, 2019), 40.

12. Cooper, *Family Values*, 36, notes, for example, that as white women were increasingly
integrated into the waged workforce and middle class, programs to support families
were increasingly associated with women of color as they were demonized and
defunded. Similarly, access to benefits linked to the wage earner (such as healthcare)
depended on legally recognized marriage for much of U.S. history, thereby excluding
queer people. Indeed, Cooper suggests that the recent acceptance of gay marriage is
less a cause for celebration and more an ongoing strategy of neoliberal policies that seek
to devolve all economic responsibility for the needy to the family unit: to expand this
structure to as many people as possible, nonheterosexual marriage and other civil
unions had to be incorporated into the family wage system.

13. Brown, *Undoing the Demos*, 44–45.

14. Brown, *Undoing the Demos*, 129, 17.

15. Max Haiven, *Cultures of Financialization: Fictitious Capital in Popular Culture and
Everyday Life* (London: Palgrave Macmillan, 2014).

16. See David Graeber, *Debt: The First 5,000 Years* (New York: Melville House, 2011); David
Harvey, *Seventeen Contradictions and the End of Capitalism* (Oxford: Oxford Univer-
sity Press, 2014); Annie McClanahan, *Dead Pledges: Debt, Crisis, and Twenty-First-
Century Culture* (Stanford, CA: Stanford University Press, 2017); Ivan Ascher, *Portfolio
Society: On the Capitalist Mode of Prediction* (New York: Zone, 2016); Nigel Dodd, *The
Social Life of Money* (Princeton, NJ: Princeton University Press, 2014).

17. Cherniavsky, *Neocitizenship*, 1.

18. Cherniavsky, *Neocitizenship*, 151, 10.

19. Cherniavsky, *Neocitizenship*, 147.

20. Cherniavsky, *Neocitizenship*, 160.

21. Cherniavsky, *Neocitizenship*, 157.

22. Amanda D. Lotz is a leading voice documenting the relevance of political economy and
other industry changes for the medium. See her *The Television Will Be Revolutionized*,
2nd ed. (2007; New York: New York University Press, 2014) and *We Now Disrupt This
Broadcast: How Cable Transformed Television and the Internet Revolutionized It All*
(Cambridge, MA: MIT Press, 2018).

23. Another relevant factor is ways of generating revenue after broadcast, from videotape
and DVD sales to syndication, streaming on secondary markets, and global distribution. All of these considerations, too, shape what television is financed and by whom.

24. Also relevant here is the fact that viewers increasingly watched both film and television across a range of devices, from large sets to small smartphone screens, with ongoing visual improvements across these devices.

25. See Shoshana Zuboff, *The Age of Surveillance Capitalism: The Fight for a Human Future
at the New Frontier of Power* (New York: PublicAffairs, 2019). It is important to note

here that every technological innovation that seems to increase consumer agency and choice is also a point of increased surveillance and capture of data for industry use.

26. Here too SF is a leader: *Babylon 5* pioneered this method of storytelling long before the prestige series, but it was not widely embraced at the time. Jason Mittell, *Complex TV: The Poetics of Contemporary Television Storytelling* (New York: New York University Press, 2015), also identifies *The X-Files* as an important early innovator of story-arc television.

27. Mittell, *Complex TV*, 52.

28. Lotz, *The Television Will Be Revolutionized*, "Navigating Convenience," chap. 2.

29. Lotz, *We Now Disrupt This Broadcast*, chap. 21.

30. Carl Freedman, *Critical Theory and Science Fiction* (Middletown, CT: Wesleyan University Press, 2000), 200.

31. E. P. Thompson, *William Morris: Romantic to Revolutionary* (London: Merlin, 1977), qtd. in Ruth Levitas, *The Concept of Utopia* (Syracuse, NY: Syracuse University Press, 1990), 141.

32. José Esteban Muñoz, *Cruising Utopia: The Then and There of Queer Futurity* (New York: New York University Press, 2009), 28.

33. Muñoz, *Cruising Utopia*, 28.

34. Mari Ruti, *The Ethics of Opting Out: Queer Theory's Defiant Subjects* (New York: Columbia University Press, 2017), 7.

35. Ruti, *The Ethics of Opting Out*, 38.

36. Douglas Kellner and Harry O'Hara, "Utopia and Marxism in Ernst Bloch," *New German Critique* 9 (1976): 16, https://doi.org/10.2307/487686.

37. Muñoz, *Cruising Utopia*, 28.

38. Phillip E. Wegner, *Shockwaves of Possibility: Essays on Science Fiction, Globalization, and Utopia* (New York: Peter Lang, 2014), xii, 50.

39. Rosemary Hennessy, *Profit and Pleasure: Sexual Identities in Late Capitalism*, 2nd ed. (New York: Routledge, 2018), xxv.

40. Hennessy, *Profit and Pleasure*, xxix.

41. Peter Drucker, *Warped: Gay Normality and Queer Anti-Capitalism* (Chicago: Haymarket, 2015), 390, 388. Other theorists have argued similarly and compellingly. Janet R. Jakobsen notes how capitalism has been reproducing itself for the last two centuries through the nuclear family: "Sex in the form of the Protestant family is one way to make human beings who value—morally as well as economically—participation in capitalism." As such, Jakobsen considers how queer and non-normative sexual intimacies, practices, and relations *might* offer opportunities for revisioning the structures that support and sustain capitalism: "But if sex cannot undo global capital, it can be an important part of the project of resisting the construction of the world in the terms most suited to the prevailing economic system. In particular, sexual perversity can help create alternative economic units to that of the autonomous individual and the household. This possibility is important in an era of neoliberal privatization, when the individual household is called on to carry ever-increasing burdens for producing social goods." Janet R. Jakobsen, "Perverse Justice," *GLQ: A Journal of Lesbian and Gay Studies* 18, no.1 (2012): 28, 32, https://doi.org/10.1215/10642684-1422125.

42. Chaput, *Market Affect and the Rhetoric of Political Economic Debates*, 50.

1. THE CHANGING SHAPE OF
SCIENCE FICTION TELEVISION

1.   The cancelation of *The X-Files* in 2002 was not only attributable to the tension between its ethos and shifts in contemporary culture. The last two years of the series were also plagued by frequent absences of its star Duchovny, who no longer wanted to commit to the long filming obligations of then-standard series lengths of twenty to twenty-six episodes a season. Most of *Star Trek Enterprise* aired after 9/11, but it is a series very out of tone with the rest of the franchise.

2.   Despite this, the series remains hugely significant for SF fans and no doubt influenced casting in *Continuum* (discussed in chapter 4). Its vision of corporations compromising governments may also be an influence on *Mr. Robot* (discussed in chapter 6).

3.   The colonialist narrative may be a carryover perhaps from the Horatio Hornblower series that partially inspired Roddenberry as well as the Golden Age SF of Heinlein and Asimov, two other influences on the original series.

4.   Interestingly, the project to send Americans to the moon was unfolding as viewers watched Keeler dream of it, but it was unfolding in the context of the Cold War, not the socialist utopia she outlines.

5.   This is the only crew, after the original, that has transitioned from television to film.

6.   The dating is of course complicated by the twenty years during which events of the original crew's film cycle take place.

7.   It also refers back to the original *Star Trek* episode "Arena" (S1E18), as in both the captain must survive on an alien planet by allying with an alien whose language he does not originally speak or understand.

8.   Here it is important to keep in mind the restrictions of the broadcast television era and its control by advertisers. The first openly gay character on network television, Ellen DeGeneres in her comedy *Ellen* (1994–1998), only came out in a season 4 episode that aired in 1997, three years after *TNG* was off the air.

9.   John Rieder, *Colonialism and the Emergence of Science Fiction* (Middleton, CT: Wesleyan University Press, 2008), 146–47.

10.   Robin Roberts, *Sexual Generations: "Star Trek: The Next Generation" and Gender* (Champaign: University of Illinois Press, 1999), 183.

11.   Roberts, *Sexual Generations*, 184.

12.   This is not to say that there will not be Star Trek films. CBS is owned by Viacom, which also owns Paramount, and this cross-platform integration of intellectual property is part of the new political economy of transmedia entertainment.

13.   There are several more new Star Trek series in development, including *Strange New Worlds*, a prequel series featuring the crew Roddenberry originally imagined, led by Pike and including a female second officer, a configuration that network executives refused to film. The animated *Lower Decks* (2020–) was just released at the time of writing.

14.   Introduced in S2E4 of the original *Star Trek*. In this series, the "evil" counterparts are clearly very different from the upstanding citizens of the *Enterprise* and the Federation.

15. See especially Daniel Bernari, *"Star Trek" and History: Race-ing Toward a White Future* (New Brunswick, NJ: Rutgers University Press, 1998). A number of works examine the military ethos of the series, including H. Bruce Franklin's *"Star Trek* in the Vietnam Era," *Science Fiction Studies* 21, no.1 (March 1994): 22–34; Steffen Hantke, *"Star Trek's* Mirror Universe Episodes and U.S. Military Culture Through the Eyes of the Other," *Science Fiction Studies* 41, no. 3 (November 2014): 562–78; Lincoln Geraghty, "A Truly American Enterprise: *Star Trek's* Post-9/11 Politics," in *New Boundaries in Political Science Fiction*, ed. Donald M. Hassler (Columbia: University of South Carolina Press, 2008), 157–66; George Gonzalez, *"Star Trek" and the Politics of Globalization* (Switzerland: Springer/Palgrave Macmillan/Palgrave Pivot, 2018); and Rick Worland, "From the New Frontier to the Final Frontier: *Star Trek* from Kennedy to Gorbachev," *Film and History* 24, no.1 (2013): 19–35. Lee F. Heller, "Persistence of Difference: Postfeminism, Popular Discourse, and Heterosexuality in *Star Trek: The Next Generation*," *Science Fiction Studies* 24, no. 2 (July 1997): 226–44, makes a similar argument about how patriarchy also persists, despite overt storylines that challenge it. The collection *Fighting for the Future: Essays on "Star Trek: Discovery*," ed. Sabrina Mittermeier and Mareike Spychala (Liverpool: Liverpool University Press, 2020), shows how *Discovery* takes on these issues from a twenty-first-century perspective.

16. Interestingly, the pandemic web series "Alone Together," which extends the storylines for *DS9* characters but also references in-world changes reflected in *Discovery* and *Picard* narratives, frames its story of the increased militarization of the Federation in terms that reflect post-9/11 America: "benevolence has taken a back seat to security" (E1). See Anthony Pascale, "Watch *Alone Together*, a 4-Part Remote Series Read by *Star Trek: Deep Space Nine* Actors in Character," *TrekMovie.com*, August 4, 2020, https://trekmovie.com/2020/08/04/watch-alone-together-a-4-part-remote-series-read-by-star-trek-deep-space-nine-actors-in-character/.

17. See Henry Jenkins, *Textual Poachers* (New York: Routledge, 2013).

18. This storyline seems influenced by the sleeper Cylons of *Battlestar Galactica*, discussed in chapter 2.

19. Steps in this direction had already been taken by *DS9* and its emphasis of Sisko's African American heritage, as well as in *Voyager* with storylines about Chakotay's Indigenous background.

2. INVENTING SCIENCE FICTION TELEVISION AS POLITICAL NARRATIVE

1. For further analysis, see Mike Milford and Robert C. Rowland, "Situated Ideological Allegory and *Battlestar Galactica*," *Western Journal of Communication* 76, no. 5 (2012): 536–51; and Mikkel Vedby Rasmussen, "Cylons in Baghdad: Experiencing Counterinsurgency in *Battlestar Galactica*," in *"Battlestar Galactica" and International Relations*, eds. Nicholas J. Kiersey and Iver B. Neumann (New York: Routledge, 2013), 167–78.

2. To give only a range of examples of this scholarship, there are two collections on *Battlestar Galactica* and philosophy: Josef Steiff and Tristan Tamplin, eds., *"Battlestar Galactica" and Philosophy: Mission Accomplished or Mission Frakked Up?* (Chicago: Open Court, 2008); and Jason T. Eberl, ed., *"Battlestar Galactica" and Philosophy: Knowledge Here Begins out There* (Malden, MA: Blackwell, 2008). Religion is considered in Kevin J. Wetmore, *The Theology of "Battlestar Galactica": American Christianity in the 2004–2009 Television Series* (Jefferson. NC: McFarland, 2012). Tiffany Potter and C. W. Marshall, eds., *Cylons in America: Critical Studies in "Battlestar Galactica"* (New York: Bloomsbury, 2007), is the best overview of many themes in the series, including important work on gender. One edited collection, Iver B. Neumann and Nicholas J. Kiersey, eds., *"Battlestar Galactica" and International Relations* (New York: Routledge, 2013); and one monograph with *BSG* as a major example, Stephen Benedict Dyson, *Otherworldly Politics* (Baltimore, MD: Johns Hopkins University Press, 2015), focus exclusively on political themes in the series.

3. Based on a fan-letter campaign, similar to that which enabled renewal of the original *Star Trek*, a spinoff *Galactica 1980* has a single season in that year about the colonists' arrival on Earth. *Caprica* (2009–2010), a single-season reboot spinoff, focused on the eponymous planet in the years during which Cylon technology was developed.

4. "Battlestar Galactica (Sci Fi)," Peabody Awards, Henry W. Grady College of Journalism and Mass Communication, 2005, https://web.archive.org/web/20100610221349 /http://www.peabody.uga.edu/winners/details.php?id=1443. *Star Trek: The Next Generation* was the only other SF series to receive a Peabody before this (for an episode, not the entire series, as in the case of *BSG*). The website also praises *BSG* for making SF "accessible to all," an elitist remark we would not endorse. More genre series have been recognized in the years since, and it is clear that *BSG* changed mainstream critics' ideas about what SF could do, opening the stores for increasingly complex series in its wake.

5. Lisa Duggan, *Twilight of Equality? Neoliberalism, Cultural Politics, and the Attack on Democracy* (Boston: Beacon, 2017), x.

6. Duggan, *Twilight*, 7.

7. The idea that love is central to reproductive capacity is borrowed from Karel Čapek's *Rossums Universal Robots*, a 1920 SF play that gave the world this term, borrowed from a Czech word analogous to "serf." Its robots are also made of flesh, and the play is a harsh critique of the dehumanization of workers by reducing their lives merely to their capacity to work. The rebellious robots in the play are dependent on humans who control the technology for their manufacture, until love enables a revolutionary pair to inaugurate a new future of robot self-generation.

8. There is, unfortunately, a chauvinistic element to the otherwise hopeful conclusion. While surveying the new planet, they notice some native hominids seen only from a distance. While it is impossible to ascertain their race, we later learn that the location is Tanzania, where the Mitochondrial Eve is eventually excavated. The settlers decide to give up their technology and live simply in this new land, and their diminished numbers will be replenished by interbreeding with the local hominids, whom they note have only primitive technology and no language. Thus, the series implies that the capacity that produced *Homo sapiens* from less-capable, earlier hominids was found not in

the indigenous African population but in the mostly white cast of the series. Hera, it should be noted, is mixed race in two senses, both human/Cylon and also partially of Asian descent, based on the fact that Cylon Model Eight is played by a Korean-Canadian actress.

9. Season 4 also has a strange hint of a queer relationship in S4E16 when Ellen (Kate Vernon), wife of Tigh (Michael Hogan), expresses her jealousy of Adama: she claims Tigh has prioritized his friendship with and military service alongside Adama over their marriage—and this despite the fact that by this point in the series we know that both Tigh and Ellen were original human creators of the Cylons, also partners in this original human life, and now part of the final five.

10. See Derek Maisonville, "So Say Who All? Cosmopolitanism, Hybridity, and Colonialism in the Reimagined Battlestar Galactica," in *"Battlestar Galactica" and International Relations*, ed. Nicholas J. Kiersey and Iver B. Neumann (New York: Routledge, 2013), 119–36, for an analysis of the persistence of liberal cosmopolitan ideals of tolerance in the series' treatment of hybridity.

11. The much-discussed Hulu series *The Handmaid's Tale* (2017–2022) is another example that could fit within this framework, in that it is a well-crafted drama that uses SF motifs that address ongoing political issues. Although we admire many things about this series and indeed have written about it elsewhere, it is not in scope for the specific idea about inequality and governance that we seek to trace in this book. *The Handmaid's Tale* addresses problems of authoritarianism, as do other series we discuss here, but through a framework focused all but exclusively on patriarchy. Our critique of the series' lack of intersectionality mirrors some of the ideas we discuss throughout this book.

12. The comic was written by Alan Moore, drawn by Dave Gibbons, and colored by John Higgins, and was serialized by DC Comics between 1986 and 1987.

13. The phrase originally comes from Juvenal's *Satires*: "*Quis custodiet ipsos custodes?*" That is, "who watches the watchmen (guards)?"

14. Rorschach is the antihero of the comic, a foil to Ozymandias, whose own heroism is compromised by his willingness to sacrifice lives he deems expendable to the end of the greater good (as he sees it). The original Rorschach believes in moral absolutism and refuses to work for the government as do some of his peers, and thus he is a criminal vigilante. Rorschach identifies with right-wing political agendas, whereas Ozymandias supports those on the left. This character was very positively received, especially his refusal to support the moral relativism of Ozymandias's plan to kill thousands in his fake attack in order to save millions from the looming threat of nuclear war. In many ways, then, his character emblematizes the limited notion of justice that fuels much American popular media, precisely what is critiqued by the miniseries.

15. Reeves was a real Black marshal in the Oklahoma Territory in the nineteenth century. The in-text serial film is in the style of contemporary serials but is invented for the miniseries.

16. *Ms. 45* is a rape revenge film about a timid woman who, after being raped twice in one day, obtains a gun and takes revenge on men. She wears a nun's habit as a disguise for some of her murders, matching the image on the cover of *Sister Night* as depicted in the miniseries.

3. 9/11 AND ITS AFTERMATHS:
THREATS OF INVASION

1. See Steffen Hantke, "Bush's America and the Return of the Cold War in Science Fiction: Alien Invasion in *Invasion, Threshold*, and *Surface*," *Journal of Popular Film and Television* 38, no. 3 (2010): 143–51, for a detailed discussion of relevant film and television titles in the early 2000s.

2. A paradigmatic text, which also takes on questions of how postwar America was being changed by the rise of consumer culture and increased urbanization, is Don Siegel's *Invasion of the Body Snatchers* (1956). The story of humans replaced by pod-grown alien imitations, this cult-classic film is the first of four film adaptations of Jack Finney's *The Body Snatchers* (New York: Dell, 1955). Frequently read as thematizing anxiety about conformist communist culture that threatened to take over America, the film speaks equally to the rigidity and uniformity of a contemporary America so afraid of communist influence that it enforced a narrow version of appropriately American life on its subjects with authoritarian zeal. This motif of people changed into alien versions of themselves—and the doubled-edged themes it conveys—shapes the texts we discuss in this chapter. In many ways, *Invasion of the Body Snatchers* is a cultural touchstone for all three series we discuss.

3. In 2001, Jack Valenti, then president of the Motion Picture Association, met with members of the Bush government to discuss ways Hollywood could contribute to the war effort. John King, "White House Sees Hollywood Role in War on Terrorism," *CNN Online*, November 8, 2001, http://www.cnn.com/2001/US/11/08/rec.bush.hollywood/.

4. Susan Sontag, "The Imagination of Disaster," *Commentary* (October 1965): 42, 47.

5. Eva Cherniavsky, *Neocitizenship: Political Culture After Democracy* (New York: New York University Press, 2017), 132.

6. Seo-young Chu, *Do Metaphors Dream of Literal Sleep?* (Cambridge, MA: Harvard University Press, 2010), argues that science fiction is best understood as a distinctive kind of realism, not as its opposite. Echoing Sontag's language about what is "inconceivable," she argues that SF depicts things that are "nonimaginary yet cognitively estranging," doing important work that renders such referents "available both for representation and for understanding" (7). Throughout this book, we read SF series in a similar way, as a kind of litmus paper that registers the ongoing erosion of liberal democratic values in American culture, even if such texts are not able to point directly to a material cause for such changes other than through the displaced images associated with science fiction.

7. It is worth noting that this series was produced by Brannon Braga, best known for his work on three Star Trek series before this; he went on to produce the antiterrorist series *24*. Braga also served as a writer for some episodes on all of these shows.

8. See Lindsay Thomas, "Forms of Duration: Preparedness, the Mars Trilogy, and the Management of Climate Change," *American Literature* 88, no. 1 (2016): 159–84, for a discussion of the speculative management of affect as accomplished by government "preparedness" scenarios as compared to the provocative use of speculation for social change enabled by science fiction.

9. In her analysis of the series as a new frontier myth, Barbara Gurr, "Masculinity, Race, and the (Re?)imagined American Frontier," in *Race, Gender, and Sexuality in Post-Apocalyptic TV and Film* (New York: Palgrave, 2015), 40, notes that a historical Mason was one of the authors of the Bill of Rights, the first amendments to the U.S. Constitution passed in 1791. Thus, Tom Mason is entitled by both his knowledge and his heritage to take on the mantle of a new founding father.

10. See John Rieder, *Colonialism and the Emergence of Science Fiction* (Middleton, CT: Wesleyan University Press, 2008), esp. chap. 1.

11. The suspense is created in part by "puzzle narratives" through which viewers, like characters, gradually find out more about the aliens and their intentions, a characteristic technique of what Jason Mittell calls "complex tv." We acknowledge the role that general changes to the medium thus play in shaping these series but nonetheless argue that the sense of menace they embody is largely linked to 9/11. *Lost* (2004–2010), the paradigmatic text that inspired this new mode of television, is generally understood as another type of response to 9/11 anxiety.

12. Jasbir Puar, *The Right to Maim: Debility, Capacity, Disability* (Durham, NC: Duke University Press, 2017), argues that attacks on infrastructure and thus on the ability to sustain life (and hence sustain forces of resistance to occupation) are now standard techniques of settler-colonial armies. Her main example is Israeli attacks on the West Bank and other Palestinian territories, but her analysis makes clear that this has also been a tactic of the U.S. so-called War on Terror (esp. 89–92).

13. The series title *Colony*, a term used synonymously with "block" for the areas of remaining human occupation, also speaks to the longer history of U.S. settler colonialism that informs both of these series. Gurr has provided a strong analysis of *Falling Skies* in this vein. We think it worth reiterating a key point she also analyzes, the use of the name Cochise to refer to an alien ally who eventually works with Mason and his militia, the Second Mass: they cannot pronounce his alien name, and this assigned name is phonetically similar. Cochise was an Apache leader who fought heroically against U.S. westward expansion. The actual person behind this name is never explained in the series, despite repeated history lessons from Tom on other topics. In this way, *Falling Skies* thus simultaneously erases indigenous presence from North America and appropriates indigenous history to position white settlers as the rightful occupiers of the land, fighting to preserve their heritage from alien invasion. *Colony* is equally culpable in failing to have indigenous characters or discussions of specific indigenous history, beyond the (also unexplained) use of the name Geronimo (another Apache leader) as the code name for an underground resistance cell in season 1. Nonetheless, we see this series in a more positive light as it does not allow all Americans to exempt themselves from complicity in the colonial suppression of indigenous communities, although once again it appropriates this history by representing its largely white cast as victims of an occupying force that confines them to reservations and sees them as resources to be exploited. There is more to say on indigeneity and both series, but that is beyond the scope of our chapter.

14. The finale goes so far as to inoculate our capacity to believe that the aliens might have a point of view on the war: Tom is finally confronted by the alien "queen" (a figure whose

femaleness underlines how deeply patriarchal the entire ethos of the series has been), whose death will ensure the death of all her minions (he is of course successful, using a bioweapon, but questions of the ethics of genocide are never even raised). This queen announces that she wants to kill humanity in revenge for humanity's murder of her daughter, sent 1,500 years ago in a first colonization effort. Beyond the absurdity of this date (do they mean 15,000 years ago, as the cave paintings in this scene might suggest?), the nonsensical logic of positing humans as the aggressors in a scenario that was self-defense parallels the series' refusal to admit any hint that previous American imperial actions had anything to do with attacks on U.S. soil. By analogy, this also prevents any complex thinking about why Muslims and others in the Middle East might resent U.S. global hegemony.

15.   The decisive governmental action depicted here resonates, however anachronistically, as we write this in the midst of the global COVID pandemic, a particular historical situation with complicated entanglements with civil liberties that we address in our conclusion.

16.   Curiously, *Falling Skies* also has a storyline about the Espheni fighting a different alien race, the Volm, who briefly become humanity's allies (Cochise is a Volm). This storyline is mainly used to reinforce human exceptionalism: a rebel faction within the Espheni is inspired to action only by seeing the unprecedented human resilience, for example, and Volm forces mostly retreat to fight elsewhere in the galaxy by season 5, ensuring the final victory is clearly a human one. Perhaps this idea of two alien races fighting their war on Earth's soil allegorizes something of the "Third World" experience of nations whose homelands became the frontlines of the United States' struggle for global hegemony against the Soviet Union, the same geopolitical struggle that seeded the antagonisms the United States now fights as the "war on terror."

17.   See "Our Mission," World Economic Forum, https://www.weforum.org/about/world -economic-forum.

18.   It is worth noting that, as shaped by whatever the Espheni did to her biology, Lexi has blond hair. Yet in dream sequences where Tom and Anne each separately reconcile with the human "side" of Alexis, she has dark hair that matches their own.

19.   Overall, *Falling Skies* has a poor record for diversity in its cast. Moon Bloodgood is partially Asian, but this is not mentioned in the series. Almost all the main cast is white. Both *Threshold* and *Colony* also have mainly white casts, with Broussard the only significant character of color in the latter.

20.   An adolescent son, kept ignorant of the war by his guardians, wants to join Tom once he learns about the fight. Yet Tom tells this particular boy, "The bravest thing you can do is stay here and protect them, the people that love you—this is what we're fighting for. We're going to win this war. We're going to rebuild America."

21.   Another telling example of the series' bad-faith relationship to history comes in the first episode of season 2, "Worlds Apart," when Karen (Jessy Schram), an infected human fully turned to the Espheni side, offers Tom a truce and sanctuary, a specific

zone "where you'd be allowed to live in peace," explaining that it is an idea Espheni have taken from Earth's history. Aggressively defending humans' rights to all land, he rejects the analogy and says one cannot proceed from the worst examples from the past. Yet for Tom the relevant antecedent is Nazi Germany; British and other colonial occupations of what is now the United States is not mentioned at all. Denial of America as a colonial nation is key to the entire series: how invasion disrupts their old lifeways is a continual motif, but their experiences of fleeing, hiding, food and other shortages, and the like are never compared to the experiences of indigenous peoples, despite Tom's frequent history lessons on other matters.

22. "Margaret Thatcher: A Life in Quotes," *Guardian*, April 8, 2013, https://www .theguardian.com/politics/2013/apr/08/margaret-thatcher-quotes; Cherniavsky, *Neocitizenship*, 10.

23. This approach is influenced by the work of Kevin Floyd, who traces the common hermeneutical roots of the development of ways of thinking about economics and sexuality that have since branched into contemporary Marxist and queer theorizing. Attempting to heal the long-standing "split" between Foucauldian and Marxist thinkers, he turns critical attention to "heteronormativity's relation to capital" and specifically offers a "rich consideration of the ways in which this relation is mediated by a range of normalizing regimes and forms of social hierarchy, including those that operate along axes of gender, race, and nation" (3). Particularly relevant for our concerns is Floyd's attention to modes of regulation. As he puts it, "Regulation theory emphasizes that the accumulation of capital, if it is to be sustained over long periods, must always be institutionally secured at a range of different levels, from corporate and governmental forms of regulation to a normalization of everyday social practices" (33). Floyd argues that while many Marxist theories help us understand various regimes of accumulation and the concentration of wealth particularly during a neoliberal time, queer theory's interest in the workings of power at the level of the social group and the individual body offers an opportunity to see the dense interrelationships between capital and identity. Heteronormativity constrains desire, but this must be grasped not merely as a repression or shaping of affective energies but also as part of a world-building impetus that shapes family structures to serve economic priorities.

24. A season 3 storyline in *Colony* more overtly suggests something similar. MacGregor (Graham McTavish), a right-wing conspiracy theorist and prepper before the war, runs a resistance camp outside the wall. He insists on seeing things in black and white, and violence is his standard tactic in all situations. He often espouses views that mirror those expressed by Tom in *Falling Skies*, but this narrative does not endorse them. Examining one of the bombs MacGregor has built, Will recognizes a design like the Oklahoma City bombings, linking this ideological stance to domestic terrorism (S3E4).

25. Wendy Brown, *Undoing the Demos: Neoliberalism's Stealth Revolution* (London: Zone, 2017), 129.

26. Ernst Bloch, *The Principle of Hope* (Oxford: Basil Blackwell, 1986), 1:12.

4. AMERICAN CIVIL WARS

1. It is also relevant that intercut with this scene we see the remaining sheriff's authorities in Jericho interrogating the Hawkins family and demanding to search their home, actions that the family protests as a violation of their civil rights and likely evidence of racial profiling, as discussed earlier.

2. It is worth noting here that there is not a hint of a queer relationship in *Jericho*, part of its small-town, family-values ethos. None of Jake's friendships reach this level of intensity, but instead affective drama centers on restoring his relationship with his high-school girlfriend. Another subplot involves his biological brother and their parents' condemnation of this brother for having an affair, rather than staying with his pregnant wife.

3. Series creator Frank Spotnitz started his career writing for *The X-Files* and other Chris Carter series, including co-writing the film *The X-Files: I Want to Believe* (2008).

4. We later learn in Smith's backstory that economic precarity and his starving infant son motivated Smith's decision to capitulate rather than join the resistance and that his own life was shaped by his banker father's losses during the Depression.

5. Its title is from the Japanese depiction of three monkeys who cover, respectively, their eyes, ears, and mouth, to convey the maxim "see no evil, hear no evil, speak no evil." The surveillance program is named for Iwazaru, the third monkey.

6. The series establishes that one can pass into another world only if one's "double" there has died. This world's John Smith was a traveling salesman who left the military after the war, finding he distrusted the lust for power leadership inculcated in him. He dies defending Juliana (who has also traveled to this world) from Reich agents sent to kill her.

7. Bloch, *The Principle of Hope*, 1:27.

8. Bloch, *The Principle of Hope*, 1:312.

9. Footage from yet another world that shows prisoners forced by Nazi authorities to enter the anomaly, echoing the use of concentration camp victims as part of von Braun's rocketry experiments in Germany. Tagomi is able to travel to other worlds by concentrating on a picture of his wife, alive in the United States but not in his world, a method reminiscent of Chris Marker's time-travel, postnuclear film *La Jetée* (1962).

10. Bloch, *The Principle of Hope*, 1:195.

11. This storyline anticipates Shoshana Zuboff's arguments in *The Age of Surveillance Capitalism: The Fight for a Human Future at the New Frontier of Power* (New York: PublicAffairs, 2019). As well as drawing attention to the privacy crisis created by how apps and smart devices track our patterns of mobility and consumption, she notes that the wealthy elites who profit from these tools also use campaign finance and other economic pressures to prevent regulation (107). She also notes a pattern of employees moving from high government office, such as the White House, into jobs at Silicon Valley firms (124). Finally, she begins to consider how the same microtargeting strategies used for advertising are also used to influence voting (280), a point Peter Pomerantsev develops at length in *This Is Not Propaganda* (New York: PublicAffairs, 2019).

5. DESIRING A DIFFERENT FUTURE:
THE 100 AND *THE EXPANSE*

1. Both *The 100* and *The Expanse* are based on novels, the former on a young adult series written by Kass Morgan and the latter on a space opera series written by James S. A. Corey (the pseudonym for the writing team of Daniel Abraham and Ty Franck). The narrative of *The 100* is almost entirely different from the television series, while *The Expanse* more closely parallels the novels. At the same time, though, the televised series *The 100* is true to its young adult dystopian roots, reminiscent of other stories such as *The Hunger Games*, in which characters face terrible choices just to survive. Such narratives stretch back to William Golding's *Lord of the Flies* (1954), a novel frequently taught in high schools and that itself seemed a more brutally realistic version of R. M. Ballantyne's nineteenth-century juvenile fiction *The Coral Island*, in which a group of stranded young people find a (mostly civilized) way to survive being shipwrecked. The thought experiment of such narratives raises questions about how different characters (and, by extension, readers) might react in extreme situations. The conflict played out in many of the contemporary TV series we have been examining in this book focuses on differences between groups seeking control over both limited resources and limited populations. *The 100* is narratively very wedded to this mode, so much so that, even when the last habitable place on Earth is bombed into oblivion—through a series of increasingly dramatic plot twists centered on conflicts between different factions battling for control—the main characters and a cadre of others are able to use a spaceship to cryogenically preserve themselves and wake up hundreds of years later at a (mostly) habitable planet, where they discover a settlement from an earlier period of human expansion into the stars. The narrative of fighting to survive then basically reboots as our main characters come into conflict with the original settlers, who too have been facing their own internal divisions and group strife. By this point in the sixth season, some characters actually comment on how frequently the characters find themselves in the same predicament. Main characters, such as Clarke, often respond by pointing out that there are few other options.

2. By using the term "racialization" here, we emphasize the fact that racist politics are human constructions that seize upon particular features of morphology and interpret them to mark ontological or ethical distinctions among humans. The categories of being "my people" or enemies as explored by *The 100* do not map allegorically onto recognized racial categories that govern real-world politics, but we seek to draw attention to the operation of a similar and false logic that undergirds such distinctions.

3. In one long-running iteration of this dialectic, the grounder culture is in some ways similar to premodern, tribal culture in Europe based on an ethos of vengeance, documented in various Viking sagas. An axiom they follow is "blood must have blood," and initially Clarke secures the first alliance by applying that maxim to her own people as well, killing Finn (Thomas McDonel), who had massacred a grounder village in his own act of misguided vengeance, believing they had kidnapped Clarke. Later Clarke convinces the grounder leader Lexa to adopt a new motto, "blood must not have blood,"

but this is to prevent Lexa from taking justifiable vengeance against the Skaikru encampment that has slaughtered part of her army, led by a rogue commander who refuses the alliance with grounders. The series thus repeatedly stages the need for— but also the difficulty of securing—community across difference.

4.   A scene in S2E10 of Bobbie seeing the ocean for the first time, which first captures her awe and then pulls back into wider frame to show her surrounded by garbage on the shore, illustrates this point sharply.

5.   Mari Ruti, *The Ethics of Opting Out: Queer Theory's Defiant Subjects* (New York: Columbia University Press, 2017), 38.

6.   Michel Foucault, *The History of Sexuality* (New York: Pantheon, 1978), 1:137.

7.   Jaha, who is among those who secured a space in the bunker, explicitly suggests that Octavia needs to return to the same harsh logic that shaped life on the Ark: "on the Ark, we made death the enemy, that is how we survived, anyone who did anything to push us closer to death we floated" (S5E2).

8.   Sylvia Wynter, "Unsettling the Coloniality of Being/Power/Truth/Freedom: Towards the Human, After Man, Its Overrepresentation—an Argument," *CR: The New Centennial Review* 3, no. 3 (Fall 2003): 260, 267.

9.   Nonetheless, *The 100* especially makes some problematic casting choices. Both Pike and Jaha, who represent the worst aggression at points, are played by African American actors, while Clarke and Bellamy, the main protagonists, are played by white actors. Yet Monty and Raven (Lindsay Morgan), core members of the inner circle, are respectively Asian and Latina, showing diversity among the main cast. And Lincoln (Ricky Whittle), a central grounder character who first bridges the two communities and who becomes the victim of Pike's racialized violence, is also played by an actor of African descent. So, while multicultural casting of characters in *The Expanse* and *The 100* might suggest that contemporary forms of racial struggle and bias are *not* a part of the futures depicted, race still resurfaces in other ways as an ongoing problematic for community building. Race—also reinscribed through other somatic differences—remains a point of conflict and division in the series.

10.   Michel Foucault, *Society Must Be Defended* (London: Penguin, 2003), 255.

11.   Achille Mbembé, "Necropolitics," *Public Culture* 15, no. 1 (Winter 2003): 21.

12.   Jasbir Puar, *The Right to Maim: Debility, Capacity, Disability* (Durham, NC: Duke University Press, 2017), 65, xviii.

6. REBOOTING DEMOCRACY AND *MR. ROBOT*

1.   See Veronica Hollinger, "Genre vs. Mode," in *The Oxford Handbook of Science Fiction*, ed. Rob Latham (Oxford: Oxford University Press, 2014), 139–154 for a discussion of this shift.

2.   Wendy Brown, *Undoing the Demos: Neoliberalism's Stealth Revolution* (London: Zone, 2017), 9, 17.

3. Retroactively, the version of Elliot we stay with throughout the series is called the Mastermind, and the finale's culminating moment is when the "real" Elliot wakes up. We will refer to the protagonist as Elliot throughout this chapter, nonetheless, as that is how he is named through almost all of the screen time.

4. Moreover, there is a SF temporality to finance capital itself. Sherryl Vint, "Promissory Futures: Reality and Imagination in Finance and Fiction," *CR: The New Centennial Review* 19, no. 1 (Spring 2019): 11–36.

5. As discussed in our introduction, this point is made in multiple recent works that theorize debt, including David Graeber, *Debt: The First 5,000 Years* (New York: Melville House, 2011); Max Haiven, *Cultures of Financialization: Fictitious Capital in Popular Culture and Everyday Life* (London: Palgrave Macmillan, 2014); Annie McClanahan, *Dead Pledges: Debt, Crisis, and Twenty-First-Century Culture* (Stanford, CA: Stanford University Press, 2017); and Joseph Vogl, *The Ascendancy of Finance*, trans. Simon Garnett (Cambridge: Polity, 2017).

6. See Maurizio Lazzarato, *The Making of Indebted Man: An Essay on the Neoliberal Condition*, repr. ed. (New York: Semiotext(e), 2012); Vogl, *The Ascendancy of Finance*; Ivan Ascher, *Portfolio Society: On the Capitalist Mode of Prediction* (New York: Zone, 2016).

7. Diegetically, the mask's design is linked to a 1980s slasher film called *The Careful Massacre of the Bourgeoisie*, included as an extra on the season 2 DVD. Its title alludes to Luis Buñuel's satirical and surreal *The Discreet Charm of the Bourgeoisie* (1972).

8. A dark-pool investment is a private securities exchange that allows elite investors the opportunity to place large orders without their trades being publicly visible, thereby preventing other market players from reacting to the trade in ways that might change the market toward adverse prices for these investors. They are nontransparent and often rely on algorithmic, high-frequency trading. Only investors with very high equity have the opportunity to use them, and thus they belie the neoliberal ideology that the market offers fair exchange, equal opportunity, and the efficiency of "perfect" information. The political machinations of this group in the conspiracy narrative of the series are consistent with the ways that economic actors (such as corporations) often appropriate or otherwise limit state sovereignty—see Vogl, *The Ascendancy of Finance*; and Katharina Pistor, *The Code of Capital: How the Law Creates Wealth and Inequality* (Princeton, NJ: Princeton University Press, 2020).

9. Michel Foucault, *The Birth of Biopolitics: Lectures at the Collège de France, 1978–1979* (New York: Picador, 2010); and Melinda Cooper, *Family Values: Between Neoliberalism and the New Social Conservatism* (New York: Zone, 2017).

10. Cyberpunk, a SF subgenre with which *Mr. Robot* is clearly in dialogue, was dubbed the "supreme *literary* expression . . . of late capitalism itself." Fredric Jameson, *Postmodernism: or, the Cultural Logic of Late Capitalism* (Durham, NC: Duke University Press, 1991), 419.

11. He breaks the fourth wall in these monologues, addressing the audience as "hello friend," an allusion to one of the earlier worm virus attacks on email and also underlining themes about loneliness and isolation.

12.   E Corp seems simultaneously a corporation that manufactures and distributes items (as per the storyline about one of their factories creating carcinogenic contaminants) and a firm offering financial services, including the Bank of E. This is figural shorthand for the financial power of corporations, of course, but perhaps also not as fictional as it might appear when one thinks about companies such as Amazon or Google that continue to branch out into new products, services, and logistical infrastructures, perhaps aspiring to become the Company (as we saw extrapolated in *Incorporated*).

13.   Darlene is with the FBI agent Dom when she redistributes the Ecoin in the finale, and Dom objects that an illegal action cannot be just. Darlene counters by emphasizing this role of the law to institutionalize inequality: "They were so powerful they wrote the laws to benefit themselves. They got away with it because they banked on us, all of us, to trust the system" (S4E10).

14.   Angela possesses leaked documents that demonstrate the company had concluded it was not "cost effective" to retool their systems as compared to dealing with lawsuits, including strategies of discrediting complainants. This corporate strategy is documented in the film *Dark Waters* (2019), based on a real case.

15.   A season 4 storyline includes a drug dealer, Vera (Elliot Villar), who wants to establish a real estate empire with his proceeds and who explicitly makes the connection between how he gained his fortune and actions in the so-called legitimate economy: "Behind every great fortune, there lies a great crime. That is the corporate motto of these United States" (S4E7).

16.   In *24/7: Late Capitalism and the Ends of Sleep* (London: Verso, 2013), Jonathan Crary traces how contemporary economic structures require that we be always on, that we not only have a huge array of consumable goods and services available to us around the clock but that we too, in turn, be ourselves available as a good, a potential service, around the clock. The expansion of work through mobile devices into leisure hours is only the most obvious example of our 24/7 life. In such a world, as Crary puts it, "The primary self-narration of one's life shifts in its fundamental composition. Instead of a formulaic sequence of places and events associated with family, work, and relationships, the main thread of one's life-story now is the electronic commodities and media services through which all experience has been filtered, recorded, or constricted" (58–59).

17.   Bloch put it this way: "Only as something brooding in an *undischarged, undeveloped, in short, utopian way* does it [the night-dream] have the power to open up in the daydream, does it attain the power not to hold itself sealed against the latter; but as such, even though only as such, it can circulate in the notions of clear road, preserved-retained ego, world-improvement, journey to the end. The insight therefore that archaic brooding can be utopian in reality finally explains the possibility of merging of night-dreams and daydreams, given *the explanation and dissolution* of a partially possible *merging of the dream-games*." Ernst Bloch, *The Principle of Hope*, trans. Neville Plaice, Stephen Plaice, and Paul Knight, 3 vols. (Oxford: Basil Blackwell, 1986), 1:102.

18.   Christopher Chitty, *Sexual Hegemony: Statecraft, Sodomy, and Capital in the Rise of the World System* (Durham, NC: Duke University Press, 2020), 145.

19. Walter Benn Michaels, "50 Shades of Libertarian Love," *LARB*, May 22, 2015, https://lareviewofbooks.org/article/50-shades-of-libertarian-love/.

20. Coming so late in the series, this revelation about a character who will become the main villain harks back to caricatures of Asian evildoers in earlier SF, such as Ming the Merciless, the hypersexualized, occasionally feminized, and decidedly Orientalist antagonist from the Flash Gordon comic books and film series, while at the same time playing on more recent American fears of Chinese economic ascendancy.

21. Sedgwick explores the theoretical and material power of the sexual secret as organizing identity in the opening chapter of *Epistemology of the Closet* (Berkeley: University of California Press, 1990); see esp. 22ff.

22. Curiously, one could trace the genealogical shifts in the X-Men narrative from its early gloss on racial divides in the comics through the films of Bryan Singer in the 1990s, which metaphorized mutant status as a kind of queerness, to its possible recasting in *Mr. Robot* as centering economic inequality and divergent approaches to remedying such.

23. Bloch, *The Principle of Hope*, 1:12.

CONCLUSION: DEMOCRACY IN CRISIS

1. Cynthia Miller-Idriss, *Hate in the Homeland: The New Global Far Right* (Princeton, NJ: Princeton University Press, 2020), 2.

2. Masha Gessen, *Surviving Autocracy* (New York: Riverhead, 2020), 53.

3. Gessen, *Surviving Autocracy*, 14. The Reichstag fire refers to an arson attack on the German parliament buildings that occurred a month after Hitler was sworn in. His administration blamed communists and used this allegation of crisis to force through legislation that suspended most civil liberties. This is often seen as the key event that paved the way for the Nazi state.

4. Wendy Brown, *In the Ruins of Neoliberalism: The Rise of Antidemocratic Politics in the West* (New York: Columbia University Press, 2019), 180.

5. Jill Lepore, *This America: The Case for the Nation* (New York: Liveright, 2019).

6. Lepore, *This America*, 73.

7. Our interest in focusing on the political and economic conditions that enabled the rise of neoliberalism has shaped our choices of series to analyze in this book. Therefore, we have not discussed *The Handmaid's Tale*, another interesting recent SF television drama. It focuses on the other side of this coin, the return of religious fundamentalism and what that means for sexual and reproductive freedoms.

8. Melinda Cooper, *Family Values: Between Neoliberalism and the New Social Conservatism* (New York: Zone, 2017), 137.

9. Eva Cherniavsky, *Neocitizenship: Political Culture After Democracy* (New York: New York University Press, 2017), 10.

10. Anne Applebaum, *Twilight of Democracy: The Seductive Lure of Authoritarianism* (New York: Doubleday, 2020), 37. Applebaum credits the historian Timothy Snyder with the

phrase "Medium-Size Lie"; Snyder has written an important book about Russian authoritarianism and what it presages for one possible US future, *The Road to Unfreedom: Russia, Europe, America* (New York: Tim Duggan, 2018).

11. Ernst Bloch, *The Principle of Hope* (Oxford: Basil Blackwell, 1986), 1:302, 1:221, 1:4.

12. Hannah Arendt, *The Origins of Totalitarianism* (New York: Harcourt, Brace, Jovanovich, 1973), 474.

13. Svetlana Boym, *The Future of Nostalgia* (New York: Basic Books, 2002), xvi.

14. Boym, *The Future of Nostalgia*, xiv.

15. Gessen, *Surviving Autocracy*, 215.

16. Cherniavsky, *Neocitizenship*, 153.

17. Cherniavsky, *Neocitizenship*, 155.

18. Miller-Idriss, *Hate in the Homeland*, 12.

BIBLIOGRAPHY

Applebaum, Anne. *Twilight of Democracy: The Seductive Lure of Authoritarianism*. New York: Doubleday, 2020.

Arendt, Hannah. *The Origins of Totalitarianism*. New York: Harcourt, Brace, Jovanovich, 1973.

Ascher, Ivan. *Portfolio Society: On the Capitalist Mode of Prediction*. New York: Zone, 2016.

Ballantyne, R. M. *The Coral Island: A Tale of the Pacific Ocean*. Scotland: Thomas Nelson, 1857.

"Battlestar Galactica." *Peabody Awards*. Henry W. Grady College of Journalism and Mass Communication, 2005. https://web.archive.org/web/20100610221349/http://www.peabody.uga.edu/winners/details.php?id=1443.

Bauman, Zygmunt. *Liquid Modernity*. Cambridge: Polity, 2000.

Bernari, Daniel. *"Star Trek" and History: Race-ing Toward a White Future*. New Brunswick, NJ: Rutgers University Press, 1998.

Bloch, Ernst. *The Principle of Hope*. Trans. Neville Plaice, Stephen Plaice, and Paul Knight. 3 vols. Oxford: Basil Blackwell, 1986.

brown, adrienne maree. *Emergent Strategy: Shaping Change, Changing Worlds*. Chico, CA: AK, 2017.

——. *Pleasure Activism: The Politics of Feeling Good*. Chico, CA: AK, 2019.

Brown, Wendy. *In the Ruins of Neoliberalism: The Rise of Antidemocratic Politics in the West*. New York: Columbia University Press, 2019.

Brown, Wendy. *Undoing the Demos: Neoliberalism's Stealth Revolution*. London: Zone, 2017.

Boym, Svetlana. *The Future of Nostalgia*. New York: Basic Books, 2002.

Bulgakov, Mikhail. *The White Guard*. Trans. Michael Glenny. New York: Melville House, 2014.

Chaput, Catherine. *Market Affect and the Rhetoric of Political Economic Debates*. Columbia: University of South Carolina Press, 2019.

Cherniavsky, Eva. *Neocitizenship: Political Culture After Democracy*. New York: New York University Press, 2017.

Chitty, Christopher. *Sexual Hegemony: Statecraft, Sodomy, and Capital in the Rise of the World System*. Durham, NC: Duke University Press, 2020.

Chu, Seo-young. *Do Metaphors Dream of Literal Sleep? A Science-Fictional Theory of Representation*. Cambridge, MA: Harvard University Press, 2010.

Collins, Suzanne. *The Hunger Games*. New York: Scholastic, 2010.

Cooper, Melinda. *Family Values: Between Neoliberalism and the New Social Conservatism*. New York: Zone, 2017.

Corey, James S. A. *Leviathan Wakes*. New York: Hachette, 2011.

Crary, Jonathan. *24/7: Late Capitalism and the Ends of Sleep*. London: Verso, 2013.

Csicsery-Ronay Jr., Istvan. *The Seven Beauties of Science Fiction*. Middletown, CT: Wesleyan University Press, 2011.

Dodd, Nigel. *The Social Life of Money*. Princeton, NJ: Princeton University Press, 2014.

Drucker, Peter. *Warped: Gay Normality and Queer Anti-Capitalism*. Chicago: Haymarket, 2015.

Duggan, Lisa. *Twilight of Equality? Neoliberalism, Cultural Politics, and the Attack on Democracy*. Boston: Beacon Press, 2017.

Dyson, Stephen Benedict. *Otherworldly Politics*. Baltimore, MD: Johns Hopkins University Press, 2015.

Eberl, Jason T., ed. *"Battlestar Galactica" and Philosophy: Knowledge Here Begins out There*. Malden, MA: Blackwell, 2008.

Edelman, Lee. *No Future: Queer Theory and the Death Drive*. Durham, NC: Duke University Press, 2004.

Floyd, Kevin. *The Reification of Desire: Toward a Queer Marxism*. Minneapolis: University of Minnesota Press, 2009.

Franklin, H. Bruce. "*Star Trek* in the Vietnam Era." *Science Fiction Studies* 21, no.1 (March 1994): 22–34.

Freedman, Carl. *Critical Theory and Science Fiction*. Middletown, CT: Wesleyan University Press, 2000.

Finney, Jack. *The Body Snatchers*. New York: Dell, 1955.

Foucault, Michel. *The Birth of Biopolitics: Lectures at the Collège de France, 1978–1979*. New York: Picador, 2010.

——. *The History of Sexuality*. Vol. 1. New York: Pantheon, 1978.

——. *Society Must Be Defended*. London: Penguin, 2003.

Geraghty, Lincoln. "A Truly American Enterprise: *Star Trek*'s Post-9/11 Politics." In *New Boundaries in Political Science Fiction*, ed. Donald M. Hassler, 157–66. Columbia: University of South Carolina Press, 2008.

Gessen, Masha. *Surviving Autocracy*. New York: Riverhead, 2020.

Giroux, Henry A. *On Critical Pedagogy*. New York: Continuum International, 2011.

Golding, William. *Lord of the Flies*. London: Faber and Faber, 1954.

Gonzalez, George. "*Star Trek*" and the Politics of Globalization*. Switzerland: Springer/Palgrave Macmillan/Palgrave Pivot, 2018.

Graeber, David. *Debt: The First 5,000 Years*. New York: Melville House, 2011.

Gurr, Barbara. "Masculinity, Race, and the (Re?)imagined American Frontier." In *Race, Gender, and Sexuality in Post-Apocalyptic TV and Film*, ed. Barbara Gurr, 31–44. New York: Palgrave, 2015.

Haiven, Max. *Cultures of Financialization: Fictitious Capital in Popular Culture and Everyday Life*. London: Palgrave Macmillan, 2014.

Hall, Stuart. *Cultural Studies 1983: A Theoretical History*. Reprint ed. Ed. Jennifer Daryl Slack and Lawrence Grossberg. Durham, NC: Duke University Press, 2016.

——. "Encoding and Decoding in the Television Discourse." In *Essential Essays*, vol. 1: *Foundations of Cultural Studies*, ed. David Morley, 257–76. Durham, NC: Duke University Press, 2018.

——. "Notes on Deconstructing 'The Popular.'" In *Essential Essays*, vol. 1: *Foundations of Cultural Studies*, ed. David Morley, 347–61. Durham, NC: Duke University Press, 2018.

Hantke, Steffen. "Bush's America and the Return of Cold War in Science Fiction: Alien Invasion in *Invasion*, *Threshold*, and *Surface*." *Journal of Popular Film and Television* 38, no. 3 (2010): 143–51.

——. "*Star Trek*'s Mirror Universe Episodes and U.S. Military Culture Through the Eyes of the Other." *Science Fiction Studies* 41, no. 3 (November 2014): 562–78.

Harvey, David. *A Brief History of Neoliberalism*. Oxford: Oxford University Press, 2005.

——. *Seventeen Contradictions and the End of Capitalism*. Oxford: Oxford University Press, 2014.

Heller, Lee F. "Persistence of Difference: Postfeminism, Popular Discourse, and Heterosexuality in *Star Trek: The Next Generation*." *Science Fiction Studies* 24, no. 2 (July 1997): 226–44.

Hennessy, Rosemary. *Profit and Pleasure: Sexual Identities in Late Capitalism*. 2nd ed. New York: Routledge, 2018.

Hollinger, Veronica. "Genre vs. Mode." In *The Oxford Handbook of Science Fiction*, ed. Rob Latham, 139–54. Oxford: Oxford University Press, 2014.

Huntington, Samuel. *The Clash of Civilizations and the Remaking of World Order*. New York: Simon and Schuster, 1996.

Jakobsen, Janet R. "Perverse Justice." *GLQ: A Journal of Lesbian and Gay Studies* 18, no. 1 (2012): 19–45. https://doi.org/10.1215/10642684-1422125.

Jameson, Fredric. *Postmodernism: or, the Cultural Logic of Late Capitalism*. Durham, NC: Duke University Press, 1991.

Jenkins, Henry. *Textual Poachers*. New York: Routledge, 2013.

Keeling, Kara. *Queer Times, Black Futures*. New York: New York University Press, 2019.

Kellner, Douglas, and Harry O'Hara. "Utopia and Marxism in Ernst Bloch." *New German Critique* 9 (1976): 11–34. https://doi.org/10.2307/487686.

King, John. "White House Sees Hollywood Role in War on Terrorism." *CNN Online*, November 8, 2001. http://www.cnn.com/2001/US/11/08/rec.bush.hollywood/.

Lazzarato, Maurizio. *The Making of Indebted Man: An Essay on the Neoliberal Condition*. Reprint ed. New York: Semiotext(e), 2012.

Lepore, Jill. *This America: The Case for the Nation*. New York: Liveright, 2019.

Levitas, Ruth. *The Concept of Utopia*. Syracuse, NY: Syracuse University Press, 1990.

——. *Utopia as Method: The Imaginary Reconstitution of Society.* London: Palgrave Macmillan, 2013.

Lotz, Amanda D. *The Television Will Be Revolutionized.* 2nd ed. New York: New York University Press, 2014.

——. *We Now Disrupt This Broadcast: How Cable Transformed Television and the Internet Revolutionized It All.* Cambridge, MA: MIT Press, 2018.

Maisonville, Derek. "So Say Who All? Cosmopolitanism, Hybridity, and Colonialism in the Reimagined *Battlestar Galactica*." In *"Battlestar Galactica" and International Relations*, ed. Nicholas J. Kiersey and Iver B. Neumann, 119–36. New York: Routledge, 2013.

Marx, Karl. *Capital: A Critique of Political Economy.* Vol. 1. Trans. Ben Fowkes. London: Penguin, 1992.

——. *Capital: A Critique of Political Economy.* Vol. 3. Trans. David Fernbach. London: Penguin, 1992.

Mbembé, Achille. "Necropolitics." *Public Culture* 15, no. 1 (Winter 2003): 11–40.

McClanahan, Annie. *Dead Pledges: Debt, Crisis, and Twenty-First-Century Culture.* Stanford, CA: Stanford University Press, 2017.

Michaels, Walter Benn. "50 Shades of Libertarian Love." *LARB*, May 22, 2015. https://lareviewofbooks.org/article/50-shades-of-libertarian-love/.

Milford, Mike, and Robert C. Rowland. "Situated Ideological Allegory and *Battlestar Galactica*." *Western Journal of Communication* 76, no. 5 (2012): 536–51.

Miller-Idriss, Cynthia. *Hate in the Homeland: The New Global Far Right.* Princeton, NJ: Princeton University Press, 2020.

Mittell, Jason. *Complex TV: The Poetics of Contemporary Television Storytelling.* New York: New York University Press, 2015.

Mittermeier, Sabrina, and Mareike Spychala, eds. *Fighting for the Future: Essays on "Star Trek: Discovery."* Liverpool: Liverpool University Press, 2020.

Moore, Alan, David Lloyd, and Tony Weare. *V for Vendetta.* New York: Vertigo/DC Comics, 1982.

Morgan, Kass. *The 100.* New York: AlloyEntertainment, 2013.

Muñoz, José Esteban. *Cruising Utopia: The Then and There of Queer Futurity.* New York: New York University Press, 2009.

Neumann, Iver B., and Nicholas J. Kiersey, eds. *"Battlestar Galactica" and International Relations.* New York: Routledge, 2013.

Orwell, George. *1984.* New York: Signet Classics, 1961.

Pascale, Anthony. "Watch *Alone Together,* a 4-Part Remote Series Read by *Star Trek: Deep Space Nine* Actors in Character." *TrekMovie.com*, August 4, 2020. https://trekmovie.com/2020/08/04/watch-alone-together-a-4-part-remote-series-read-by-star-trek-deep-space-nine-actors-in-character/.

Pistor, Katharina. *The Code of Capital: How the Law Creates Wealth and Inequality.* Princeton, NJ: Princeton University Press, 2020.

Pomersantsev, Peter. *This Is Not Propaganda: Adventures in the War Against Reality.* New York: PublicAffairs, 2019.

Potter, Tiffany, and C. W. Marshall, eds. *Cylons in America: Critical Studies in "Battlestar Galactica."* New York: Bloomsbury, 2007.

Puar, Jasbir. *The Right to Maim: Debility, Capacity, Disability.* Durham, NC: Duke University Press, 2017.

Rasmussen, Mikkel Vedby. "Cylons in Baghdad: Experiencing Counterinsurgency in *Battlestar Galactica.*" In *"Battlestar Galactica" and International Relations,* ed. Nicholas J. Kiersey and Iver B. Neumann, 167–78. New York: Routledge, 2013.

Rieder, John. *Colonialism and the Emergence of Science Fiction.* Middleton, CT: Wesleyan University Press, 2008.

Roberts, Robin. *Sexual Generations: "Star Trek: The Next Generation" and Gender.* Champaign: University of Illinois Press, 1999.

Ruti, Mari. *The Ethics of Opting Out: Queer Theory's Defiant Subjects.* New York: Columbia University Press, 2017.

Sedgwick, Eve Kosofsky. *Epistemology of the Closet.* Berkeley: University of California Press, 1990.

Sontag, Susan. "The Imagination of Disaster." *Commentary,* October 1965, 42–48.

Spiegel, Lynn. *Make Room for TV: Television and the Family Ideal in Postwar America.* Chicago: University of Chicago Press, 1992.

Steiff, Josef, and Tristan Tamplin, eds. *"Battlestar Galactica" and Philosophy: Mission Accomplished or Mission Frakked Up?* Chicago: Open Court, 2008.

Snyder, Timothy. *The Road to Unfreedom: Russia, Europe, America.* New York: Tim Duggan Books, 2018.

Thomas, Lindsay. "Forms of Duration: Preparedness, the *Mars* Trilogy, and the Management of Climate Change." *American Literature* 88, no. 1 (2016): 159–84.

Thompson, E. P. *William Morris: Romantic to Revolutionary.* London: Merlin, 1977.

Vint, Sherryl. "Promissory Futures: Reality and Imagination in Finance and Fiction." *CR: The New Centennial Review* 19, vol. 1 (Spring 2019): 11–36.

Vogl, Joseph. *The Ascendancy of Finance.* Trans. Simon Garnett. Cambridge: Polity, 2017.

Wegner, Phillip E. *Shockwaves of Possibility: Essays on Science Fiction, Globalization, and Utopia.* New York: Peter Lang, 2014.

Wetmore, Kevin J. *The Theology of "Battlestar Galactica": American Christianity in the 2004–2009 Television Series.* Jefferson, NC: McFarland, 2012.

Worland, Rick. "From the New Frontier to the Final Frontier: *Star Trek* from Kennedy to Gorbachev." *Film and History* 24, no. 1 (2013): 19–35.

Wynter, Sylvia. "Unsettling the Coloniality of Being/Power/Truth/Freedom: Towards the Human, After Man, Its Overrepresentation—An Argument," *CR: The New Centennial Review* 3, no. 3 (Fall 2003): 257–337.

Yaszek, Lisa. *Galactic Suburbia: Recovering Women's Science Fiction.* Columbus: Ohio State University Press, 2008.

Zuboff, Shoshana. *The Age of Surveillance Capitalism: The Fight for a Human Future at the New Frontier of Power.* New York: PublicAffairs, 2019.

FILMOGRAPHY

Buñuel, Luis, dir. *The Discreet Charm of the Bourgeoisie*. 1972; 20th Century Fox.

"Careful Massacre of the Bourgeoisie, The." *Mr. Robot: Season 2*, 2017; Universal Pictures. DVD.

Carson, David, dir. *Star Trek Generations*. 1994; Paramount.

Colony (2016–2018). Season 1, episode 1, "Pilot." Aired January 14, 2016, USA.

——. Season 2, episode 1, "Eleven.Thirteen." Aired January 12, 2017, USA.

——. Season 2, episode 4, "Panopticon." Aired February 2, 2017, USA.

——. Season 2, episode 6, "Fallout." Aired February 16, 2017, USA.

——. Season 2, episode 11, "Lost Boy." Aired March 23, 2017, USA.

——. Season 3, episode 4, "Hospitium." Aired May 23, 2018, USA.

——. Season 3, episode 8, "Lazarus." Aired June 20, 2018, USA.

——. Season 3, episode 11, "Disposable Heroes." Aired July 11, 2018, USA.

Continuum (2012–2015). Season 1, episode 1, "A Stitch in Time." Aired January 14, 2013, Showcase.

——. Season 1, episode 4, "Matter of Time." Aired February 4, 2013, Showcase.

——. Season 1, episode 6, "Time's Up." Aired February 18, 2013, Showcase.

——. Season 1, episode 9, "Family Time." Aired July 29, 2012, Showcase.

——. Season 2, episode 9, "Seconds." Aired July 7, 2013, Showcase.

——. Season 3, episode 4, "Minute Changes." Aired April 25, 2014, Showcase.

——. Season 3, episode 6, "Wasted Minute." Aired May 9, 2014, Showcase.

——. Season 4, episode 6, "Final Hour." Aired October 16, 2015, Showcase.

Expanse, The (2015–). Season 1, episode 1, "Dulcinea." Aired November 23, 2015, SyFy.

——. Season 1, episode 5, "Back to the Butcher." Aired January 5, 2016, SyFy.

——. Season 1, episode 6, "Rock Bottom." Aired January 12, 2016, SyFy.

——. Season 2, episode 7, "The Seventh Man." Aired March 8, 2017, SyFy.

——. Season 2, episode 10, "Cascade." Aired March 29, 2017, SyFy.

——. Season 2, episode 12, "The Monster and the Rocket." Aired April 12, 2017, SyFy.

——. Season 3, episode 12, "Congregation." Aired June 27, 2018, SyFy.

Falling Skies (2011–2015). Season 1, episode 1, "Live and Learn." Aired June 19, 2011, TNT.

——. Season 1, episode 2, "The Armory." Aired June 19, 2011, TNT.

——. Season 1, episode 7, "Sanctuary: Part 2." Aired July 24, 2011, TNT.

——. Season 2, episode 1, "Worlds Apart." Aired June 17, 2012, TNT.

——. Season 2, episode 9, "The Price of Greatness." Aired August 12, 2012, TNT.

——. Season 3, episode 7, "The Pickett Line." Aired July 14, 2013, TNT.

——. Season 5, episode 6, "Respite." Aired August 2, 2015, TNT.

——. Season 5, episode 8, "Stalag 14th Virginia." Aired August 16, 2015, TNT.

——. Season 5, episode 10, "Reborn." Aired August 30, 2015, TNT.

Harron, Mary, dir. *American Psycho.* 2000; Lions Gate Films.

Hayes, Todd, dir. *Dark Waters.* 2019; Focus Features.

Incorporated (2016–2017). Season 1, episode 2, "Downsizing." Aired December 7, 2016, SyFy.

——. Season 1, episode 4, "Cost Containment." Aired December 21, 2016, SyFy.

——. Season 1, episode 5, "Profit and Loss." Aired December 28, 2016, SyFy.

——. Season 1, episode 7, "Executables." Aired January 11, 2017, SyFy.

Jericho (2006–2008). Season 1, episode 8, "Rogue River." Aired November 8, 2006, CBS.

——. Season 1, episode 9, "Crossroads." Aired November 14, 2006, CBS.

——. Season 1, episode 22, "Why We Fight." Aired May 9, 2007, CBS.

——. Season 2, episode 1, "Reconstruction." Aired February 12, 2008, CBS.

——. Season 2, episode 3, "Jennings & Rall." Aired February 26, 2008, CBS.

——. Season 2, episode 4, "Oversight." Aired March 4, 2008, CBS.

The Man in the High Castle (2015–2019). Season 1, episode 1, "The New World." Aired January 15, 2015, Prime Video.

——. Season 1, episode 2, "Sunrise." Aired October 23, 2015, Prime Video.

——. Season 1, episode 6, "Three Monkeys." Aired November 20, 2015, Prime Video.

——. Season 2, episode 1, "The Tiger's Cave." Aired December 16, 2016, Prime Video.

——. Season 2, episode 4, "Escalation." Aired December 16, 2016, Prime Video.

——. Season 2, episode 10, "Fallout." Aired December 16, 2016, Prime Video.

——. Season 3, episode 7, "Excess Animus." Aired October 5, 2018, Prime Video.

——. Season 3, episode 8, "Kasumi (Through the Mists)." Aired October 5, 2018, Prime Video.

——. Season 4, episode 6, "All Serious Daring." Aired November 15, 2019, Prime Video.

——. Season 4, episode 10, "Fire from the Gods." Aired November 15, 2019, Prime Video.

Marker, Chris, dir. *La Jetée.* 1962; Argos Films.

Mr. Robot (2015–2019). Season 1, episode 1, "eps1.0_hellofriend.mov." Aired June 24, 2015, USA.

——. Season 1, episode 3, "eps1.2_d3bug.mkv." Aired July 8, 2015, USA.

——. Season 1, episode 7, "eps1.6_v1ew-source.flv." Aired August 5, 2015, USA.

——. Season 1, episode 9, "eps1.8_m1rror1ng.qt." Aired August 19, 2015, USA.

——. Season 1, episode 10, "eps1.9_zero-day.avi." Aired September 2, 2015, USA.

——. Season 2, episode 1, "eps2.0_unm4sk-pt1.tc." Aired July 10, 2016, USA.

——. Season 2, episode 2, "eps2.0_unm4sk-pt2.tc." Aired July 13, 2016, USA.

——. Season 2, episode 4, "eps2.2_init_1.asec." Aired July 27, 2016, USA.

——. Season 2, episode 6, "eps2.4_m4ster-s1ave.aes." Aired August 10, 2016, USA.

——. Season 2, episode 7, "eps2.5_h4ndshake.sme." Aired August 17, 2016, USA.

——. Season 2, episode 9, "eps2.7_init_5.fve." Aired August 31, 2016, USA.

——. Season 2, episode 11, "eps2.9_python-pt1.p7z." Aired September 14, 2016, USA.

——. Season 3, episode 1, "eps3.0_power-saver-mode.h." Aired October 11, 2017, USA.

——. Season 3, episode 6, "eps3.5_kill-process.inc." Aired November 15, 2017, USA.

——. Season 3, episode 7, "eps3.6_fredrick+tanya.chk." Aired November 22, 2017, USA.

——. Season 3, episode 10, "shutdown -r." Aired December 13, 2017, USA.

——. Season 4, episode 2, "402 Payment Required." Aired October 13, 2019, USA.

——. Season 4, episode 3, "403 Forbidden." Aired October 20, 2019, USA.

——. Season 4, episode 6, "406 Not Acceptable." Aired November 10, 2019, USA.

——. Season 4, episode 7, "407 Proxy Authentication Required." Aired November 17, 2019, USA.

——. Season 4, episode 10, "410 Gone." Aired December 8, 2019, USA.

——. Season 4, episode 13, "Hello, Elliot." Aired December 22, 2019, USA.

Nygard, Roger, dir. *Trekkies*. 1997; Paramount.

100, The. Season 1, episode 1, "Pilot." Aired March 19, 2014, The CW.

——. Season 1, episode 7, "Contents Under Pressure." Aired April 30, 2014, The CW.

——. Season 2, episode 5, "Human Trials." Aired November 19, 2014, The CW.

——. Season 3, episode 3, "Ye Who Enter Here." Aired February 4, 2016, The CW.

——. Season 4, episode 8, "God Complex." Aired March 29, 2017, The CW.

——. Season 5, episode 2, "Red Queen." Aired May 1, 2018, The CW.

——. Season 7, episode 3, "False Gods." Aired June 3, 2020, The CW.

Ra, Sun. *Space Is the Place*. Dir. John Coney. 1974.

Revolution (2012–2014). Season 2, episode 17, "Why We Fight." Aired March 19, 2014, NBC.

"Scary Details, The." *Threshold: The Complete Series*, 2006; Paramount. DVD.

Siegel, Don, dir. *Invasion of the Body Snatchers*. 1956; Allied Artists.

Spotnitz, Frank. *The X-Files: I Want to Believe*. Dir. Chris Carter. 2008; 20th Century Fox.

Star Trek: Deep Space Nine (1993–1999). Season 6, episode 13, "Far Beyond the Stars." Aired February 11, 1998, Syndication.

Star Trek: Discovery (2017–). Season 1, episode 12, "Vaulting Ambition." Aired January 21, 2018, CBS.

——. Season 1, episode 15, "Will You Take My Hand?" Aired February 11, 2018, CBS.

——. Season 2, episode 1, "Brother." Aired January 17, 2019, CBS.

——. Season 2, episode 6, "The Sound of Thunder." Aired February 21, 2019, CBS.

Star Trek: Enterprise (2001–2005). Season 4, episode 20, "Demons." Aired May 6, 2005, UPN.

——. Season 4, episode 21, "Terra Prime." Aired May 13, 2005, UPN.

Star Trek: The Next Generation (1987–1994). Season 1, episode 3, "Code of Honor." Aired October 10, 1987, First-run syndication.

——. Season 2, episode 9, "The Measure of a Man." Aired February 11, 1989, First-run syndication.

——. Season 3, episode 16, "The Offspring." Aired March 10, 1990, First-run syndication.

——. Season 3, episode 26, "The Best of Both Worlds." Aired June 16, 1990, First-run syndication.

——. Season 4, episode 1, "The Best of Both Worlds: Part II." Aired September 22, 1990, First-run syndication.

——. Season 4, episode 23, "The Host." Aired May 11, 1991, First-run syndication.

——. Season 5, episode 2, "Darmok." Aired September 28, 1991, First-run syndication.

——. Season 5, episode 17, "The Outcast." Aired March 14, 1992, First-run syndication.

——. Season 5, episode 23, "I Borg." Aired May 9, 1992, First-run syndication.

——. Season 5, episode 25, "The Inner Light." Aired May 30, 1992, First-run syndication.

——. Season 6, episode 9, "The Quality of Life." Aired November 14, 1992, First-run syndication.

——. Season 6, episode 10, "Chain of Command, Part I." Aired December 12, 1992, First-run syndication.

——. Season 6, episode 11, "Chain of Command, Part II." Aired December 19, 1992, First-run syndication.

Star Trek: The Original Series (1966–1969). Season 1, episode 18, "Arena." Aired January 19, 1967, NBC.

——. Season 1, episode 28, "The City on the Edge of Forever." Aired April 6, 1967, NBC.

——. Season 2, episode 4, "Mirror, Mirror." Aired October 6, 1967, NBC.

Star Trek: Picard (2020–). Season 1, episode 1, "Remembrance." Aired January 23, 2020, CBS.

Star Trek: Voyager (1995–2001). Season 3, episode 6, "Remember." Aired October 9, 1996, UPN.

——. Season 4, episode 4, "Nemesis." Aired September 24, 1997, UPN.

Threshold (2005–2006). Season 1, episode 1, "Trees Made of Glass: Part 1." Aired September 16, 2005, CBS.

——. Season 1, episode 13, "Alienville." Aired February 1, 2006, CBS.

X-Files, The (1993–2018). Season 11, episode 4, "The Lost Art of Forehead Sweat." Aired January 24, 2018, Fox.

INDEX